Religious Imaginations

How Narratives of Faith are Shaping Today's World

Edited by James Walters

GINGKO

First published in 2018 by
Gingko Library
4 Molasses Row
London SW11 3UX

ISBN 978-1-909942-20-2
eISBN 978-1-909942-23-3

Typeset in Times by MacGuru Ltd
Printed in Spain

www.gingko.org.uk
@GingkoLibrary

Contents

Re-imagining Belief

Religion and Sustainability

From Imagination to Religious Practice

Acknowledgements

This book arises from the Religious Imaginations and Global Transitions conference we hosted at LSE in June 2017. I would like to thank all who contributed to that conference, including our partners at the Foreign and Commonwealth Office and Mena Mark Hanna, Dean of the Barenboim-Said Akademie. Many worked hard to make the conference a success including Edward Lewis and Harry Hall from Gingko and Esther Kersley and Angharad Thain from the LSE Faith Centre. In turning this event into a book, I have relied heavily on Aida Bahrami at Gingko and Daniel Coyne at LSE. But most of all I would like to acknowledge my gratitude to the indefatigable Barbara Schwepcke for first approaching me about this project and for making it all possible. She is the kind of energetic bridge-builder across cultures that our fractured world desperately needs.

James Walters
London, October 2018

Introduction

James Walters

The imaginations we live by

None of us look at the world purely empirically. We all perceive and interpret the physical world around us through the various imaginative frameworks that we have inherited and which organise our thoughts and attitudes. One such framework may be that of nation state borders and of the social contract among those living within them. Through the course of history such concepts have shaped people's sense of identity and their actions towards others, compelling them *in extremis* to fight fellow human beings and give their lives in wars. On this basis, the American theologian William Cavanaugh has argued that politics is fundamentally a practice of the imagination: 'We are often fooled by the seeming solidity of the materials of politics, its armies and officers, into forgetting that these materials are marshalled by acts of the imagination.'[1] Alternatively our thoughts and perceptions may be shaped by an over-optimistic imagination of social progress and of the ability of science and technology to eliminate human want and suffering on their own. These ideas have come to dominate the Western imagination since the Enlightenment and, in spite of the crises of our times, persist in hubristic accounts of humanist potential such as Steven Pinker's 2018 book *Enlightenment Now*.[2] None of these imaginative frameworks represent demonstrable or proven descriptions of the world as it actually is, but they are organising paradigms through which we make sense of everything. The philosopher Mary Midgley, whose work attends

---

1 William T Cavanaugh, *Theopolitical Imagination: Discovering the Liturgy as a Political Act in an Age of Global Consumerism* (London: T&T Clark, 2002), p. 1.
2 Steven Pinker, *Enlightenment Now: The Case for Science, Reason, Humanism and Progress* (London: Allen Lane, 2018).

particularly to the imaginative frameworks of science, terms these structures 'the myths we live by' and argues that the way in which we imagine the world 'determines what we think important in it, what we select for our attention among the welter of facts that constantly flood in upon us'.[3]

For the vast majority of the world's population, religion plays a major part in this organising imagination. Well over 80 percent of human beings follow one of the main religious traditions. This is not to say that religious beliefs are necessarily the only or even dominant motivating forces in their lives. However, religious traditions are powerful symbolic systems that shape both collective memory and our vision of the future. As such they form individuals and communities in their personal habits, social attitudes and political beliefs in multiple ways. Scriptural texts, practices of prayer and collective acts of worship build a picture of the world and the place and purposes of the believer within it. The fact that these narratives and practices are concerned with ultimate, transcendent realities elevate their significance beyond the merely pragmatic or utilitarian frameworks of much scientific or political thinking. The religious imagination engages life and death, material and metaphysical, earthly and heavenly.

Western theories of international relations and global order have tended to overlook this significance. They have grown out of the European tradition of the apparent relegation of religion to private life. When the early modern Wars of Religion were resolved in the Treaties of Westphalia, religious sectarianism was subordinated to a regulating nation state, which came to be seen as secular in nature. Religion was viewed as a matter of personal, private choice, largely inconsequential to citizenship and public life. This approach was combined with another unempirical imaginative assumption: the conviction that the spread of science, education and affluence would progressively erode religious affiliation. Theorists of global order and political economy who were informed by this enduring assumption could not conceive that religion was (let alone would remain) a major force in global movements, conflicts and alliances.

The realist and neo-realist schools of international relations see violence and power as the principal drivers in foreign policy. They see nation states as the primary actors and religion as a mere epiphenomenon resulting from failure of states to control the inherent anarchy of the international system. Meanwhile, liberal and neo-liberal schools see economics as the main driver. Working primarily from Max Weber's secularisation thesis,[4] they view religion as irrelevant

---

3 Mary Midgley, *The Myths We Live By* (London: Routledge, 2004).
4 See: Max Weber, *Science as a Vocation* (1917).

to the motivations of states within a global system that evolves as a rational process, forging agreements on international law and trade. None of the dominant schools of thought have considered religion to be a serious force in international relations, in large part because they begin with the modern Western-European understanding of religion as an essentially private matter – personal rather than social, spiritual rather than political, supplementary rather than fundamental to everyday life.

Recovering the religious imagination

The conference convened at the London School of Economics in June 2017 by Gingko, the Foreign and Commonwealth Office and LSE Faith Centre was a recognition that these realist and liberal schools which underplay the significance of religion are not helping us to understand and address some major currents in the global transitions of our time. In all corners of the world, religious narratives are coming to the fore and becoming complexly interwoven with the main geopolitical forces that are shaping today's world. Hindu Nationalism has become the dominant force in a formerly much more plural Indian politics. Jewish and Muslim narratives are more explicit than ever before in the rhetoric on both sides of the Israeli-Palestinian conflict. The power of the Russian state has become increasingly fused with the spiritual authority of Russian Orthodox Christianity. And certain forms of Jihadist Islam are becoming a reactionary and destabilising force in many parts of the world. Even in an increasingly secular Europe, the influx of migrants of predominantly Muslim background has made religion and the 'defence of Christian Europe' a far stronger concern in the public consciousness than most mainstream media would suggest.

A few weeks before our conference, President Donald Trump made his first diplomatic visit overseas. It cannot have been incidental that his first three destinations were Jerusalem (ancient centre of all three Abrahamic faiths), Riyadh (capital of Saudi Arabia, the heartland of Islam) and Rome (centre of Western Christianity for 2000 years). The carefully choreographed gestures of this visit – praying in a *kippah* at the Western Wall, shaking the Pope's hand in the Vatican, receiving hospitality from the Wahhabi House of Saud – tap into powerful narratives of meaning, both ancient and very contemporary, in America and across the world. Consciously or unconsciously, this populist presidency appears to recognise something of the power of religious imagination, both among the American Christians who form his core supporters and in the key international challenges of our time.

The example of this presidential visit illustrates three important dimensions of the religious imagination in today's world. The first is the *legacy* of ancient religious imaginations. Part of the modern secular conceit has been to deny the enduring power of religious symbols, even among societies that have shifted away from religious observance. France is perhaps Europe's most self-consciously secular country. It has embraced a programmatic marginalisation of religion in the name of *laïcité* and claimed that Enlightenment ideals have displaced superstitious religiosity in its national character. And yet there is a blindness to the multiple ways Catholic culture continues to pervade French society, from the celebration of Catholic holidays to the deep sense of national outrage and grievance that was felt at the murder of Fr Jacques Hamel in 2016. The realist and liberal European schools of international relations have projected this blindness onto the global arena, refusing to see the power and significance of religious narratives in different peoples' history and collective memory. Drawing attention to this blind spot in our approach to many regions of the world is perhaps the primary purpose of this book. From areas as diverse as the arts (Hanna, Chapter 6) and post-conflict reconciliation (Shore, Chapter 17), ancient religious narratives and symbols remain potent. The religious traditions which spread from the historic cities on the itinerary of this presidential visit (to mention only the Abrahamic faiths) continue to influence the character of societies and individuals in all corners of today's world.

Second, we see how religious imaginations are *evolving*. The dispensationalist evangelical theology that is driving much of President Trump's support for the state of Israel is a relatively new development in the history of Christianity. It has its roots in the nineteenth century and espouses a theology of God's purposes in history that is quite at odds with that of the ancient churches present in the Middle East itself. Similarly, the puritan form of Sunni Islam formulated by Muhammad ibn Abd al-Wahhab in the eighteenth century represented a radical departure from conventional religious traditions that had a profound impact on Islamic practice in Saudi Arabia and continues to have ramifications throughout the world today. Religious traditions are not static. Reformers and iconoclasts alike bring about evolutions and revolutions and provoke fierce debates about the balance of change and continuity. Traditions evolve and new religious movements emerge (Barker, Chapter 11).

One of the most significant evolutions in religious imaginations, which constitutes an important dimension of this book, is the emergence of a global religious consciousness. As travel, technology and communications have developed a truly global awareness, the realities and challenges of religious pluralism have become a major theme in religious thinking. While attempts at accommodating multiple religious imaginations have mostly operated on Western universalist assumptions (Fahy, Chapter 8), the challenges have also been addressed by other non-Western traditions (Abdelnour, Chapter 7) and this is now a practical task to be taken up in diverse communities around the world (Robertson, Chapter 18).

Third, we can see how these evolving religious imaginations are forming new *interactions* and *engagements* with the global transitions we see in all other walks of life: political, economic, ecological, social. Religious teachings about the proper use of money in practices of debt and lending are engaging with the legacy of the 2008 financial crisis and the realities of increasingly indebted societies. New understandings of gender and sexuality are prompting both conservative reactions and re-evaluations of traditional teaching in queer theology and inclusive new religious communities. And increasingly, faith traditions are drawing on their theologies of the natural world to address the challenges of environmental crises. It is a striking feature of religious imagination in our times that media coverage of the meeting between President Trump and Pope Francis focussed on their divergent positions on climate change, the Pope's encyclical *Laudato Si* being one of the most effective calls to action on this issue that we have seen. As we explore in this book, addressing the challenges of global warming is a major form of engagement that religious thinkers and activists are taking up in Christianity (Gordon, Chapter 14), Islam (Karagiannis, Chapter 16), Sikhism (Singh, Chapter 15) and other traditions.

Imagining the future

Whether we consider religious narratives in terms of their legacies, their evolutions or their contemporary interactions, the power of the religious imagination might be said to lie in its opening up of the unseen. Jean-Paul Sartre defined the imagination as the ability to think of (the image of) what is not. This is how imagination (of what is not) amounts to more than mere perception (of what is).[5] For religious people this may include the willingness to attribute agency to unseen dimensions of the real (angels and demons, the communion of saints, the miraculous). But most especially imagination comprises the ability to think of what is not *yet*, that is to say, what is to come. Theologians call this eschatology, a vision of God's purposes for the future that shapes the believer's present. For a Christian to pray, 'Thy Kingdom come on earth as it is in heaven' is for them to invoke a rich picture of God's future purposes for justice, peace and restoration which informs

---

5 Jean-Paul Sartre, *The Imagination* (Abingdon: Routledge, 2012).

their actions today. The twentieth-century philosopher and politician Alexandre Kojève saw this primacy of the future in human imagination as constituting the fundamental capacity for social change. He saw this idea as being fully recognised in Hegel's *The Phenomenology of Mind*.[6] In pre-Hegelian philosophy, the movement of time went from the past to the future by way of the present. For Hegel, however, the movement is 'engendered in the Future and goes towards the Present by way of the Past: Future → Past → Present (→ Future)'.[7] Kojève, in common with other twentieth-century French interpreters of Hegel and those influenced by them (e.g. Alexandre Koyré, Judith Butler), identifies this initiative of the future in a movement that arises from desire. Desire is the creative human capacity that brings into existence that which does not yet exist. 'Desire is the presence of an absence.'[8] This historical agency of desire is explored in Chapter Four of *The Phenomenology of Mind* where the parable of the Lord and the Bondsman serves to illustrate that the struggle for recognition forms the dynamic principle of all historical progress. Desire is therefore the instrument of freedom, seeking to bring into being a new reality. The primacy of the future leads to transformation of the present through the identification and realisation of what is desired. Quoting Hegel's maxim, 'Geist ist Zeit' (Spirit is Time), Kojève presents the whole historical process as driven by the future as time realised through desire.

We can understand the potency of the religious imagination in its forming desire for the future among believers of different kinds. This may be particularly true of the Abrahamic faiths for whom the linearity of time is the condition of salvation history. It is integral, for example, to the English Idealism (also influenced by Hegelian thought) that fed into Anglican social visions of the betterment of society. The desires of Christian Socialists and social reformers were shaped by a vision of God's creation of a New Jerusalem where poverty, want and pain

---

6 G W F Hegel, *The Phenomenology of Mind* (Mineola: Dover Classics, 2003).

7 Alexandre Kojève, *Introduction to the Reading of Hegel* (New York: Basic Books, 1969), p. 134. Michael Roth discusses the ironic twist that Kojève, in fact, held that historical progress had come to an end and that he was living in a post-historical world where nothing really new occurred; see *Knowing and History: Appropriations of Hegel in Twentieth-Century France* (Ithaca: Cornell University Press, 1988), chp. 4. Kojève's writings on this topic appear to have inspired Francis Fukuyama's subsequent declaration of the 'End of History'; see, *The End of History and the Last Man* (London: Hamish Hamilton, 1992). Roth sees a contradiction, noting that 'the content of his discourse seems to be at odds with the form and the point of this pedagogy' (p. 84). But surely Kojève seeks to theorise from Hegel a dynamic account of the future in order to overcome the political impasses of the present, as Roth states, 'to think through the ways in which action can be meaningful both because of its orientation toward the future and because of the fact of human finitude' (p. 84).

8 Kojève, *Introduction to the Reading of Hegel*, p. 134.

are eliminated. Eschatology also features strongly in the Islamic imagination. A major factor in the significance of the Al-Aqsa Mosque and the Haram al-Sharif for Muslims around the world is the role that they believe it will play in the End Times. Muslims believe that Jesus (Isa) will return to Jerusalem to set about the chain of events that lead to the Last Judgement. Some sources even argue that the Kaaba will be brought from Mecca to Jerusalem. So relinquishing the significance of Al-Aqsa (such as many feel that current political pressure is asking of them) would constitute the ultimate religious betrayal: an abandonment of God's future purposes for the world. Little wonder the cry to 'Save Al-Aqsa' reverberates around the Muslim world.

While the linear salvation histories of the Abrahamic faiths may encourage this eschatological orientation, imaginative visions of the future also exist in the cyclic traditions of the East. In the Theravada Buddhist tradition, it is believed that the teachings of the Buddha will pass away after five thousand years. At this point a degenerate human society will see the advent of a new Buddha, embodying wisdom, goodness, happiness and knowledge. He will rule over an earthly paradise and teach virtue to humanity.[9] In its theory of reincarnation, Buddhism shares with Hinduism and Sikhism a more personal imagining of the future as the eventual liberation from rebirths through moral progress. The believer is oriented towards a utopian future toward which they are already journeying.

So, across faith traditions, the fundamental orientation of the religious imagination is towards the future. And this has such immediate import because it is about what human beings are formed to desire, be that virtuous ideals of social harmony and peace or the more dangerous apocalyptic visions of the dispensationalists or the so-called Islamic State.[10] Religious imagination shapes the believer's vision of the world and the ideals for which they will pray, work and even die.

The opening section of the book comprises four of the keynote addresses from the conference, a talk on religious musical traditions given before the conference concert and an additional essay from Ophir Yarden, a regular contributor to LSE Faith Centre programmes. In Chapter One, Craig Calhoun takes us much further into reflections on religious imagination and the transformations currently taking place in the world. He explores both how religious traditions are being

---

9 See: John S Strong, 'Buddhist Relics in Comparative Perspective: Beyond the Parallels', in D Germano and K Trainor, eds., *Embodying the Dharma: Buddhist Relic Veneration in Asia* (Albany: State University of New York Press, 2004), pp. 27–50.

10 See, John Gray, *Black Mass: Apocalyptic Religion and the Death of Utopia* (London: Allen Lane, 2007), for a discussion of the dangers of religious eschatology.

transformed and how they themselves continue to exert a transformative influence on social movements and political systems. He highlights the extraordinary
technological challenges of the future and asks what contribution religious imaginations might yet make to the challenging of instrumentalist logics evident in the
politics of migration, markets and crime, as well as the impersonal interaction of
social media.

The subsequent three chapters are contributions from the religious imaginations
of the three Abrahamic faith traditions. They are, of course, single perspectives
from within internally diverse traditions, and yet they come from imaginative
thinkers seeking to speak from the depths of their own tradition in order to make
connections with the multiple imaginations of today's world. Mona Siddiqui
reflects on the imagination from the Islamic perspective and beyond. She laments
an impoverishment of conversations about religion (particularly Islam) and also of
the religious imagination itself in the post-colonial and postmodern era. She calls
for a deepening of the ethical imagination to address the challenges of the conflicts
in the Middle East and of mass migration to Europe. Archbishop Angaelos also
speaks of these conflicts, as both a practitioner, leading the Coptic Christian community in the United Kingdom, and as a wise commentator on the global struggles
of religious minorities. He draws on the New Testament for a Christian imagination to face terrorism with fortitude and forgiveness. Defending the stranger in our
midst is also central, argues Ophir Yarden, to the Jewish imagination, rooted in
the experience of the Hebrew people as 'strangers in the land of Egypt'. He sees
the centenary of the Balfour Declaration, with its provision 'that nothing shall be
done which may prejudice the civil and religious rights of existing non-Jewish
communities in Palestine', as an opportunity to reimagine how people might live
together in the contemporary state of Israel.

John Casson has been navigating these religious imaginations in his career as
a diplomat and particularly in his role as Her Majesty's Ambassador to Egypt.
His chapter shares practical wisdom from a region where religion and diplomacy
unavoidably encroach on each other's space. He cautions against compartmentalising or instrumentalising religion and goes so far as to suggest that diplomats
should 'draw on the resources of faith to refresh our imaginations'. Mena Mark
Hanna is a practitioner of a different kind, a musician and Dean of the Barenboim-
Said Akademie which forms musicians from across the Middle East and North
Africa in a spirit of mutual learning and reconciliation. He explores the crucial
role that music can play in uniting the believer with God, in binding believers
together, and in drawing a divided humanity together.

The remaining chapters comprise many of the shorter papers given at the conference, loosely grouped into four sections. Mohammad Gamal Abdelnour and John Fahy confront the challenges of engaging across religious traditions in our globalised world. Abdelnour is one of the Al-Azhar scholars to which Casson refers in Chapter Five. His work explores the writings of a twentieth century Muslim Egyptian thinker, Muhammad abu Zahra, to see how the critical approach he developed might be applied to a contemporary theology of religions. John Fahy sets out the bigger picture of the interfaith enterprise as it developed through the nineteenth and twentieth centuries and as it is perceived in the Middle East today. Also examining the meaning of President Trump's visit, Fahy explores the inescapable tensions between theology and politics in interfaith dialogue and peacebuilding.

The next section explores the reimagining of belief systems themselves. Kamran Bashir looks at how debates about the interpretation of early Islam underpin attempts to reform contemporary Islam, such as those of Pakistani scholar Javed Ahmad Ghamidi, as well as efforts to resist reform. Abby Day presents her fieldwork on lived belief within the transitional context of Egypt's Arab Spring, comparing her findings to earlier work in the UK. She draws attention to the contextual reimagining of belief as practice in different times and locations. Distinguished sociologist Eileen Barker also attends to the lived realities of faith for adherents of the thousands of new religious movements found in the UK and around the world today. While attention has focused on the developments within the ancient traditions, new religions are coming into being all the time and, as well as engendering fear among outsiders, they make significant and varied contribution to wider society, Barker points out. Jenna Reinbold extends the boundaries of religious imagination yet further to consider how the secular discourse of human rights might also be considered a 'narrative of faith', opening up questions of distinction between religious and non-religious belief systems. It is essential to do so, she argues, to understand the current religious pushback against the hegemony of human rights as a universalised quasi-religious framework. Finally, in this section, Thahir Jamal looks at the re-imagination of Islam within the social movements of South India, seeing such organic practice as a legitimate custodian of Qur'anic interpretation.

The next three chapters address questions of religion's engagement with environmental sustainability. In contrast to those who present the Judeo-Christian tradition as an ideological driver of environmental exploitation ('fill the earth and subdue it', Genesis 1:28), Caleb Gordon sees ecologically-conscious Christianity as a faithful continuation of an evolving tradition. But extending Christian ethics beyond a narrow attention to the individual is what is at stake here. As Gordon puts it, 'when we wonder what it looks like to love a neighbour, we are asking a question about the physical world.' Khushwant Singh argues that the Sikh tradition is perhaps better equipped for this as custodian of a spiritual wisdom that points to beyond material consumption. He identifies 'the poison of hubris' as a critical obstacle to our human flourishing and presents Sikh spiritual practice as a source of global renewal, beginning with a radically different approach to education. But if this integrated vision appears more foundational in Eastern thought, Emmanuel Karagiannis argues that the Islamic tradition also contains the theological tools necessary to reconnect humanity and the environment. It is possible, he argues, to maintain the common religious belief that humanity is at the heart of God's creation while associating this with a meaningful and demanding sense of guardianship for the natural order.

The final two chapters are illustrations of how the religious imagination can be drawn into practical engagement. Megan Shore looks at how the Christian imagination shaped post-conflict South Africa through the influence of religious leaders. Rather than sentimentalise the process enacted by the Truth and Reconciliation Commission she assesses why religious communities were able to fill the political vacuum with their organisational capacity and ability to build bridges and she looks at the criticisms and limitations of this faith-led approach. A broader understanding of religion among politicians and diplomats would, she argues, open up other possibilities for religious input into conflict resolution, strengthened by the lessons learned from the South African experience. Catriona Robertson's examples are from the UK and she offers reflections from her unparalleled experience in leading wide-ranging community interfaith work. She describes what might be termed a 'post-secular turn' in the public sphere as statutory provision for community cohesion and welfare has broken down and both local and national government look increasingly to those motivated to engage with society by their religious commitments. Robertson highlights the eschatological inspiration I described earlier: 'They want to make a difference because they can imagine a world without famine, without injustice, without ill health, without violence and suffering.' Her closing remarks echo Calhoun's opening chapter in observing how the religious imagination speaks into a society increasingly defined by market logic with a deeper sense of value, dignity and trust. At a time when political and social imagination seem lacking, religious imagination is powerful.

Some of these essays, therefore, address the problems associated with religion in a world where potentially violent intolerance of other faiths is clearly on the rise.[11] But overwhelmingly the contributors to this volume demonstrate not only

---

11 See: Pew Research Center, *Global Restrictions on Religion Rise Modestly in 2015, Reversing Downward Trend* (April 2017), available at: http://www.pewresearch.org/.

how an understanding of religious imagination is beneficial to those seeking to shape today's world, but also how religious imaginations constitute an enormous resource for the constructive shaping of the global transitions that affect us all. Several chapters draw on Charles Taylor's use of the term 'social imaginary'[12] to explore religion's ability to galvanise a collective vision at a time when individualism and social atomisation render us incapable of addressing common concerns and challenges. Some also allude to the power of the religious imagination for the individual in an age when personal resilience and determination need continuous renewal. To address today's complex global transitions 'demands virtue', argues Casson, 'and wisdom of the heart and soul as well as of the head'. This volume is offered as a small contribution to that multifaceted pursuit of wisdom to further understanding of the self and the world in an age when the religious imagination can no longer be ignored.

Bibliography

Cavanaugh, William T, *Theopolitical Imagination: Discovering the Liturgy as a Political Act in an Age of Global Consumerism* (London: T&T Clark, 2002).

Fukuyama, Francis, *The End of History and the Last Man* (London: Hamish Hamilton, 1992).

Gray, John, *Black Mass: Apocalyptic Religion and the Death of Utopia* (London: Allen Lane, 2007).

Hegel, G W F, *The Phenomenology of Mind* (Mineola: Dover Classics, 2003).

Kojève, Alexandre, *Introduction to the Reading of Hegel* (New York: Basic Books, 1969).

Midgley, Mary, *The Myths We Live By* (London: Routledge, 2004).

Pew Research Center, *Global Restrictions on Religion Rise Modestly in 2015, Reversing Downward Trend* (April 2017), available at: http://www.pewresearch.org/.

Pinker, Steven, *Enlightenment Now: The Case for Science, Reason, Humanism and Progress* (London: Allen Lane, 2018).

Roth, Michael, *Knowing and History: Appropriations of Hegel in Twentieth-Century France* (Ithaca: Cornell University Press, 1988).

Sartre, Jean-Paul, *The Imagination* (Abingdon: Routledge, 2012).

Strong, John S, 'Buddhist Relics in Comparative Perspective: Beyond the Parallels', in D Germano and K Trainor, eds., *Embodying the Dharma:*

---

12 Charles Taylor, *A Secular Age* (Cambridge, MA: Belknap Press, 2007), esp. p. 146fn.

Buddhist Relic Veneration in Asia (Albany: State University of New York Press, 2004).

Taylor, Charles, *A Secular Age* (Cambridge, MA: Belknap Press, 2007).

Weber, Max, *Science as a Vocation* (1917).

ENGAGING
THE RELIGIOUS
IMAGINATION

1

Religious Imaginations in a Changing World

Craig Calhoun

In an earlier era of transformation and upheaval, amid crisis in the Roman Empire and after the Visigoths sacked Rome itself, St. Augustine imagined a City of God.[1] This was focused on eternal truths rather than the greedy pursuit of pleasure in sensual earthly existence. But though its truths were eternal, the City of God was also a historical project, part of a struggle between God and the Devil in which human beings could take part. Augustine's imagination was informed by visions of a New Jerusalem proclaimed by prophets from Ezekiel to John of Patmos. It was informed by Rome, which was not just the Earthly City of iniquity but at the same time part of the path to the City of God. And it in turn informed the Roman Empire, the history of Christianity, and countless efforts to build a better world into our own time.

Today we live in another era of transformation and upheaval. Responses continue to be informed by the visions of Ezekiel and John of Patmos, and by Augustine's effort to distinguish the good that is higher and eternal from the more evanescent apparent goods of earthly acquisition and experience. But with a wider global consciousness we recognise that these are but a narrow fraction of the sources shaping contemporary religious imaginations.

Nor are religious imaginations limited to otherworldly evocation of the City of God. They have material implications. Religious imaginations bring a message

---

1 Augustine of Hippo, *The City of God against the Pagans* (Cambridge: Cambridge University Press, 1998) [among many translations].

of healing the world and building community. They inform ferocious ethnic and nationalist conflicts. They inspire fear. They inspire hope. And indeed, they inspire social movements that are not themselves explicitly religious but nonetheless try to bring utopia into human history.

I

Though some seek in religion the transcendence of worldly existence or escape from the sinfulness of a fallen world, others mobilise religion to engage the world. Religion figures in the politics of nation states and moral projects such as attempts to defend the sanctity of marriage or life itself. It motivates humanitarian action to relieve the human suffering brought by human conflict, technological failures, or natural disasters. Religion is part of a global social ecology in which change in one element affects others.

Globalisation has reshaped national cultures as well as the reach of markets, the processes of capital accumulation, and the ability of states to claim complete sovereignty. After long seeming almost an evolutionary inevitability, democracy has been unsettled by shifting media, weakened political parties, polarisation and the populist appeal of demagogues. New technologies have brought upheavals alongside conveniences and capacities we barely contemplated but now find it hard to live without. Some of these technologies raise not just material questions about employment or privacy. They raise existential questions about what it means to be human and whether what we value in humanity will long survive. Though hope is widespread for technological solutions to the impending crisis of climate change, technology at least as prominently joins climate change as another source of uncertainty and anxiety about the future. It transforms employment and poses cataclysmic risks.

In this context, many rely on religion as a source of security and confidence in the eternal. Yet religion does not remain stable while the world around it changes. Augustine tried to align Christianity with the eternal truths of God and thus make it a source of stability against a secular world of constant change. Indeed, one of the most fundamental meanings of 'secular' is concern with the temporal world in which history and change are basic. But at the same time, Augustine was part of a re-imagining of religion – indeed the very creation of Christianity.

Religion has been transformed not least by the processes loosely called secularisation: declining participation, assertive atheism, reliance on scientific (and other) efforts to explain all there is by only what is visible or at least experimentally verifiable, and simple worldliness. Religion has also been transformed by

renewed religious engagements in politics, movements of revitalisation and sometimes purification, a resurgent 'prosperity gospel', and intensified engagement in
eschatology. Democracy and nationalism have each been approached as though
they offered secular salvation.

Religious participation may be declining in the West, but not without excep-
tions and influential political engagements. Elsewhere, the picture is even more
varied. Religions shape and influence each other in new ways, including by new
alliances among peoples of different faiths, by new or renewed lines of conflict,
and by mediated force of example.

This takes place in intimate personal life and devotion as well as on the grand
scale of global affairs. And it takes place not simply in schools of divinity or in
some separate part of life called 'religion' but also in politics, economics, family
life, genetic engineering, and war. And if religion is transformed, religious traditions and imaginations also give shape to the ways people understand all these
other dimensions of life.

Religion today is not well symbolised by monks in contemplative retreat. In
this sense, large parts, indeed dominant dimensions, of most religions are themselves secular, engaged in the world. Judaism has informed both the creation of
the state of Israel, and recent efforts to make it more explicitly, exclusively, and
religiously Jewish. Movements of renewal and purification in Islam have joined
with efforts to seek power as well as defence against what has seemed a world
hostile to the faith, and the clash of Sunni and Shia religious imaginations has
brought war. Evangelical Christianity has been transformed by a new emphasis
on action – including politics – in this temporal and material world.[2] Some Evangelical Christians even engage in the world to hasten its end, supporting Israel
and notably its claim to Jerusalem in order to fulfil End Days prophesies from the
Book of Revelations, secure the conditions for Armageddon, and hasten deliver-
ance from this sad world.[3] Worldliness need not mean a simple love of the world.

All of this suggests that to understand religion today, or indeed to benefit from
religion today, it is best not to approach it simply as a matter of settled doctrines.
I don't mean simply that there is contestation and innovation in every religious

---

2 See James Davison Hunter's illuminating consideration in *To Change the World: The
Irony, Tragedy, and Possibility of Christianity in the Late Modern World* (Oxford: Oxford
University Press, 2010).
3 Examples in this paper come mainly from the Christian tradition, but this is a reflection
of where my knowledge is greater not an intention for the argument to apply only narrowly.
I have tried to give enough other examples to make this clear, though not alas to be 'fair' to
other traditions.

tradition, though this is true. I mean that we should embrace imagination as a central dimension of religion, making important contributions to the actively religious and also to the world at large. And I mean also that in the contemporary world we may need to reimagine religion itself.

II

To stress imagination is not simply to assert that we can think whatever we want. On the contrary, what we are able to imagine is itself shaped and channelled by received categories, available examples, and personal inhibitions. We imagine the world – and the question of what is beyond the world of sensible appearances – not in a completely open way, but influenced by what we have learned of how people imagined it before, what resources we have for imagination, and what we think possible.

We can term the more or less routinely available and shared ways of imagining the world 'social imaginaries'. Charles Taylor has, for example, described how we imagine democracy and markets through imaginaries of serial individual actions, voting, buying and selling.[4] These produce imaginations that are neither false, nor perfectly correct descriptions. They are constitutive. They help to make the reality by enabling millions of dispersed individuals to not only perform the required actions, but to think the reality of the larger system. At the same time, they can be limiting. Democracy is much more than voting, and markets are shaped by structures of power and constraint beyond the voluntary choices of individual consumers.

Taylor's account of social imaginaries draws on Benedict Anderson's analysis of nations as 'imagined communities'.[5] Anderson evoked a range of practices and institutions like censuses, maps and museums that help reproduce the powerful salience of nations. He suggested that the ways in which novels entwine multiple biographies into shared narratives helps facilitate the imagining of multiple, more individual narratives as part of shared national stories. To say that nations are imagined communities is not to contrast them to 'real' communities but rather

---

4 Charles Taylor, *New Social Imaginaries* (Durham, NC: Duke University Press, 2003). See also: D Gaonkar and B Lee, eds., *New Social Imaginaries,* special issue of *Public Culture* (Duke University Press, 2002), and C Calhoun, D Gaonkar, B Lee, C Taylor, and M Warner, eds., 'Modern Social Imaginaries Revisited: A Conversation', in *Social Imaginaries* 1.1 (2015).
5 Benedict Anderson, *Imagined Communities* (London: Verso, 2006).

to identify the way in which they became real.[6] This involves the production of a shared national imaginary inside countries but also a transnational nationalist imaginary that reproduces the tacit but influential view of the world as a world of nations (as we imagine the division of the globe's landmasses into the sharply demarcated pink, grey and yellow territories on maps). All this depends not just on unconstrained individual creativity in imagination, but on the social reproduction of ways of imagining.

Religion has figured in national imaginaries, but religion is also shaped by its own imaginaries. Muslims imagine Islam through quotidian rituals like prayer that help to organise time itself, but also through an image of the actually or potentially unified Ummah. They may remember past Caliphates or civilisational insults. Learning the Qur'an integrates images of the lives of Muhammad and his followers with both ideals and questions about life today. Divergent tracings of Islamic (and secular) history join with (partially) different ritual practices and calendars and a different sense of location in the world in separating Shia from Sunni and hindering the integration of the imagined Ummah. Islam may be imagined in rich historical detail and nuanced Qur'anic scholarship or in simpler ways. There are specific occasions and practices, like fasts and feasts, a religious calendar, lunar cycles, *zakat* as obligatory charity, Islamic finance, the Hajj. And so it is, with varied specifics, for Buddhism, Christianity, and all the world's religions.

So it is too for imagining religion as such, distinct from any one faith or tradition, somehow a common denominator or connection among all. Most imagining of a category of religion focuses manifestly on the distinctions and common denominators among religions. A list is offered, similarities and differences noted. But latent in this same project is the implication that religion is distinct from the rest of life, that it is one aspect of a way of life and not the whole of it. Or, perhaps better put, that ways of life can be carved up into their different aspects and each of these studied (or lived) more or less autonomously. This is of course a basis for academic disciplines, but it is not obviously or simply a reflection of reality as distinct from a way of imagining it. Is religion (or politics or economics) whole unto itself?

Trying to demarcate religion and non-religion is fundamental to the cultural construction of modernity.[7] Religion must be sharply distinct from the secular,

---

6 C Calhoun, 'The Importance of Imagined Communities – and Benedict Anderson', in *Debats* 130.1 (2016), pp. 11–16.

7 This is of a piece, for example, with Max Weber's notion of the differentiation of value spheres. See: *Economy and Society* (Berkeley: University of California Press, 1968). This remains important, and indeed definitive of modernity, in the work of Jürgen Habermas. See his *Theory of Communicative Action* (Boston: Beacon, 1984).

and in particular from science. Religion is private and should not be public (or publicly regulated or managed). Religion should be celebrated on Sundays and left behind on weekdays or provide a framework for holidays and the management of exceptional moments like weddings and funerals. Clergy who have little public voice most of the time should appear when needed for a coronation, or the mourning of lost soldiers, or the effort to reclaim community after an attack. Or so a misleading normative framework suggests.

In fact, in the contemporary world, religions are entwined with nationalism, philanthropy, higher education institutions, money and markets, local community life, networks of mutual assistance, prisons, and terrorism. Religion informs militarism and pacifism. It is enlisted by those who cause wars and it motivates those who put their lives at risk as humanitarians trying to reduce suffering. It is invoked in support of the human right to exploit nature and the human responsibility for stewardship. It matters in public because it matters in private and vice versa.

III

The idea of religions, as the plural tokens of a singular type, comes not from within any one religion but from their interaction. What Karl Jaspers described as the 'axial age' in which many world religions took shape – roughly from the 8th to the 3rd centuries BCE – was not just a period of great religious innovation, but of great mutual influence among religions.[8] So were the years of early Christianity and early Islam. From the point of view of each, the others were generally primitive, false, or heretical. Only rarely, if at all, were they simply others – other examples of the same larger class of phenomena, of faiths as we might say now. Islam was distinctive in granting both Judaism and Christianity special status as fellow 'religions of the book'.

From the point of view of the Roman Empire, non-Roman religions could more readily be seen in this classificatory way – as instances of a common phenomenon. And so generally empires have recognised the beliefs, rituals and sacred texts of multiple religions (with greater or lesser claim that one of these was true and right). Empires distinctively needed to be able to imagine religion as a category with plural exemplars in order to rule over peoples who were differently religious. Some modern nation states have embraced a similar pluralism.

---

8 Jaspers analysed the 'axial age' of roughly the 8th to the 3rd Centuries BCE as a period of great religious ferment and the formation of enduring faiths and philosophies from the Mediterranean through Asia. See: *Origin and Goal of History* (Oxford: Routledge, 2011).

But if this established a category of religions, it did not settle very precisely just what counted as a religion, and the entire academic field of comparative religion grew to address this question and situate each exemplar in relation to others.[9] In the 19th century, especially, the European colonial project of accounting for and managing non-Western religions was complemented by the continued history of missionary activity and the development of various forms of scholarship. European Christianity was taken as a primary and sometimes distorting exemplar (with of course its own internal divisions). Older efforts at classification informed divisions like that which divided 'religions of the book' or the 'great religious traditions' from 'folk religions'.

This effort at classification reflected the long European Christian struggle for doctrinal purity and against 'superstition'. Throughout its history, Christianity has been shaped by efforts to establish internal doctrinal conformity and boundaries against innovations, deviations, and rivals. Already a theme in the Biblical letters of Paul, this became central to the Patristic era and the great Councils by which the early Church decided core tenets of faith and questions like which texts should be included as books of the authorised Bible. Settling such questions and maintaining orthodoxy was an important reason for the growth of priestly hierarchy inside the Church. It helped to make a field of struggles for religious authority.[10] Never absent through the Middle Ages, struggle within this field was dramatically renewed in the early modern era.

Both the articulation of heterodox views and efforts to secure orthodoxy and heterodoxy were intensified. Religious imaginaries began to include a new level of codification and explicit pedagogy. Among both Protestants and Catholics this era brought high standards for personal devotion. This meant imposing standards of religious practice previously reserved for clergy and monastics on lay people. It meant developing 'high' traditions of theology, doctrine and critical inquiry. It meant centring religion around 'belief' rather than only practice – though it could include intense emotion as well. Ironically, these developments internal to religion may have helped to set the stage not just for secularism but for explicit atheism.

In addition to the doctrinal struggles between those who came to be divided as Protestants and Catholics, there was a struggle for doctrinal and devotional purity

---

9 Tomoko Masuzawa, *The Invention of World Religions* (Chicago: University of Chicago Press, 2005).

10 See Pierre Bourdieu's interesting sociological account which among other things stresses the difference of both orthodoxy and heterodoxy from a more 'doxic' attitude of unchallenged acceptance as distinct from belief amid challenge; 'Genesis and Structure of the Religious Field', in *Comparative Social Research* 13 (1991), pp. 1–43.

against residua of European folk religion – against 'doxic' or less reflexively lived religion. Some older traditions would return in new, semi-Christianised garb, like Saint Nicholas as Santa Claus. Others were repressed or marginalised. But a key point is that the imagining of what counted as religion was at stake, not only what counted as the 'true religion' of Christianity. Witches were not granted the status of practitioners of an alternative legitimate religion, not even as much as persecuted Jews.

This became part of the imaginary of the larger field of religion – and non-religion – that European Christians took into their encounters with religion, ritual, and worship in colonial settings. Imagining was informed by accounts of polytheism and monotheism, efforts to construct evolutionary hierarchies, and questions like whether religion had to involve belief in supernatural beings. For some, texts and explicitly stated beliefs were crucial; for others ritual practice or spiritual expression loomed larger. But always, imagining religion meant not only internal classification but opposition to practices deemed not to rise to the level of religion proper.[11]

IV

My intention here is not to enter the perilous waters of trying to define religion. Rather, I want to suggest the reflexive character of religious imaginations in the modern world. There was already reflexivity and mutual observation in the axial age and other earlier times, but today it is all but impossible for a religion to imagine itself entirely in and of itself, with no reference to other religions. The others may be considered legitimate, despised as enemies, or condemned as heretics. We may learn much or little about them. But to imagine one's own religion is inescapably to imagine it in relation to a field of religions.

Outside of both governments and academia, the project of identifying and recognising religions was embodied in the 1893 World Parliament of Religions and its successors. Like the United Nations, such organisations had to decide which potential members to recognise. In the case of the UN, recognition turns not just on the socio-cultural attributes of nations – language, say, collective identity, solidarity or a tradition of folk dress; it is based importantly on representation by a state. Organised representation matters in the case of religions, as well, though

---

11 Atheism was seldom the form of unbelief with which either the promoters of orthodoxy or the classifiers of religion and non-religion were concerned. Rather, they worried about animism, ancestor worship, and a host of 'quasi-religious' heterodoxies.

not all have churches, clergy, or their analogues in quite the same sense. Dealing with other religions and seeking recognition gives an incentive to formalisation or finding plausible substitutes. And the idea of 'world religions' placed a premium on being large-scale, supra-local, and/or transportable.

Note that all of this involves imagining and reimagining both the category of religion and specific religions. Religions are not simply external phenomena available to be found. They are not simply available as neutral facts. How we imagine them, individually or collectively, is always shaped by perspective, examples, and personal understandings or commitments. And it always has stakes. The way we imagine religion shapes how we value it, rely on it or fear it. It may be biased, but it is also a starting point for access to and understanding of the religions of others. Imagining religion is not something that starts over afresh every time we ask a question. There are established practices and habits and what amount to instruction manuals for imagining religion.

The instruction manuals are not just academic treatises. They include legal doctrines, like those on which the US Internal Revenue Service relies in determining what organisations and activities are religious enough to merit tax exemption.[12] They involve norms, like just what is 'too much' religion for a secular politician to bring into matters of state. Even more profoundly, guidance in imagining religion is embedded in music, art, and ritual. Choral music immediately evokes spiritual significance for some. A steeple, a stained glass window or a soaring nave may do the same in architecture. More basically, the imagining of religion may rely on the simple presence of buildings dedicated to some sort of observance or practice, be they simple, ancient mosques, multi-coloured and multi-tiered Hindu shrines, or modernist Jewish temples rendered in glass and concrete. The architecture and the sites can cross religions, as Muslims repurposed the once-Christian Hagia Sophia and Buddhists the once-Hindu Angkor Wat. The reproduction of social imaginaries makes thoughts and reality graspable – and memorable and moving – by rendering them in images.

V

Because reality comes to us partly through imagination, it is always open to creative re-imagining. No religion is thus merely a fixed inheritance, nor is any imagining of the category of religions. This is not to say that no one defends hard views

---

12 See: Deborah Podus, 'Churches, Tax-Exemption, and the Social Organization of Religion', in *Comparative Social Research* 13 (1991).

of doctrine as received and immutable truth. But contrary to what some assert, even seemingly fixed statements of doctrine take on new significance in changed contexts. Even more, the fabric connecting doctrine to action, feeling, and understanding is continually rewoven.

In short, religions are recurrently invented and reinvented. The 'great world religions' were themselves once new. As noted, they were formed amid waves of religious innovation and experimentation. Their early years involved the absorption of multiple influences. But they also engaged in the formation of doctrinal and other approaches to internal cohesion and boundary formation. They worked to make themselves.

There are innumerable 'green shoots' of new religious practices today. Some are absorbed into existing religious traditions. Some form syncretistic mixtures, as bits of the religious practices and ideas of the peoples who preceded Europeans in North America are drawn into versions of Christianity or New Age spiritualism. Some may become bases for enduring new religions. In the meantime, all are part of a spiritual supernova, in Charles Taylor's phrase.[13] Amid decline in adherence to some established religions there is an explosion of explorations and inventions of new ways of being religious. There are seekers after spiritual satisfaction who wander among religions. This may issue in new assertions of orthodoxy but it is also a process of change.

Innovation is hardly limited to the early years of a religious tradition. Judaism, for example, has both preserved commonalties and been reshaped in a variety of diasporic contexts. From the Biblical stories of exile in Babylon and Egypt forward through the celebration of Passover around the world this became a feature of Jewish self-reflection. Their faith – and certain key practices – endured in Arab empires and it became European and was renewed and reshaped in each context; it was enduringly reshaped when transplanted into North American settings.[14] And of course Judaism has been reshaped by the creation of the state of Israel and its subsequent history.

So basic was the theme of diaspora to Judaism that the very term was long treated as specific to Jews.[15] In the contemporary global context, we readily

---

13 Charles Taylor, *A Secular Age* (Cambridge, MA: Harvard University Press, 2007).
14 The ethnographic as distinct from theological dimension is nicely explored in Ewa Morawska, 'Small Town, Slow Pace: Transformations of the Religious Life in the Jewish Community of Johnstown, Pennsylvania (1920–1940)', in *Comparative Social Research* 13 (1991), pp. 127–178.
15 William Safran, 'The Jewish Diaspora in a Comparative and Theoretical Perspective', in *Israeli Studies* 10.1 (2005), pp. 36–60.

recognise a range of diasporas including Sikh, Buddhist, and Ismaili Muslim. Religious expulsions occasion some and religions identities unify each. The fusion of religion with ethnicity, in-marriage and common descent may be more or less strong.

Beyond diasporas narrowly understood, religion is a central feature of global migrations. This is not new. The Ummah was expanded through Asia by sea-faring Arab traders and trade routes became in many cases migration routes.[16] European missions and colonialism spread Christianity and relocated Europeans.

Migrants may spread religions; they may be more insular and stay minorities. Religion often gives them unity both within new contexts and across such contexts. But migration also reshapes 'host' cultures including religion. Hispanics migrating to the US have boosted the number of Catholics, predictably, but have surprised researchers more because of how many have left Catholicism for Evangelical Christianity and how they in turn are reshaping this tradition.[17] Religion itself is reimagined as it becomes trans-local and is subjected to new cultural influences.

VI

As important as the reimagining of religion are the religious ways of imagining the world and religious contributions to broader or more secular imaginations of the world. We can see the former in the missionary orientation that shaped how Westerners understood the non-Western world throughout much of moder-nity. The latter is explicit in projects like promoting peace and justice, celebrating family, or seeing God in all things and protecting nature.

In the context of globalisation, thus, different religions (or sub-religions like Catholic, Protestant and Orthodox Christians or Reform, Conservative, and Ortho-dox Jews) are not just competing interest groups. They are sources of different perspectives on the rest of the world and different motivations for action in it.

Religious imaginations shape projects that are not immediately or only reli-gious. This is evident in humanitarianism. A mission to care for all people and mitigate their suffering is a religious expression for many. People of faith are over-represented in both formal organisations that undertake humanitarian action and informal, immediate responses to disasters. The volunteers who tended to

---

16 See: Engseng Ho, *The Graves of Tarim: Genealogy and Mobility across the Indian Ocean* (Berkeley: University of California Press, 2006); Leif Manger, *The Hadrami Diaspora: Community-Building on the Indian Ocean Rim* (Oxford: Bergahn Books, 2010).
17 See: Peggy Levitt, *God Needs No Passport: How Immigrants are Changing the American Religious Landscape* (New York: The New Press, 2007).

migrants camped in the 'Jungle' of Calais in 2016 were commonly organised by churches. Those who give succour to refugees in the Middle East are often devout Muslims who see it as a duty. We recognise the religious roots of both the Red Cross and the Red Crescent.

Care may be offered primarily to co-religionists, Christians caring for other Christians, Jews seeking to save Jews, Muslims trying to help their brothers in need. But a strong theme in humanitarianism is reaching beyond this. For Christians the Parable of the Good Samaritan informs the sense of an obligation to strangers and those outside one's own group or faith. Christianity deeply informed the notion that humanity was and should be a common object of concern. Humanism took shape in Spanish Catholic debates about the souls, developmental potential, and proper treatment of the natives of the Spanish colonies in the New World.[18] Promotion of human unity remained a project for both religious and secular intellectuals through the Enlightenment into modernity. Modern humanitarian action, from joining Catholic Relief Services to making a donation to Partners in Health or Oxfam draws on this heritage.

But the idea of a clash of civilisations has at least as deep a grounding in religious imaginations. So do many of the specific clashes that create humanitarian disasters. Religious imagination can be fierce as well as pacific; it can be joined with nationalist or tribal understandings of self or 'us' against others.

The idea of civilisation itself is deeply informed by religious imagination. Indeed, from Max Weber to Samuel Huntington the most influential categorisations of different civilisations have been at least partially based on religions: Christian, Islamic, Hindu, Buddhist, and so forth. Chinese civilisation is the most important possible exception – depending on whether Confucianism is considered a religion. It offers an encompassing system of morality but is not centred on ideas of the divine (though they are not entirely absent from the Confucian tradition and still less from the rest of Chinese civilisation).

In any case, when we think of religion as central to civilisation, as distinct from personal devotion or theology, we stress the ways religious imagination informs a broader culture and understanding of the world. Crucially, this includes horizons of value, the basic evaluative commitments that put others into perspective.

Jewish and Christian religion played important roles in the development of

---

18 On the famous Valladolid debates, see Lewis Hanke, *All Mankind is One: A study of the Disputation Between Bartolomé de Las Casas and Juan Ginés de Sepúlveda in 1550 on the Intellectual and Religious Capacity of the American Indian* (Illinois: Northern Illinois University Press, 1974).

Western civilisation's emphasis on the significantly autonomous individual. Themes included the prioritisation of guilt and innocence over honour and shame that was already prominent in medieval Europe. This informed the pursuit of witches and a succession of moral panics as we developed elaborate legal systems. Reinforced by the idea of individual souls, it informed the Renaissance and early modern humanism already mentioned, and through it ideas of human rights as well as the notion of a universal duty of care informing humanitarianism.

Ideas developed in one religious and/or civilisational context can of course be adopted and adapted in others. Judeo-Christian ideas of humanity have influenced the whole world, but they also propose challenges, not least for imagining the world as a connected whole. Buddhism and Asian religions more generally have stressed the 'implicate order' that joins all life. For many non-Buddhists this has been helpful in imagining nature and other forms of life not as resources for human exploitation but as part of an interconnected order of intrinsic value.

VII

Different religious imaginations foreground different themes and foster different sensibilities. They reveal different notions of what is the higher Good against which mere material goods and pleasures may be judged. But, as Gaia and Taylor's imagery of 'fullness' suggest, there are commonalties. And there are dimensions of life to which religious imaginaries may distinctively orient us, and which we may miss without them.

Transcendence is a way of referring to many of these. Religions call on us to transcend our narrow selfishness, and to transcend a view limited to the everyday and immediate. Holidays, fasts, and feasts are all reminders of a 'higher' reality – sacred rather than profane. The ideas of Good and Evil – as distinct from mere material goods or pleasures and bads or pains – suggest something of that higher reality. It is one in which moral horizons are clearer and less utilitarian. This, in turn, is one reason why religious imaginations sometimes have the power to move people in ways far beyond what seems in ordinary terms to 'make sense'. The movement may be to self-sacrifice – in the service of causes that we may deem good or bad, Good or Evil.

Religions call on us to recognise the 'not present, not now'. They commonly emphasise a vision of the world in which the merely evident isn't everything. This is in stark contrast to the dominant 'immanent frame' of our secular, scientific civilisation, the notion that all that matters is materially present.[19] But imaginaries themselves are not materially present in quite the same sense, even if they are materially powerful. Neither are traditions that orient us in relation to a meaningful world, a sense of past and future, and ways of understanding. Religions not only reproduce such traditions, they call on adherents to 'curate' and reinterpret them, to be their stewards.

Religious imaginations may call our attention not just to the eternal, or even to attaining the Kingdom of God, but to creativity or what Hannah Arendt called 'natality'. As for Arendt, remembering great acts of politics like the founding of the United States may be at least as important as religious celebration of natality. But religious imaginations do, in varying degree, recall to us that there is always a possibility of newness in the world. This may involve creativity or art or literature or philosophy – or indeed war or cruelty. Most basically, it involves the creation of new human beings. And with this creativity comes not only the potential for things to be better in the future, but important obligations to future generations, and indeed, to the Earth.

As the example makes clear, the issue is not just science versus other ways of learning. It is a kind of reductionism that may be adopted or reinforced by some scientists but is not intrinsic to science. For science may also give us tools for seeing farther and more clearly into the past and future that would be conceivable without it. But reductionism – and presentism – are widespread features of our secular civilisation. Religious imaginations help us to be articulate about what we may lack or be missing.

It is important to recognise that secularism is not simply the absence of religion. It is itself a way of imagining the world and thereby shaping it.[20] One feature of the secular imaginary, in fact, is what Taylor has called the 'subtraction story'.[21] This presents contemporary secularism as simply the removal of religion – myth, superstition – while the rest of thought and reality are unchanged. But this is radically misleading, treating ideas as far more separate and less

---

19 The phrase is Taylor's, from chapter 10 of *Secular Age*.
20 Old usage in the Catholic Church distinguished secular priests – those who ministered in the world – from members of religious orders who tried to sustain a purer life separate from it. On the complexities of considering secularism as a phenomenon in itself, not just the absence of religion, see C Calhoun, M Juergensmeyer, and J VanAntwerpen, eds., *Rethinking Secularism* (Oxford: Oxford University Press, 2011); C Taylor, *A Secular Age* (Cambridge, MA: Harvard University Press, 2007); and M Warner, J VanAntwerpen, and C Calhoun, eds., *Secularism in A Secular Age* (Cambridge, MA: Harvard University Press, 2010).
21 Taylor, *Secular Age*.

interconnected than they are. Removing (or attempting to remove) religion from politics, economics, education, healthcare and other social institutions is also transformative.

In the past, religious imaginations were sometimes hindrances compared with the secular understandings that followed. The point is not that religious thought is always better. It is, rather, that secularisation involves transformation not subtraction, change of perspective not simply truth. There may be improvements of understanding, or knowledge or practice – just as there can be when religious engagements with a changing world produce transformations in religion. But shifts in perspective commonly bring new obscurities as well as new revelations.

Secularisation as subtraction informs the approach to neutrality that has led many to try to banish religion from the public sphere. It is one thing to say that public decisions should not be made on the basis of religious partisanship and quite another to say that religiously informed arguments should not be admissible.[22] Attempts in the tradition of French *laïcité* to banish all religious symbolism from public places go still further down the path of subtraction. But still, the secular or *laïc* is part of its own imaginary, not simply the removal of superstition to reveal unvarnished truth.

As has been observed, all secularisms involve their own imaginative representation of religion. The secularisms of India, Senegal, France, and the US are accordingly somewhat different because they face different configurations of religion as well as other differences in public institutions.[23] More generally, secular imaginaries present faith as merely one option among many, and often as one particularly beyond the reach of logic and evidence. They commonly emphasise instrumentality over meaning. Resisting religious imaginations of the interconnection of everything, they often overstate separateness of what to other ways of thinking are parts of larger wholes. Individuals and their autonomous interests may be privileged in relation to community (though actually existing community is at least as much a secular as a religious phenomenon). The very notion of an individual may be asocial, neglecting for example how much each of us can exist – and think – only on the basis of what we share, like language.

---

22 See the considerations in Eduardo Mendieta and Jonathan VanAntwerpen, *The Power of Religion in the Public Sphere* (New York: Columbia University Press, 2011).

23 This was a theme emphasised importantly by the late Alfred Stepan. See among many, 'The multiple secularisms of modern democracies and autocracies', in C Calhoun, M Juergensmeyer, and J VanAntwerpen, eds., *Rethinking Secularism* (Oxford: Oxford University Press, 2011).

VIII

In short, religious imaginations can speak to contemporary secular predicaments, to political upheavals, global transformations, and the challenges of new technologies. But how they do this is not a settled matter of sacred texts, doctrinal elaborations, or inherited perspectives. Traditions will change as they are renewed. Religions will be reimagined.

The common condition is a combination of connections and plurality – both among religions and among forms of unbelief. We influence each other but we do not become the same or feel as one. Themes like community, or peace, or the value of life are not unique to religion, but religious imaginations are important sources and reminders.

Where religion matters less, we need to ask how ideas or institutions have been reconfigured and what has filled gaps – or not. Religious vocabulary and imagination have often lost their purchase without fully being replaced. Speaking of salvation, sin, soul, and redemption has never become entirely secularised. Even where the words are used more secularly the religious roots are close at hand. This is why secular thinkers like Jürgen Habermas point to the capacities for renewal of radical vision and motivation offered by religious vocabularies.[24]

Religious imaginaries are commonly expressed in stories, narratives, images, and evocations of characters. Michael Walzer has called attention to the way the story of Exodus has informed not only Jewish and Christian traditions but also secular imaginations, even of revolution.[25] The story of Job evokes struggles between doubt and faith. And in other traditions the *Bhagavad Gita* and Muhammad's Night Journey are powerful bearers of religious imagination. Narrative is hardly the unique property of religion, and indeed these instances illustrate the power of imaginative literature as well as the power of specifically religious imaginations. But in each case, they point to ways in which religious imaginations exercise an influence that cannot be reduced to propositional logic, a set of truth-statements somehow alternative to those of science.

The strength of religious imaginations is not in any sense an alternative to science. It lies in support for efforts to establish higher values, moral orientations, and understandings of what the world means – as distinct from how it works

---

24 Jürgen Habermas, *Between naturalism and religion. Philosophical essays*, transl. C Cronin (Cambridge: Polity Press, 2010); and see Habermas's *Philosophical Introductions: Five Approaches to Communicative Reason* (New Jersey: Wiley, 2018). Also, C Calhoun, E Mendieta, and J VanAntwerpen, eds., *Habermas and Religion* (Cambridge: Polity, 2013).
25 Michael Walzer, *Exodus and Revolution* (New York: Basic Books, 1995).

technically. Such understandings can be the products of creativity as much as tradition. And they can speak to the deep challenges of the contemporary era.

To start with, we live in an era where intensified globalisation is met with renewed assertions of national belonging and resistance. This is partly due to demagogues who fan flames of fear and resentment. It is partly due to the extent to which national and international politics and global institutions have all failed to manage an unbridled pursuit of wealth. This has brought not only inequality but degradation of nature and upheavals in social and cultural life. Wealthy and powerful corporations keep expanding markets and technological systems that seem at once as irresistible and as precarious as forces of nature.

Clashing religious projects and identities are sources of division. But religious imaginations can be counterbalancing sources of connection and unity. This need not take the form of merger and overcoming difference. Rather, it can be a matter of developing the orientations and understandings needed for communication and collaboration across lines of difference.

The same is often true with regard to nationalism. Religion can be an exacerbator of anxieties about global threats to national identity. But it can also be a resource for imagining ways to relate to people in different settings, with different identities. The 'great world religions' all encompass multiple nationalities and far-reaching diasporas. They have an interest in peaceful co-existence, though it remains a question whether religious actors will choose that over more conflictual projects. Both globally and in specific national settings, religious imaginations are potential resources for developing mutual understanding and ways of working and living together.

Technology is not only part of the story of a globalisation that currently fuels pessimism more than optimism. New technologies are themselves sources of upheaval. Jobs will likely be lost in large numbers and not replaced with alternatives as desirable. Communities are undermined. For many, a basic sense of belonging is challenging. Existential insecurity is real.

The challenges of new technology are not only economic or matters of risk from hacking and systemic failures. They include basic questions of value, understanding, and social solidarity. Will machines in some sense be 'like' people, sensate creatures that should be seen as a source of value in themselves? Or, does artificial intelligence mean that human beings will become irrelevant? Will 'superintelligence' mean machines dispensing with people?[26] The world of AI is

---

26 Nick Bostrom, *Superintelligence: Paths, dangers, Strategies* (Oxford: Oxford University Press, 2014).

full of breathless predictions and hype, but this doesn't mean that the issues are not momentous.

Religious imaginations will be called on to integrate these new realities into religious understanding and teaching. They will also be resources for more secular, or cross-religious, efforts to make sense of new possibilities and ethical conundrums. For example, debates over the nature of the soul long provided occasions for thinking about what is crucially valuable about human beings and why all human beings have a spark of the divine or are created in God's image. Will they be renewed to try to understand the possibility of sentient machines or artificially designed babies? Or can religious or secular imaginations provide other, better frameworks for considering these questions? At present, we are troublingly inarticulate.

Has the advancement of technology made human beings like gods, as Yuval Noah Harari asserts?[27] And if so which human beings, backed up by what structures of power and authority? Will we be content to say, as Harari does, that most of humanity will simply be redundant in the new era of artificial intelligence and technologically enhanced life? Or, will we perhaps discern reasons still to value humanity as such? Will we, perhaps, still commit ourselves to the idea of God, an uncreated Creator, as the horizon of value?

These questions bear not just on the standing of human beings as somehow 'higher' than animals or 'different' from machines. They matter for whether we will continue to accept statements like 'all human beings are created equal' or 'one person, one vote'. They will inform understandings of human rights, citizenship, justice, and economic entitlement and inequality. They will affect the ways we form relations of solidarity with others, forge communities, establish collegial relations at work.

To some extent globalisation already poses similar questions about how we should relate to those different from ourselves. Some people and some countries have been exemplary at certain times. But it is not clear that we are passing the test with flying colours. We have a hard time achieving an 'I/Thou' relationship with other people, as Martin Buber urged, suggesting all human relationships are also relations with God.[28] We are apt to treat others instrumentally, as objects for our own projects, not ends in themselves (to switch to a Kantian way of speaking). And if we achieve the I/thou in directly interpersonal bonds and communication, we have a hard time extending it to larger scales. Especially when we categorise

---

27 Yuval Noah Harari, *Homo Deus* (New York: Harper Collins, 2017).
28 Martin Buber, *I and Thou* (New York: Scribner's, 1937).

others as different, when we learn of their existence only through the media, or when we think of them in terms of statistics from crime rates to market demand to migration numbers we are apt to adopt the attitude Buber described as 'I/it'.

Not least of all, in any catalogue of global challenges, humanity faces the risk that processes it has helped initiate but failed to control will annihilate us all and perhaps even life itself. If so, we have become as gods only to preside over suicidal destruction.

Whether we understand it through the quasi-religious imagery of Gaia or in some other way, we face potentially apocalyptic transformation of Earth's climate and degradation of nature. At the very least, we must live under a new climate regime, with more heat waves, more floods, more fires. Whether it will also bring more famines and massive forced migration remains to be seen.

So far, human beings and different cultures have not succeeded very well in imagining the scale of the crisis of climate change. Religious imaginations have been engaged, a little, but have so far not contributed enough. We might expect more from religious imaginations, for what is involved is at the epic scale.[29] Beginnings are being made in better imagining what it means to endanger the Earth and imperil life.[30] Beginnings are being made at articulating the moral demands this places on humanity and on individual nations and persons. Beginnings are being made at building the better relations necessary for more effective action. But beginnings only, and against a tremendous weight of inertia in global capitalism and national projects of economic growth. And against the deterioration of global institutions and transnational structures of cooperation.

In summary, we face fundamental challenges of globalisation, technological transformation, and potentially the most momentous upheaval of all with climate change. If this is not to be the age in which humanity ends, we are likely to see renewal of both religious and non-religious imaginations – and material projects. These will attempt not merely to help us cope but to guide us through a future that is at once hard to discern and yet in considerable degree ours to choose. But

---

29 Indeed, both the temporal and the geographic scale of climate change are impediments to literary imagination as well as religious. So far there is no climate change epic. On the difficulty of rendering this drama without protagonists, see: Amitav Ghosh, *The Great Derangement: Climate Change and the Unthinkable* (Chicago: University of Chicago Press, 2016).

30 *Laudato si'*, Pope Francis's 2015 encyclical on climate change and 'care for our common home' is one such forward step, itself based on the work of numerous scientists and theologians.

we will of course choose our future through a scale of interdependent action that none of us can control.

We see renewal of religious efforts to grasp our predicament but not yet a renewal of religious imaginations adequate to address it. We see strengthening of religious and religio-nationalist identities. Seeking stability amid upheaval, these are too often coupled with rigid appropriations of tradition. We see, too often, the deployment of religious imagination in ways that block us from meeting the challenges before us.

But we do also see imagination transformed by recognition of other civilisations and traditions, both religious and secular, and seeking bases for better cooperation and mutual engagement. We see secular imaginations shaped by engagement with religion. And we must hope for more. Imagination is crucial because we have no choice but to try to remake the world, not just find rules for navigating within the world as it exists.

Bibliography

Anderson, Benedict, *Imagined Communities* (London: Verso, 2006).

Augustine of Hippo, *The City of God against the Pagans* (Cambridge: Cambridge University Press, 1998).

Bostrom, Nick, *Superintelligence: Paths, dangers, Strategies* (Oxford: Oxford University Press, 2014).

Bourdieu, Pierre, 'Genesis and Structure of the Religious Field', in *Comparative Social Research* 13 (1991), pp. 1–43.

Buber, Martin, *I and Thou* (New York: Scribner's, 1937).

Calhoun, C, 'The Importance of Imagined Communities – and Benedict Anderson,' in *Debats* 130.1 (2016), pp. 11–16.

Calhoun, C, Gaonkar, D, Lee, B, Taylor, C, and M Warner, eds., 'Modern Social Imaginaries Revisited: A Conversation', in *Social Imaginaries* 1.1 (2015).

Calhoun, C, Juergensmeyer, M and J VanAntwerpen, eds., *Rethinking Secularism* (Oxford: Oxford University Press, 2011)

Calhoun, C, Mendieta, E and J VanAntwerpen, eds., *Habermas and Religion* (Cambridge: Polity, 2013).

Davison Hunter, James, *To Change the World: The Irony, Tragedy, and Possibility of Christianity in the Late Modern World* (Oxford: Oxford University Press, 2010).

Gaonkar, D and B Lee, eds., *New Social Imaginaries*, special issue of *Public Culture* (Durham, NC: Duke University Press, 2002).

Ghosh, Amitav, *The Great Derangement: Climate Change and the Unthinkable* (Chicago: University of Chicago Press, 2016).

Habermas, Jürgen, *Between naturalism and religion. Philosophical essays*, transl. C Cronin (Cambridge: Polity Press, 2010).

Habermas, Jürgen, *Philosophical Introductions: Five Approaches to Communicative Reason* (New Jersey: Wiley, 2018).

Habermas, Jürgen, *Theory of Communicative Action* (Boston: Beacon, 1984).

Hanke, Lewis, *All Mankind is One: A study of the Disputation Between Bartolomé de Las Casas and Juan Ginés de Sepúlveda in 1550 on the Intellectual and Religious Capacity of the American Indian* (Illinois: Northern Illinois University Press, 1974).

Harari, Yuval Noah, *Homo Deus* (New York: Harper Collins, 2017).

Ho, Engseng, *The Graves of Tarim: Genealogy and Mobility across the Indian Ocean* (Berkeley: University of California Press, 2006).

Jaspers, Karl, *Origin and Goal of History* (Oxford: Routledge, 2011).

Levitt, Peggy, *God Needs No Passport: How Immigrants are Changing the American Religious Landscape* (New York: The New Press, 2007).

Manger, Leif, *The Hadrami Diaspora: Community-Building on the Indian Ocean Rim* (Oxford: Bergahn Books, 2010).

Masuzawa, Tomoko, *The Invention of World Religions* (Chicago: University of Chicago Press, 2005).

Mendieta, Eduardo and Jonathan VanAntwerpen, *The Power of Religion in the Public Sphere* (New York: Columbia University Press, 2011).

Morawska, Ewa, 'Small Town, Slow Pace: Transformations of the Religious Life in the Jewish Community of Johnstown, Pennsylvania (1920–1940)', in *Comparative Social Research* 13 (1991), pp. 127–178.

Podus, Deborah, 'Churches, Tax-Exemption, and the Social Organization of Religion', in *Comparative Social Research* 13 (1991).

Safran, William, 'The Jewish Diaspora in a Comparative and Theoretical Perspective', in *Israeli Studies* 10.1 (2005), pp. 36–60.

Taylor, Charles, *New Social Imaginaries* (Durham, NC: Duke University Press, 2003).

Taylor, Charles, *A Secular Age* (Cambridge, MA: Harvard University Press, 2009).

Walzer, Michael, *Exodus and Revolution* (New York: Basic Books, 1995).

Warner, M, VanAntwerpen, J, and C Calhoun, eds., *Secularism in A Secular Age* (Cambridge, MA: Harvard University Press, 2010).

Weber, Max, *Economy and Society* (Berkeley: University of California Press, 1968).

2

Imagination and the Ethics of Religious Narratives

Mona Siddiqui

'A map of the world that does not include Utopia is not even worth glancing at, for it leaves out the one country at which Humanity is always landing. And when Humanity lands there, it looks out, and, seeing a better country, sets sail. Progress is the realisation of Utopias.'

Oscar Wilde, 1854–1900

It is said that utopias exist in our imagination as better futures. Human beings become who they are and develop their view of the world through the interplay of will, imagination and reason. The vast literature on imagination shows that the word often provokes conflicting or contradictory assumptions and traditions within the philosophy of mind, aesthetics, psychology, literature, theology. Furthermore, human will and imagination have often been closely associated. According to Claes G Ryn's theory of imagination, our will is 'the generic, categorical name for that infinity and variety of impulse that orients the individual to particular tasks'. Our will informs our character and behaviour, but the direction which our will takes is informed by imagination. It is the imagination which both shapes and is shaped by will/desire.[1] It is most fundamentally through imagination

---

1 Claes G Ryn, *Will, Imagination and Reason: Irving Babbitt and the Problem of Reality* (New Brunswick, NJ: Transaction Publishers, 1997), p. 147. See, Joshua James Bowman, *Arcadian Exile: The Imaginative Tension in Henry David Thoreau's Political Thought*, PhD Thesis (2016), pp. 27–28.

that an individual or group of people hold an intuitive sense of what is real, right, wrong, good, true and beautiful. In the end, it is our imagination which gives us the sense of possibilities.

The Islamic story of Adam and Eve, in which Adam's transgression means his destiny on earth is fully sealed, has been interpreted as a story of disobedience but also of human desire to know and to give into the imaginative impulse. Banished from paradise Adam must now experience distance from God in order to understand what nearness means, and while this might lie at the root of human struggle, it is also a route to human development. In fact, some Muslim thinkers saw a positive ray in the first human act of disobedience. The Indian philosopher poet Muhammad Iqbal saw the creation of man as the creation of a being who, driven by desire and passion, would tear away all veils:

> Desire, resting in the lap of life
> And forgetful of itself,
> Opened its eyes, and a new world was born.
> Life said, 'Through all my years
> I lay in the dust and convulsed
> Until at last a door appeared
> In this ancient dome.'[2]

For Iqbal, Adam's transgression was not a loss and 'not an act of moral depravity', but 'man's transition from simple consciousness to the first flash of self-consciousness, a kind of waking from the dream of nature'.[3]

For many philosophers and political theorists, imagination and hope for a better world inspire and drive many not only to search for happiness in the present but to enterprise for change in the future. Imagination is about seeing and understanding the world and this is inherently a moral activity. It is through observation that we become aware of human freedom to think and act, of our relational existence, of a moral impulse to make things better. Without effort and change, things do not improve and as Bertrand Russell wrote, 'It is not a finished Utopia that we ought to desire, but a world where imagination and hope are alive and active.'[4]

The power of the imagination lies in its potential to persuade and provoke.

---

2 Muhammad Iqbal, *Tulip in the Desert, A Selection of Poetry*, transl. Mustansir Mir (London: Hurst & Company Publishers, 2000), p. 26.
3 Muhammad Iqbal, *The Reconstruction of Religious Thought in Islam* (Lahore: Ashraf Press, 1934), p. 85.
4 Bertrand Russell, *Political Ideals* (New York: The Century Co., 1917), p. 23.

Herein lies its ambivalence so that there is arguably both good imagination and bad imagination, and it matters what we commit ourselves to imagining. It is not simply about the means but also the ends, not just about making things happen but what is worth pursuing to begin with. Thus, imagination is bound up with ethical consciousness.

For those with a religious faith, religion can hold several competing claims on our lives. For some it is truth, history and fact told in multiple narratives, through multiple voices. Religion is God and goodness, poetry and prophecy told and retold in worship, stories and artistic renditions over the centuries. For others, despite the imaginative impulse behind all religion, religious faith has been confined largely to doctrines and dogmas, rituals and practices many of which struggle to remain meaningful in peoples' lives today. Yet in our increasingly pluralist societies, faith in God should be a vessel for a shared imagination. This requires thinking beyond our personal struggle of achieving a good and happy life, thinking beyond our personal salvation. Rather it should be seen as a collective struggle where we retain a reverence for the desires and truths of others alongside our own hopes. Thus, the transcendent and the human social are intertwined. Yet to some extent it seems that imagination has lost its place in our daily life – we have lost the art of thinking, speaking and doing imaginatively in our political and moral discourse. Imagination should be central to the very ethic which allows us to think of different worlds, different justices, different kinds of knowledge.

A central question for scholars of religion is how we should restore to the humanities and the social sciences a sense of transcendent moral purpose. Why should any artistic quest or interest, including writing, be about transformation of the self and society? For most, any pursuit of the arts, especially literature, engages our inner life, the inner life where most of us live our lives. All narrative is a kind of storytelling, what we choose to think about and the spaces which we create to invite others in. Literature, like most arts, elevates society above its purely practical needs. It gives value to human existence, it ponders on the desires and restlessness which make us fully human. Literature, like so many art forms, throws light on the emotions we cannot explain or understand, the metaphors of our existence, which add colour and life to our everyday flat world language of numbers, efficiency and performance.

James Smith describes this as the 'ultimate love' of that which we pledge allegiance to, that which we worship, and states that, 'it's not what I think that shapes my life from the bottom up; it is what I desire, what I love, that animates my passion.' For human beings, things matter because in ways that we cannot often articulate:

There is a sort of drive that pushes (or pulls) us to act in certain ways, develop certain relationships, pursue certain goods, make certain sacrifices, enjoy certain things. And at the end of the day, if asked why we do this, ultimately we run up against the limits of articulation even though we 'know' why we do it: it's because of what we love.[5]

For Smith, the *telos* to which our love is aimed is not a 'list of ideas and propositions or doctrines, disembodied concepts of values'. Rather, it is an imagined and aesthetic picture communicated through stories and plays, novels and films. It is our imagination that is captivated by what forms the good life, the life of human flourishing, and it is our teleological love which orients us to particular ways of envisioning the good life.[6] It is argued that an appeal to the imagination also supports tolerance, because an imaginative claim is less confrontational than an analytical claim. When a religion presents its claims in a narrative (poetic) and visual (aesthetic) form, it leaves the audience more room for interpretation and greater freedom to absorb the information at its own pace. Appeals to the imagination come across as less imposing and therefore engender a more tolerant environment.[7]

And all narrative, the written and the spoken word shapes our attitude to one another; thus we cannot escape the moral and intellectual impulse behind so much of what we say or do. This commitment to expression should not be thought of in the simplistic and binary terms of the religious and the secular, as these categories make for false distinctions when we reflect on civilisational progress. The English historian Arnold Toynbee believed that civilisations are always confronted with challenges and that societies either flourish or flounder and ultimately fall, based on whether a creative minority crafts the right responses to those challenges. Many Muslim scholars decry the gradual decline of philosophy and metaphysics in the Islamic world both of which ask how is it that we perceive the world. They argue that Muslims no longer do abstraction, rather reduce all faith to conformity and conviction. Ethics is impoverished when metaphysics is ignored.

Yet, for many, religious faith rings hollow and disenchantment permeates peoples' lives. In the 1970s, Christopher Lasch spoke of our changing sensibilities and argued that in the 1960s 'radical politics filled empty lives, provided a sense of meaning and purpose'. But today, he states:

---

5 James K A Smith, *Desiring the Kingdom* (Grand Rapids, Michigan: Baker Academic, 2009), pp. 51–52.
6 Smith, *Desiring*, p. 53.
7 Andrew V Abela, 'Appealing to the Imagination: Effective and Ethical Marketing of Religion', in *Journal of Business Research* 67.2 (2014), p. 54.

The contemporary climate is therapeutic, not religious. People today hunger
not for personal salvation, let alone for the restoration of an earlier golden age,
but for the feeling, the momentary illusion, of personal wellbeing, health, and
psychic security.[8]

It seems that as a society we struggle to talk of spiritual matters of our internal
world, even as we realise that the material life, the life of the here and now, is never
completely fulfilling. The truth is that our real learning takes place when we are
confronted and challenged by the stuff that is not material, that is not about goals
and targets, that cannot be measured, packaged or commodified, that is unsettling,
and this is what really gives shape and discernment to our lives as individuals and
to the moral judgements we make as a society. In our metaphysical age philosophy
no longer pretends to have answers to questions regarding the personal, or even the
collective, conduct of life. Philosophy, especially in its classical form, was focused
on teaching the good life, the just society, but today the role of philosophers is dis-
puted. Theodore Adorno lamented in his famous *Minima Moralia* that contemporary philosophers were too occupied with the minutiae of method and that in place
of robust doctrines about the good life, philosophy has become the melancholy
science allowing at best only scattered aphoristic reflections from damaged life.[9]

And yet while philosophical thinking on what makes for the good life for
human flourishing and for good human relations are still appealing, Ryn writes
that appeals to the imagination is an ethic in itself; such appeals are poetic, they
convey information intuitively rather than analytically. Poetic information adds
to the general intuitive grasp of life that human beings hold: human beings did
not have to wait for philosophers to know something substantial about their own
existence. They always had an immediate intuition of the nature of the whole, an
awareness to which story-tellers, poets, and other artists contributed. Thus our
moral visions for life are most compelling when they say something about how
all of us relate to one another in the here and now. The subtext for moral sources
cannot always be theism when we live in an increasingly secular society. But
imagination at its best brings all aspects of life, desires, faith character into an
intricate whole, showing us the strength and complexity of human interconnec-
tedness. For educationalists like the American Irving Babbit, the true purpose of

---

8 Christopher Lasch, *The Culture of Narcissism* (New York: W. W. Norton & Inc, 1991),
p. 7.
9 Robert Louden, 'Meaningful but Immoral Lives', in Beatrix Himmelman, ed., *On meaning
in Life* (Berlin: Walter de Gruyter, Inc., 2013), p. 23.

education was to assimilate the wisdom of the ages through the right use of the human imagination. Art was essential to creating community:

> What creates community – what advances civilization and the happiness of the human person – is that which takes the individual away from his impulsive, natural, self-conceit and offers a larger reality revealed through the lessons of the ages. These lessons, exemplified in great works of literature and history, communicate the larger world and stimulate the moral imagination of the student with reference to a shared, humane center.[10]

Whenever we write, we are saying something about our world, so the question is with what eyes should we see the world? In his 2010 book, *The Christian Imagination*, Yale theologian Willie Jennings pays tribute in his acknowledgment to his parents who, he writes, 'taught me to see the world with Christian eyes'. As a writer, I contend that all vision is not about seeing the world but a certain way of reflecting on the world which uses story, metaphor, thought and action. 'The concepts that govern our thoughts are not just matters of the intellect,' write George Lakoff and Mark Johnson. 'They also govern our everyday functioning. Our concepts structure what we perceive, how we get around in the world, and how we relate to other people.'[11]

Stories have great significance to human life because people create stories to understand the world around them and, as many cultural theorists have concluded, human thought has the structural form of a narrative. For Jennings, who writes as a black theologian and who lives in and outside a particular story, 'Christianity in the western world lives and moves within a diseased social imagination'. He sees the history of Christian theological imagination as woven into 'processes of colonial dominance'. In this respect, he writes:

> Indeed it is as though Christianity, wherever it went in the modern colonies, inverted its sense of hospitality. It claimed to be the host, the owner of the spaces it entered, and demanded native peoples enter its cultural logics, its way of being in the world and its conceptualities.[12]

---

10 Glenn Davis, *Moral Imagination and Progressive Education*, available at: http://www. theimaginativeconservative.org/2010/08/irving-babbitt-moral-imagination-and.html.
11 George Lakoff and Mark Johnson, *Metaphors We Live By* (Chicago: The University of Chicago Press, 1980), p. 3.
12 Willie James Jennings, *The Christian Imagination* (New Haven: Yale University Press, 2010), p. 8.

The underlying question for Jennings is why Christianity, which claims to be a religion based on brotherly love, has failed to heal all kinds of social and racial divisions, in fact it came to be defined with these very divisions; the social imaginary of which he speaks is the lived realities of peoples' lives. If we then go to the Islamic world, we can see a similar issue, that Muslims who continually defend Islam as a religion of peace, have to contend with the historical conflicts and current wars, both political and sectarian, which continue to plague large parts of the Muslim world. The defence that this is not the real Islam, much like the Christianity which propped up racial division etc. is not the real Christianity, wears thin when we see that neither narrative is reflected in the complex religiosity of both communities of people. The postcolonial lens makes for a complex understanding of histories, and while it is morally wrong to essentialise religions and civilisations, it is important to work with a few realities and perspectives which continue to challenge us about the narratives we read, believe and then pass down. This is all against a particular angst of the modern age where postmodernism itself is based on the internal distrust of meta-narratives of society and knowledge.

Our discourse around religion takes place largely through a Eurocentric prism. It is not only a postcolonial world, it is a world where for some history seems to be irrelevant. We live in a new world of speed and progress where history neither needs to be remembered nor honoured. In his thoughtful epilogue to *Lost History*, Michael Morgan contemplates the 'what ifs' of history as follows:

> History might have taken another course. At that moment of rare equipoise between China, India and the Muslim world, and Europe in the late 15th and 16th centuries, any one of Europe's rivals could have made the same fateful decisions that Spain, Portugal and England undertook to support voyages of exploration and conquest. The Chinese could have easily sailed the Pacific and the Ottoman Turks might have controlled the Atlantic.

But the Muslims did not lead the Age of Discovery and Imperialism; the Christian Europeans undertook this chapter in history. And so, the past continues to divide the present. As Morgan says, many others are not seduced by the power of the present, the 'past for them remains a source of anger, resentment, vendetta. They will not rest until they correct the real or imagined crimes of the past'.[13]

Religion and politics have never been separate throughout history. But the rise

---

13 Michael Morgan, *Lost History* (Washington DC: National Geographic Society, 2008), pp. 289–290.

of the secular public space in much of western Europe means that religion has lost its public hold. In much of western Europe, in industrialised states, institutional religion has declined as a singular cohesive force, a force which traditionally gave meaning and stability to communities. Religion may still have its connective and collective attraction, binding people together, but society is now one in which 'faith, even for the staunchest believer, is one possibility among others', as Charles Taylor states.[14] Despite the decline of institutional religion, religious discourse in the public sphere has been reawakened.

Our conversations are often not so much about religion itself but about the possible reach of religion and how to protect the perceived secular space. Here religious faith often appears as a problem to be resolved through discussions on pluralism or diversity, or a problem exacerbated by superficial and often stereotypical analysis of the unreasonable demands of religious people. Religions are frequently presented as monoliths, faith in God often stripped of meaning and fulfilment but seen rather as a perpetual, social and political source of angst. That religion is a central feature of human life, giving shape and meaning to our existence is often lost in the frequent media attention given to contesting whether religion is a force for good or bad in the modern world. Here, religious faith, especially theistic faith, is often seen as something which directs us to an intolerant past, whereas secularism and liberalism grounds us in individual freedom and orients us towards a hopeful future. Politics and religion are seen as separate spheres. The debate has a simple premise which is that a gradual secularisation of most of the western world has been realised through a conscious and enlightened distance between church and state, especially after the bloody religious wars of early modern Europe, leading eventually to healthy, liberal democracies. The separation of church and state is not however the same as the separation of religion and politics which led many, like Mark Lilla, to reflect on the continuing appeal of religion and its excesses:

> We are disturbed and confused. We find it incomprehensible that theological
> ideas still inflame the minds of men, stirring up messianic passions that leave
> societies in ruin. We assumed that this was no longer possible, that human
> beings had learned to separate religious questions from political ones, that
> fanaticism was dead. We were wrong.[15]

---

14 Charles Taylor, *A Secular Age* (Cambridge, MA: Belknap Press, 2007).
15 Mark Lilla, *The Stillborn God: Religion, Politics and the Modern West* (New York: Knopf, 2003), p. 3.

In recent years the new atheism debates accuse religion as a failed science. For the new atheists, all major religions are bad but Islam is seen by some as uniquely dangerous to civilisation, or as Sam Harris says in *The End of Faith*, 'Islam has makings of the cult of death.' Their perspectives are made bold by statistics and surveys which show that many religious communities encourage fundamentalist theologies, readings of scripture which are often intolerant of other views, and thus promote a narrow ethics and a narrow vision of human coexistence and flourishing.

Public discourse on religions maintains a cautious approach to the power of theological language which in the age of the internet and globalisation can travel thousands of miles in seconds, so that what happens in the caves of Yemen, the neighbourhoods of Mosul, the trendy malls of Dubai, and the streets of Cairo have consequences on the roads and boulevards of London, Paris and Berlin. Events can bring people together or tear communities apart. Nowhere has this been more vocal in recent times than in the current focus on militant jihadism or Islamism, a vocabulary constructed to qualify sporadic yet sustained acts of violence, executed by Muslims who try to create new religious narratives through destroying that most fundamental of human virtues: empathy. Whenever a killing or a plot has been identified as terrorism, social media reflects the societal divisions which threaten decades of coexistence, from 'love not hate' slogans to appeals to internment and deportation. Time and space collapse as the distance between cultures, languages and ideologies is bridged through the power of technology. This process of technological globalisation has immediate local impact in multicultural societies, so much so that how we understand the world may be influenced by how we understand our neighbour.

For Chiara Bottici, this resurrection of the public role of religion has been the result of the reduction of politics and imagination:

> The current resurrection of religion in the public sphere is linked to a deep
> transformation of political imagination which has its roots in the double
> process of the reduction of politics to mere administration, on the one hand,
> and to spectacle, on the other. In an epoch when politics is said to be simply
> a question of 'good governance', of good administration within a neo-liberal
> consensus, the paradox is that of a lack of political imagination which goes
> hand in hand with its hypertrophy through the media.[16]

16 Chiara Bottici, 'The Politics of Imagination and the Public Role of Religion', in *Philosophy and Social Criticism* 35.8 (2009), p. 985.

For many people, the individualisation of religion, not as a transcendental experience but as value-laden normative ethics, has become the most important phenomenon of religion today. Other than a few works, classical Islam did not have systematic treatises on ethics as the subject was subsumed under law and worship. The juridical literature also gives us some insight as to the dilemmas of whether Muslims could actively participate in non-Islamic societies, but these premodern texts are not conclusive by any means. More importantly they do not contain within themselves the appropriate equivalents of words like liberalism, human rights, or democratic pluralism, the global vocabulary of the modern age. Fundamentalism has been added to the public and academic lexicon at a time when the global (dis)order with its cosmopolitanisms, relativisms, pluralisms and movement of people and ideas across the world has contributed to an excessive concern with identity, authenticity and ultimate values – the fundamentals of existence. These conditions precipitate a renewed quest for understanding what it means to live and believe. One of the effects of globalisation is that in most Muslim societies, globalisation has led to the erosion of traditional methods of knowledge production and dissemination. Mass communication and literacy have led to diverse ways of democratising knowledge even though the decentrality of knowledge has always been part of the Islamic world. Now, discussion forums involve imams, muftis and various lay and trained scholars who all become part of the public voice of Islam, all vying for the same authority. They will all claim that they do not begin with politics, they begin with ontology.

On the one hand, the dialectic of Islam and modernity seems insurmountable, as it is so pervasive throughout Muslim majority states and the West, who in different ways posit both as irreconcilable entities. However, a broader definition of modernity could simply denote adaptation and change, which occurs at all times and in all places.[17] Thus there are multifarious, organic versions of modernity, rather than a linear progression made by one group. Islam is also a term which can be negotiated. It can be conceived broadly as an effort to instigate a 'moral community' which looks to an ethical ideal in the Qur'an, with a recognition that God ultimately knows best. The late Muhammad Arkoun wished to create broader, more inclusive definitions which reconcile the two.

For Arkoun, the 'West' as a singular entity proposes one way of running the market, science and politics. It is 'devoted to secular, rational, universalist ideals'. Islamic countries were forcibly inundated with these ideals in the nineteenth and twentieth centuries. This led many of the elites in these countries to consider the

17 Michel Hoebink, *Thinking about Renewal in Islam* (Leiden: Brill, 1999), p. 29.

West as the central beacon of civilisation, whilst their own societies were deemed backward and irrelevant on the world stage. Arkoun grapples with these complex issues, rejecting Muslim apologists on the ground that 'tyranny of faith' was as toxic as 'tyranny of reason'.

Arkoun maintained that liberalism does not have to be cleaved from religion to be acceptable. Muslim scholars, he argued, need to 'initiate a process of new thinking on Islam with tools such as history of thought rather than political events or fixed parameters; to make unthinkable notions – a historical rather than a religious postulate – thinkable; and to relate secularism, religion, and culture to contemporary challenges rather than substituting one for the other'. Thoughts have their own life force and no dominating ideology can encapsulate the richness of Islam. In other words, what is needed is the freedom to think the unthought. For Arkoun, Islam as a revelation is only one attempt to emancipate human beings from the natural limitations of their biological, historical and linguistic condition. In his critique of the varying polemics recently directed against Orientalism, Arkoun argued that what intellectual Islam needs today is a new epistemological perspective for the comparative study of cultures. It needs a new dynamism and however limited the influence of thinkers, writers, artists, scholars and economic producers might be in injecting new dynamism into Islamic thought where traditions have a long and deeply rooted history, this enterprise is necessary. Intellectuals must be committed to this project. 'Some, at least, could survive and break through the wall of uncontrolled beliefs and dominating ideologies.'[18] The project of thinking Islam is basically a response to two major needs: 1) the particular need of Muslim societies to think, for the first time, about their own problems, made unthinkable by the triumph of orthodox scholastic thought; and 2) the need of contemporary thought in general to open new fields and discover new horizons of knowledge, through a systematic cross-cultural approach to the fundamental problems of human existence. Muslim thinking on so many issues has historically been confined to interpretations, albeit varying, from the classical sources. Yet modern social and political complexities require bold new ways of thinking about dramatically different frameworks of life. This demands new language and sensibilities about human coexistence. This approach does not advocate disregarding the traditional sources, but it does entail reviving them in new ways which keep them meaningful to contemporary concerns in all areas of life. The discursive

---

18 Mohammed Arkoun, 'Rethinking Islam Today', in *Annals of the American Academy of Political and Social Science*, 588 (July 2003), pp. 21–24, Islam: Enduring Myths and Changing Realities.

nature of religious piety must be kept alive so that religious faith does not turn into a fundamentalist ideology where there is only one official interpretation of text and one kind of clergy who posit 'official' interpretations.

Sometimes however, place and politics come together to create an issue of global significance. In 2003, the historian Karl Schlögel's groundbreaking work, *Im Raume lesen Wir die Zeit*, was published. In it he wrote, 'History is set not only in time but also in space,'[19] that history is not just a series of events in a linear order, it is not generalities or abstraction, it is specifics of people and places. Space and geography matter in how we give meaning to events. Perhaps nowhere has this become more relevant in recent years than in the current movement of people from east to west. Lives and landscapes have been transformed in days. The recent flow of refugees and migrants from the Middle East and North Africa into Europe has led to political and cultural soulsearching in the West, and reignited religious and civilisational debates along the binary of Islam and the West. How to end the conflicts of the Middle East and deal with the vast flow of refugees with compassion but realism, may be the most urgent ethical question bridging global politics and Islam today. There are no simple solutions to a problem which so far has been met with little political resolve but requires a profound ethical imagination.

Bibliography

Abela, Andrew V, 'Appealing to the Imagination: Effective and Ethical Marketing of Religion', in *Journal of Business Research* 67.2 (2014), pp. 50–58.

Arkoun, Mohammad, 'Rethinking Islam Today', in *Annals of the American Academy of Political and Social Science* 588 (July 2003), pp. 18–39, Islam: Enduring Myths and Changing Realities.

Bottici, Chiara, 'The Politics of Imagination and the Public Role of Religion', in *Philosophy and Social Criticism* 35.8 (2009), pp. 985–1005.

Bowman, Joshua James, *Arcadian Exile: The Imaginative Tension in Henry David Thoreau's Political Thought*, PhD Thesis (2016).

Davis, Glenn, *Moral Imagination and Progressive Education*, available at: http://www.theimaginativeconservative.org/2010/08/irving-babbitt-moral-imagination-and.html.

Hoebink, Michel, *Thinking about Renewal in Islam* (Leiden: Brill, 1999).

---

19 Karl Schlögel, *Im Raume lessen Wir die Zeit* (Munich: Carl Hanser Verlag, 2003), p. xvii.

Jennings, Willie James, *The Christian Imagination* (New Haven: Yale University Press, 2010).

Lakoff, George and Mark Johnson, *Metaphors We Live By* (Chicago: The University of Chicago Press, 1980).

Lasch, Christopher, *The Culture of Narcissism* (New York: W. W. Norton & Inc, 1991).

Lilla, Mark, *The Stillborn God: Religion, Politics and the Modern West* (New York: Knopf, 2003).

Louden, Robert, 'Meaningful but Immoral Lives', in Beatrix Himmelman, ed., *On meaning in Life* (Berlin: Walter de Gruyter, Inc., 2013).

Iqbal, Muhammad, *The Reconstruction of Religious Thought in Islam* (Lahore: Ashraf Press, 1934).

Iqbal, Muhammad, *Tulip in the Desert, A Selection of Poetry*, transl. Mustansir Mir (London: Hurst & Company Publishers, 2000).

Morgan, Michael, *Lost History* (Washington DC: National Geographic Society, 2008).

Russell, Bertrand, *Political Ideals* (New York: The Century Co., 1917).

Ryn, Claes G, *Will, Imagination and Reason: Irving Babbitt and the Problem of Reality* (New Brunswick, NJ: Transaction Publishers, 1997).

Schlögel, Karl, *Im Raume lessen Wir die Zeit* (Munich: Carl Hanser Verlag, 2003).

Smith, James K A, *Desiring the Kingdom* (Grand Rapids, Michigan: Baker Academic, 2009).

3

Christian Imagination in an Age of Terror[1]

Anba Angaelos

It is difficult to speak of the Christian imagination in an age of terror without coming across as triumphalist, overemphasising Christian forgiveness and resilience; or defeatist, focussing purely on pain and suffering. The reality however is that the situation facing Christians, particularly in the Middle East and across Africa, is very complex. It involves geopolitics, global economics, EU economics and borders, state and regional security, as well as an increasingly volatile region. It is a situation that is not only difficult to read, but to envision any long-term solution for. What we must try to avoid of course, in our own wisdom from the comfort of our own armchairs, is to export our own models to the Middle East, claiming, '*this* is what you need' or '*this* is what would be good for you'. I am sure some, if not all, of you would agree that it is the export of those very models that has contributed to a great deal of harm in the Middle East, particularly in the past six or so years, where we have tried to impose our understanding of democracy.

Democracy is a wonderful thing, but it is also multifaceted. Even if you look at the situation in the West and compare the British model to the French, German, American, and Canadian models, democracy looks very different in each country. Its application is different; sometimes even its ethical benchmarks are different. We therefore need, before we speak, to listen, and to listen faithfully. If you are anything like me, sometimes you listen selectively or prejudicially: either I listen

1 This text is a direct transcript of the speech Archbishop Angaelos gave at the Religious Imaginations and Global Transitions conference at LSE in June 2017.

and only hear what I want to hear, or I listen with an agenda to hear what I want to hear, the way I want to hear it. One of the biggest problems we have is that of expression and recognition. It is very easy to look at those coming from war-torn, conflict-ridden, near-anarchic states, who come and speak with passion, as those who are just looking to rant. It is a normal human trait that when someone rants we stop listening, because we want nice, measured, rational, logical conversation. Unfortunately, when your life and that of your closest family members depends on the issues at hand, measured, calm conversation is not always an option. What we must do, and do faithfully, is to listen sensitively, to what is said rather than focusing our attention on just the way it is being said. We need to listen to emotions and context, not just the words and intonation.

What we see in our world today is a world shaped by terror. It has been a particularly painful year for me as a Coptic clergyman in London because I have almost been toing and froing with the attacks. It started with the bombing of our Cairo cathedral precinct in December, then the Westminster attack, then the Palm Sunday bombings in Egypt, then Manchester, the Minya Province attack on pilgrims going to the monastery, and finally Borough Market and Southwark. This is a dynamic that is tragically our new reality. As I have previously mentioned on Twitter, it is amazing to see how situations like terror attacks bring us together – but it is equally amazing how quickly we forget and part ways to go our own way again.

We need a very nuanced perspective; a nuanced way of addressing this issue; a nuanced way of listening and then presenting what might be of assistance in the way people need it. If we are speaking in the context of the Coptic Orthodox Church, a first century Church within Egypt, we realise that Egypt, whether you are Christian or Muslim, is a deeply religious country. That is not a bad thing; I have no problem at all living amongst and interacting with devout Muslims. I respect their depth of faith. Yet when that faith in some respects starts to overstep and affect the freedoms, entitlements and security of others, then it is crossing the boundaries of what is acceptable.

One significant frustration I feel at the moment is that whenever we speak about terror attacks, the first thing that is brought up to challenge the Christians is: 'what about the Crusades?' I had this conversation recently in a consultation where I was part of the World Council of Churches delegation. I can look at my Scriptures and say, 'That was wrong.' I need to look at my Scriptures and take ownership of my beliefs. I am not going to wait for somebody else to say, 'These Christians are really nice people; you should not misunderstand them,' because at the end of the day, this is my Faith. I am going to take responsibility for it. I would say that the Crusades were actually purely political, and a manipulation and misapplication of Scripture – it was wrong. When, a few years ago, we were horrified to hear of an American pastor wanting to burn the Qur'an, we all stood up and said, 'Not in our name.' My Faith does not tell me to dishonour others. My Faith tells me to love all, including those who consider themselves my enemies. Furthermore, if we are trying to put something up against these evil, horrific campaigns – ones involving killing, maiming, burning alive, burying people alive and selling women and children into modern day sexual slavery – and if we are trying to balance those by talking about something that happened hundreds of years ago, when humanity was in a very different place, I do not think that argument goes very far, or is in any way helpful. As religious leaders, we must take responsibility and ownership for ourselves, our teachings and our people.

What we have experienced through recent terror attacks in England is something that Christians in countries like Egypt have been experiencing for centuries. It is only now much closer to home. So the question is, how do Christians forgive? I know that one of the benchmark historic accounts was that of twenty Coptic Orthodox Christians and their Ghanaian friend who were slaughtered by the Caliphate in Libya. Twenty-one men from poor villages who were just trying to work to earn money for their families. They never, for a moment, thought they would become martyrs or symbols, or particularly significant for that matter, but they did, and they continue to be. They have become a symbol of modern day martyrdom. Their murderers, who disseminated video images of their execution around the world to instil fear, actually affirmed them as symbols of strength, resolve and faithfulness. They knelt, repeating the words of their Christian faith as others stood over them with deadly weapons. It makes one think about what 'power' actually means. Does it belong to the perpetrator of the crime who holds the physical weapon, or is it with those men who had no weapons but demonstrated their true faith even unto death? This power was also evident in their families who had the strength to genuinely say 'we forgive you' to the perpetrators.

You may notice that I wear a Coventry Cross of nails. I do so because when Coventry Cathedral was bombed in the Second World War, Provost Howard, the Dean of the Cathedral, went into the rubble and found three nails, bound them in the shape of a cross and put them on the altar. From that time onward they dedicated their ministry to reconciliation, and I feel that there was such a parallel between that and what happened in Egypt in 2013 when there was an orchestrated attack on 100 churches and places of Christian ministry in the space of 48 hours.

While it was miraculous that no-one was injured or killed, what was more miraculous was that there was not a single incident of retaliation or revenge. Not a single one. Some say that the plan at the time was to replicate what was happening in Iraq and Syria and instigate a civil war by leading Christians to retaliate these attacks. What they did not understand was that the Christians were not going to retaliate, and you simply could not have a civil war in Egypt. Not because Egypt is better than anywhere else, but because the population of Egypt is not tribal. It is a single community with a single distinction: Christian and Muslim. If you only have two groupings – and by and large the relations are peaceful – if you have the fringe of one group lashing out at the other but the other will not retaliate, how are you going to start a civil war? The Christians of Egypt were not going to retaliate. Their forgiveness, their resilience and their faithfulness changed the dynamic.

I am always conscious of trying to remind people that freedom of any kind, including religion or belief, is given to humanity by God when He said in Genesis, 'Let us create man according to Our image and our likeness.' We were created free, but when we speak about international treaties and agreements, those are merely human manifestations that enshrine that God-given right; and that is the difference.

God Himself does not force us to believe in Him. In fact, He gives us the absolute right to even reject Him, but that does not mean He will not wait for us to repent and return to Him, for the Scriptures tell us that the Heaven rejoices over one sinner who returns. It does not mean that He will not, as the Good Shepherd, leave the 99 to go after the one, or that as the Incarnate Word, He did not leave His disciples and go all the way to a hostile territory in Samaria and sit at a well and speak to a woman He 'should not' have spoken to just to give her hope. He does not force us; so surely we have the obligation to allow one another to believe, or indeed, not believe. That does not mean I cannot share my Faith, because I feel I should. I do not share it because I get a bonus when I enter the Kingdom since I have more converts than others. I do not get greater distinction if I have brought more people to Christ. I believe that, because it is a loving message, I present it as a loving message, but then I leave people to decide. One of the principles of Christianity is that the work of faith is like planting a seed, where one sows, one tends, and one reaps. In this model, I do not have to see the product of my work; all I do is sow a seed, and I leave it to grow, but it should not ever be forced. As religious leaders, we need to address within us a tendency that will drive us to discredit not only ourselves, but all that we stand for, because if we present our religions as vehicles for hatred, aggression and violence, then we dishonour and discredit them.

I have spoken to many friends about what is happening in the Middle East where some are deciding to kill for religion. I, like you, know many Muslims and

I, like you, am sure, beyond a shadow of a doubt, that the vast majority of Muslims absolutely condemn such actions. I also realise however that all those who kill in this manner do so based on their interpretation and application of religious texts. I am not a Muslim scholar, so it is not my place to say whether an interpretation or an application is right or wrong. That must come from Muslims scholars who must say one of two things – either 'my brother/sister, you are wrong, these texts do not exist', or 'my sister/brother, these texts do exist but we need to read them in a nuanced manner and interpret them differently'. What other solutions could there be? If those who perpetrate these crimes are using religious justification, then surely that religious justification needs to be taken away by a religious expression. More and more I notice there is a decreasing appetite for the expression, 'this is not Islam', without any explanation of what it actually is. To my Muslim friends, and in particular Muslim scholars and leaders, I say please speak to the people, explain why this is wrong as only you can.

We must take account and ownership of our world and of our history. What we see happening now is the result of years, even decades, of similar acts in the Middle East that have gone unchallenged. The terrorist attacks we are now seeing in the West have been suffered by Christians and minority groups, like the Yazidis and so many others in the Middle East, for a long time. There has been a direct and/or indirect persecution, marginalisation and eradication in some places for decades. In Egypt, for instance, there has been an undeniable glass ceiling for Christians in prominent positions, whether it is the national football team or indeed any high-ranking position in the public sector. There has been an intrinsic institutional alienation. As a result, the Christians have not disappeared, but have gone into the private sector where they have become very successful, and then they have subsequently once again become a target because of this success. That is the dynamic that needs to be looked at. What we are seeing is infringements on the rights of individuals. We saw the leader of a democratically backed political party in the UK resign because he could not speak of his Faith, or if he did, he was targeted and marginalised, yet we speak of having, cherishing and protecting 'religious freedom'.

I do not think states should be religious. A state is a state. What states must do is respect all faiths equally. They should give opportunity to everyone equally, be blind to faith, but be respectful of the humanity we all share. What we sometimes see however is a positive discrimination. If we are going to be blind to faith, we should be blind to all faith. If we are going to stand up for religious freedom, then we must do so for all equally. If God looks at us all equally, then we must also look at each other in the same way.

I suppose I do not need to remind you of Einstein's definition of insanity as doing the same thing over and over while expecting a different result, but that is precisely what we do when trying to superficially and cosmetically address matters of reconciliation and social cohesion. In Egypt we have regularly seen what is referred to as 'reconciliation sessions', where a Christian family or group that has been persecuted and attacked is asked to sit with a Muslim individual or group that has attacked them, to have them reconcile miraculously before a television camera, shake hands and hug, and the world seems to have become a better place. This actually does not work. It does not resolve the subliminal sense of intolerance. That word in itself needs a lot of care. We speak of being a 'tolerant' society. As a Christian, I recognise that 'tolerance' is not the benchmark. To tolerate or merely be tolerated is not what we are aiming for. What we are aiming for is acceptance, respect, and dignity. It is not just to be alive, but to live with dignity. Not just to make do, but to live in prosperity; not just to be protected, but to be safe. That is what we need to address.

I put two things before you. I am always told as a clergyman to not 'do politics'. I do not think I do. There is however a difference between politics and advocacy. Politics has its people and its agenda, but if we look at the Gospel of Luke, chapter four, a prophecy that is given of our Lord Jesus Christ Himself, it reads, 'He has anointed me to preach the gospel to the poor; He has sent Me to heal the brokenhearted, to proclaim liberty to the captives and recovery of sight to the blind, to set at liberty those who are oppressed.' So, if He as the Chief Advocate has this role, then I also have the same role: to advocate for all.

To demonstrate, we do an immense amount of work here with the Baha'i community because the situation of the Baha'i community in Iran is similar, if not even more intense, than that of Christians in Egypt. As a Christian, I cannot possibly be tribal and sectarian, only looking after my own; which would be the most un-Christian thing I can possibly do. We need to be a voice of advocacy and look at the world in a different way. There was a time when we could all live very comfortably with a clear conscience in our silos because that is the way the world was. One could be a Coptic Christian in Egypt and never see anybody else throughout his or her life. The nature of our world today, a world of multinationals, travel, working across countries, social media platforms, and integration is one in which we are quite literally in each other's lives and must deal with each other within that context. We need to be with each other, and in that context, we need to advocate for one another. Speaking of the Baha'i community, I remember some years back they had seven of their religious leaders imprisoned. As a result, there was a campaign to write and present a letter to the UK Foreign Office. The friends involved asked, 'Will you come with us?' and I said, 'Of course.' Then they asked a couple of days later, 'Will you lead the delegation of faith leaders and representatives?' and I said, 'Yes, of course.' Then they asked, 'Actually, at the meeting, will you deliver the letter to the minister on our behalf?' So there we were, as an interreligious group going with our Baha'i brothers and sisters, saying, 'These, our Baha'i brothers and sisters have a problem. We feel with and for them. This is what they want to say to you.' I am sure that this was an infinitely more effective approach than if Baha'is, Copts, or indeed any other group, had gone by themselves.

I would like to share a quote of St Cyril of Jerusalem with you. Speaking of our Lord Jesus Christ, he says, 'Everywhere He became all things to all. To the hungry He became bread; to the thirsty, He became water; to the dead, He became resurrection; to the sick, He became a physician; to the sinners, He became redemption.' Now surely, that is what we need to be as well! To the persecuted and alienated, we need to become advocates. To the hungry, we need to become those who provide sustenance. To the marginalised, we need to become empowerment. There is so much that we can, and should, do in our world for the whole of humanity. Again, in Scripture, we are reminded in the epistle to the Galatians[2] that, beyond tribal visions, where we speak about the family of humanity, there are no divisions between Greek and Jew, slave and freeman, male and female. The image of Christ, the image of God, is the same in all of us and so we must respect and cherish that.

Of course, one thing we are all dealing with globally is internal and external displacement; it is horrific. I see people working with displaced peoples and think it must be so daunting to work with so many people who have nothing. Following the Grenfell Tower fire, we saw 120 families suddenly deprived of a home to go back to at night. Our system here means they will have shelters and provision; we saw the number of people who ran to their aid. If you think this is happening daily, in multiples, in many countries around the world, it is such an incredible thing to be witnessing.

Our response to refugees and displacement also needs to be addressed. Again, in our Old Testament Scripture, God speaks to His people, saying, 'The foreigners who come among you – treat them as yourselves; provide for them as yourselves, because you yourselves were once travellers and I looked after you.'[3] We need to realise that we are not beyond human weakness and limitation. We need to look

---

2 Galatians 3:28, NKJV.
3 Leviticus 19:34, NKJV.

at these issues with graciousness. There is this great debate: are these economic immigrants, or are they refugees? Semantics. These are semantics. I have said time and time again that these are not upwardly mobile families deciding to move from one suburb to a greener, more leafy one with better schools. They are people leaving war-torn, violence riddled, anarchic states where they are fighting for their lives. Call them migrants. Call them refugees. Just understand their undeniable humanity.

In closing, I have given you a really, really difficult impression of what the world is like for Christians in the Middle East, but one thing we have is hope. One thing I am sure of, is that we must be light, and there is no greater need for light than in the most crippling and suffocating darkness. That is where light becomes most relevant and hope becomes more relevant. I want to conclude with a passage from the Second Book of Corinthians: 'We are hard-pressed on every side, yet not crushed; we are perplexed, but not in despair; persecuted, but not forsaken; struck down, but not destroyed.'[4]

---

4 2 Corinthians 4:8, NKJV.

4

The Balfour Declaration: From Imagining a State to Re-imagining Majority-Minority Relations in Jewish Thought and the Jewish State

Ophir Yarden

Introduction

In 2017 we noted the 100th anniversary of the Balfour Declaration. Many in Israel, the Jewish world and some beyond celebrated it; some in Palestine – and beyond – lamented it. Beyond doubt, the declaration is one of the 20th century's most significant documents and I will explore some of that significance in this essay.

The Balfour Declaration is a letter sent by Arthur James Balfour, Foreign Secretary of His Majesty's government in London, to Lord Walter Rothschild, representing the Zionist Federation. As this brief document is at the centre of our discussion, I commence by citing it in its entirety:

> Dear Lord Rothschild,
> I have much pleasure in conveying to you, on behalf of His Majesty's Govern-ment, the following declaration of sympathy with Jewish Zionist aspirations which has been submitted to, and approved by, the Cabinet:
>   His Majesty's government view with favour the establishment in Palestine of a national home for the Jewish people, and will use their best endeavours to facilitate the achievement of this object, it being clearly understood that nothing shall be done which may prejudice the civil and religious rights of existing non-Jewish communities in Palestine, or the rights and political status enjoyed by Jews in any other country.

I should be grateful if you would bring this declaration to the knowledge of the Zionist Federation.

Yours sincerely,
Arthur James Balfour[1]

Foreign Office,

November 2nd, 1917.

Dear Lord Rothschild,

      I have much pleasure in conveying to you, on behalf of His Majesty's Government, the following declaration of sympathy with Jewish Zionist aspirations which has been submitted to, and approved by, the Cabinet

      "His Majesty's Government view with favour the establishment in Palestine of a national home for the Jewish people, and will use their best endeavours to facilitate the achievement of this object, it being clearly understood that nothing shall be done which may prejudice the civil and religious rights of existing non-Jewish communities in Palestine, or the rights and political status enjoyed by Jews in any other country"

      I should be grateful if you would bring this declaration to the knowledge of the Zionist Federation.

---

1 The British Library, available at: http://www.bl.uk/manuscripts/FullDisplay.aspx?ref=Add_MS_41178_A.

Before we place the Declaration in its historical context and explore its genesis let us commence with an anecdote. At a dinner on 15 November 1917, at which Lord Rothschild read the Declaration, two weeks after the letter was sent and one week after its publication, Nahum Sokolow, the Zionist diplomat who had been central to the Declaration's coming into existence joked about a letter to a private person as the vehicle for such a significant Declaration. Sokolow remarked that it had been 'sent to the Lord and not to the Jewish people because they had no address, whereas the Lord had a very fine one'.[2]

Indeed, the Jewish people not having an address was the heart of the matter.

The international status of the Balfour Declaration

As the letter states, the Balfour Declaration was a pronouncement of Britain's sympathy with Jewish Zionist aspirations and a promise to work towards the fulfilment of these aspirations. This promise is sometimes seen alongside two other promises as a result of which some have spoken of the 'Thrice-Promised Land', the land promised three times and to three different recipients.[3] The other two promises, in chronological order, are:

- The McMahon-Hussein Correspondence
- The Sykes-Picot Agreement

The McMahon-Hussein Correspondence was an exchange of letters in 1915–1916 between Hussein bin Ali, Sharif of Mecca, and Lieutenant Colonel Sir Henry McMahon, British High Commissioner in Egypt. Great Britain promised Arab independence in exchange for bin Ali's support in the war against the Turks.

The Sykes-Picot Agreement between Britain and France (and also Russia) divided parts of the to-be-conquered Ottoman empire into areas of control and spheres of influence for Britain and France.

These two promises were mutually exclusive even before the penning of the Balfour Declaration which supported a Jewish homeland in some of these same geographical regions. The secrecy of the agreements, their contradictions and the diplomatic duplicity involved were exposed after the Russian revolution. When

---

2 Cited in Martin Kramer, 'The Forgotten Truth about the Balfour Declaration', in *Mosaic Magazine*, 5 June 2017, available at: https://mosaicmagazine.com/essay/2017/06/the-forgotten-truth-about-the-balfour-declaration.

3 Arnold J Toynbee, 'The Present Situation in Palestine', in *International Affairs* 10.1 (1931), p. 45.

the Sykes-Picot agreement was made public on 23 November, 'the British were embarrassed, the Arabs dismayed and the Turks delighted'.[4]

As the Balfour Declaration and its sisters were contentious in their day, so the Declaration has remained over the last century. It has been variously called 'one of the greatest acts of Western statesmanship in the 20th century',[5] the 'original sin' against Palestinian Arabs,[6] and is sometimes summed up as a case where 'one nation solemnly promised to a second nation the country of a third'.[7]

In truth, the Declaration was extremely well founded in international law in an era preceding the League of Nations (or the UN). The Declaration was not the whimsical and unilateral act of one country acting alone. It rather represents 'the carefully calibrated consensus of the nascent international community circa 1917':[8]

- The Declaration represented pre-existing consensus of several nations when it was delivered
- It was delivered in public and was not part of secret diplomacy
- It was confirmed subsequently by supporting nations
- A Zionist delegation took part in the Paris Peace Talks at Versailles and subsequent conferences
- The Declaration was incorporated into the Treaty of Sèvres and the San Remo Resolution (1920)
- It was incorporated into the League of Nation's Mandate for Palestine

There were other considerations and factors in the origin of the Declaration ranging from Christian Zionism to national politics. Having acknowledged these factors, I will leave them behind as they are beyond the scope of the present discussion.

I shall now pursue two parallel stories. First I will explore the international support garnered by Zionist diplomacy for the Declaration. Second I will examine

4 Peter Mansfield, 'Lawrence and his Legacy', in *The British Empire Magazine* 76, available at: https://www.britishempire.co.uk/maproom/lawrenceandhislegacy.htm.

5 Richard Crossman, M.P., Lord President of the Council and Leader of the House of Commons, 1967.

6 Sharif Nashashibi, 'Balfour: Britain's original sin', in *Aljazeera*, 4 November 2014, available at: https://www.aljazeera.com/indepth/opinion/2014/11/balfour-britain-original-sin-201411472940231416.html.

7 Arthur Koestler, *Promise and Fulfilment: Palestine 1917–1949* (New York: Macmillan, 1949), available at: https://archive.org/stream/promiseandfulfil006754mbp/promiseandfulfil006754mbp_djvu.txt.

8 Kramer, 'The Forgotten Truth about the Balfour Declaration'.

the evolving drafts of what came to be the Balfour Declaration and explore the profound significance of some of the concepts included therein.

Chaim Weizmann, later the first President of the State of Israel, was central in attaining the Declaration from Britain. But a lesser known Zionist diplomat was the central force in obtaining assent from other countries. Nahum Sokolow was a Polish Jew who attended the First Zionist Congress in Basel in 1897. He became a follower of Theodor Herzl, the founder of modern political Zionism, and translated his utopian Zionist novel *Alteneuland* into Hebrew, calling it *Tel-Aviv*, Tel of Spring, which echoed the old and the new. Shortly after Herzl's death in 1904, Sokolow became the secretary general of the World Zionist Congress. In the spring and summer of 1917, he obtained the assent of the French and Italian governments, and even that of the pope, to a Jewish 'national home'.

Following Sokolow's lobbying, on 4 June 1917, Jules Cambon, secretary-general of the French foreign ministry, sent him a letter of support affirming the French government's 'sympathy for your cause whose triumph is linked to that of the Allies'. Working in tandem with the British diplomat Mark Sykes (of the 'Sykes-Picot' agreement) and with the support of the French, Sokolow travelled to Rome. On 4 May 1917, in an audience with Pope Benedict XV which was sympathetically coordinated by Monsignor Eugenio Pacelli (later to be Pope Pius XII) and Vatican Secretary of State Cardinal Pietro Gasparri, Benedict told Sokolow:

> The return of the Jews to Palestine is a miraculous event. It is providential; God has willed it... I believe that we shall be good neighbors.[9]

Some background is necessary to appreciate the significance of this, perhaps surprising, statement. Sokolow was not the first Zionist activist to seek the Vatican's endorsement. Herzl had met Pope Pius X in 1904 and was disappointed by the Pontiff's response to his Zionist plea. Pius told Herzl: 'the Jews have not recognized our Lord, therefore we cannot recognize the Jewish people.' It was quite a volte-face from 'cannot recognize' to 'God has willed it'![10]

---

9 Sergio Minerbi, *The Vatican and Zionism: Conflict in the Holy Land, 1895–1925* (New York: Oxford University Press, 1990), p. 111.
10 Raymond Cohen has analysed this exchange in the backdrop of International Relations. As the Vatican was in possession of significant capitulations from the Ottomans then controlling Palestine, it would have been politically foolish to endorse the Zionist aspirations for a Jewish State. (Personal communication.) See Raymond Cohen, 'Was Theology to Blame? The Holy See and Israel's Stony Path to Normalization', in Emma O'Donnell

Weizmann summed the situation up well when, speaking to a conference of the English Zionist Federation in London on 20 May, he said: 'The support of the British government, when given, will be in conjunction and agreement with the Allied powers.'[11] And so it was. With the most important support from France, along with those of the Vatican, Italy and the US all in place by June 1917, on behalf of the government of David Lloyd George, Balfour invited Lord Rothschild and Weizmann to submit a draft proposal for a declaration of support. Just two weeks after Balfour sent the letter to Lord Rothschild, a new government, that of Georges Clemenceau, took office in Paris. Sokolow sought French reassurances that their policy was unchanged and was able to receive them in writing (like all the others, save from Wilson). Stephen Pichon, foreign minister of the new government, wrote to Sokolow on 14 February 1918:

> [T]he understanding is complete between the French and British governments concerning the question of a Jewish national home in Palestine (*un foyer national juif en Palestine*).[12]

Italy followed suit on 9 May 1918 with a pledge to help 'facilitate the establishment in Palestine of a Jewish national center (*centro nazionale ebraico*)'.[13] On the heels of Italy, came the US with President Wilson expressing 'satisfaction in the progress of the Zionist movement… since the declaration of Mr. Balfour', in a letter sent to American Zionist leader Rabbi Stephen Wise on 31 August 1918 in which he quoted the Balfour Declaration verbatim.[14]

It is significant that between Wilson's quiet support in October 1917 and his powerful public statement in August 1918, he had given his famous 'self-determination' speech (11 February 1918) and added this principle to his previously enunciated Fourteen Points (January 1918). In his speech, Wilson said:

Polyakov, ed., *Antisemitism, Islamophobia, and Interreligious Hermeneutics: Ways of Seeing the Religious Other* (Leiden: Brill/Rodopi, Forthcoming).

11 *The Letters and Papers of Chaim Weizmann: Volume I, Series B, August 1898-July 1931*, ed. Barnet Litvinoff (New Jersey: Transaction, 1983), p. 158.

12 Cited in Ministere des Affaires Etrangeres, ed., *Documents diplomatiques français: 1921 (Annexes 10 janvier 1920–31 décembre 1921)* (Oxford: Peter Lang, 2005), p. 165.

13 Rita Campus, 'The comparison between Zionists and Catholics in the pages of "Israel" during the 1920s', in Luciano Martini, ed., *Giorgio La Pira e la vocazione di Israele* 26, p. 42.

14 R S Baker and W E Dodd, eds., *The Public Papers of Woodrow Wilson, War and Peace*, vol. I (New York: Harper, 1927), p. 243.

National aspirations must be respected; people may now be dominated and governed only by their own consent. Self-determination is not a mere phrase; it is an imperative principle of action...[15]

Clearly Wilson saw Zionism as consistent with self-determination. Endorsements from other countries continued. Five months later in January 1919, Japan informed Weizmann that 'the Japanese Government gladly take note of the Zionist aspirations to establish in Palestine a national home for the Jewish people and they look forward with a sympathetic interest to the realization of such desire'.[16]

The international assent to the Zionist aspiration of establishing a Jewish national home in Palestine was not limited to the pronouncements of individual countries. A Zionist delegation presented a draft resolution enumerating Zionist aims to the Paris Peace Conference. To this document, submitted in Versailles, were appended the Balfour Declaration itself and the endorsements of the governments of Italy, Japan, Greece, Serbia, China, and Siam. An outcome of Versailles was the Treaty of Sèvres (10 August 1920) which states the intention to establish a mandatory regime in Palestine[17] (parallel to those in Syria, Lebanon and Iraq), tasked with implementing the Declaration. The penultimate point was the San Remo Conference of April 1920, attended by Great Britain, France, Italy, and Japan (with the United States as a neutral observer). Weizmann and Sokolow attended the conference as well. They presented a memorandum to the British delegation stating the Zionist objectives. The article concerning Palestine was debated on 24 April and the next day it was resolved to incorporate the Balfour Declaration in Britain's mandate for Palestine. The Mandate Document, in its final version, specifies that:

> ... recognition has thereby been given to the historical connection of the Jewish people with Palestine and to the grounds for reconstituting their national home in that country...[18]

From this point onward the Balfour Declaration acquired standing in international law.

---

15 Available at: http://www.gwpda.org/1918/wilpeace.html.
16 World Zionist Organization, Central Zionist Archives, Jerusalem, Copy Z4/2039.
17 Article 95, available at: https://wwi.lib.byu.edu/index.php/Section_I,_Articles_1_-_260.
18 The preamble of The Palestine Mandate of July 1922 references 'the declaration originally made on November 2nd, 1917, by the Government of His Britannic Majesty...'. The Palestine Mandate, available at: http://avalon.law.yale.edu/20th_century/palmanda.asp.

The US subsequently bolstered the Declaration. Not a member of the League of Nations, the US was unable to support the Mandate, but on 21 September 1922, the 67th US Congress unanimously adopted the Lodge-Fish Resolution.[19]

The evolution of the text of the Balfour Declaration

As we have seen, His Majesty's government was inclined to issue a statement supporting Zionism and by June 1917, with the support of her allies, had resolved to do so. Lord Rothschild had been invited to submit a draft of such a declaration, and in July 1917, he proposed the following points:

1. His Majesty's Government accepts the principle that Palestine should be reconstituted as the national home of the Jewish people.
2. His Majesty's Government will use its best endeavours to secure the achievement of this object and will discuss the necessary methods and means with the Zionist Organisation.

This draft was based upon, but more modest in its demands than, a version initially outlined by Sokolow and others with reference to the French Cambon letter. Perhaps the most significant aspect of this draft – and one which survived through to the final version – was the inclusion of the phrase 'national home of the Jewish people'. The Jews were recognised as a national entity rather than as a religious community. This accorded well with the genesis of modern political Zionism which was far more cultural-national than religious in impetus.

There were to be four subsequent drafts of the text. We shall not examine all versions, some of which include minute changes. The draft which Balfour produced in August was quite similar. Significant changes were introduced by Alfred Milner. Milner was an influential member of Lloyd George's War Cabinet and he is sometimes credited as the main author of the 'Balfour' Declaration and one of its key proponents.[20] Lord Milner was an experienced colonial administrator, having served as High Commissioner for Southern Africa. His emendations of the previous draft were delicate but of great significance. First, he eliminated the phrase 'Palestine should be reconstituted as the national home of the Jewish

---

19 'Joint Resolution Favoring the establishment in Palestine of a national home for the Jewish people.' Available at: https://www.loc.gov/law/help/statutes-at-large/67th-congress/Session%202/c67s2ch372.pdf.
20 Carroll Quigley, *The Anglo-American Establishment* (New York: Books in Focus, 1981), p. 169.

people', and replaced it with 'home for the Jewish people in Palestine', hence omitting the words 'reconstituted' and 'national'. These alterations downgraded the recognition of the national aspect of Jewish identity and eliminated the acknowledgement of the Jewish people's roots in the Land of Israel/Palestine. The second change would be reversed, but the term 'reconstituted' did not appear in the final version.[21] Milner also added the preposition 'in', which is small but of huge significance. The draft no longer spoke of Palestine *as* the homeland, but of a home for the Jews *in* Palestine, which would pave the way for the interpretation that the intention was to indicate an area less than the entire region of Palestine.

Leopold Amery, an Assistant Secretary to the British war cabinet in 1917, joined Lord Milner in producing the next draft. Some believe Amery to be the main drafter of the Declaration[22] and Amery's additions to the draft are of interest to our discussion. The Milner-Amery draft of 4 October 1917 sought to address two concerns that had been raised, one by Jews and one by and on behalf of the non-Jewish residents of Palestine. As Amery put it, the draft was adjusted to include 'something which would go a reasonable distance to meeting the objectors, both Jewish and Arab, without impairing the substance of the proposed declaration'.[23] It must be remembered that not all Jews were enthusiastic supporters of Zionism. While there were several reasons for this, I will present only two:

(1) Traditional Jewish belief held that Jews lived in exile from the land of Israel as punishment for their sins, which were the cause of the destruction of the Second Temple in the year 70 CE. Jewish liturgy states: 'Because of our sins we were exiled from our land and driven far from our country...'[24] This same prayer presents the traditional solution thus:

> May it be Your will, Lord our God... that you have mercy on us... Bring back our scattered ones from among the nations and gather our dispersed people from the ends of the earth. Lead us to Zion, Your city, in jubilation, and to Jerusalem, home of Your Temple, with everlasting joy.

---

21 Though it was added to the Mandate document.

22 William D Rubinstein, 'The Secret of Leopold Amery', in *Historical Research* 73.181 (2000), pp. 175–196.

23 Leopold S Amery, *My Political Life: War and peace, 1914–1929* (London: Hutchinson, 1953), p. 116.

24 *'Amida* prayer for *Musaf* service on festivals. See, *The Koren Siddur*, transl. Jonathan Sacks (Jerusalem: Koren, 2009), pp. 812–814.

The return to Zion was to be an act of God and His Messiah, not a worldly political development. Taking the restoration into human hands was a rebellion against the Kingdom of Heaven.

(2) The second Jewish ideology that rejected Zionism had a very different motivation. Since the Emancipation of French Jewry following the French Revolution, Jews had achieved a status of which they had never before dreamed. Citizenship and *de jure* equality bordered on the utopian for many Jews. As a Parisian Jew put it in a letter to *La Chronique de Paris* in 1791, 'France... is our Palestine, its mountains are our Zion, its rivers our Jordan. Let us drink the water of these sources; it is the water of liberty...!'[25] Palestine was hence redefined as a state of being rather than a geographical entity. There was no longer any need for the Land of Israel/Palestine. Rabbi Sir Philip Magnus made the claim that ever since the Roman exile, the Jewish people ceased being a political body and shared only a religion and as such did not have a national aspiration in the Land of Israel.[26] Some influential members of the Anglo-Jewish community and their ideological cousins elsewhere felt that Zionism and a Jewish national home in Palestine could endanger their hard-won improved status bringing about, *inter alia*, questions regarding (dual) loyalty. A letter to *The Times* on 24 May 1917 entitled 'Views of Anglo-Jewry', stated:

> [T]he establishment of a Jewish nationality in Palestine, founded on this theory of homelessness, must have the effect throughout the world of stamping the Jews as strangers in their native lands, and of undermining their hard-won position as citizens and nationals of these lands.

Edwin Samuel Montagu, the Jewish Secretary of State for India, condemned the idea in even stronger terms:

> When Jews are told that Palestine is a national home every country will immediately desire to get rid of its Jewish citizens... When the Jews have a national home surely it follows that the impetus to deprive us of rights of British citizenship must be enormously increased.[27]

---

25 Emmanuel Navon, 'La France vue d'Israël: illusions perdues', in *Outre-Terre* 2.3 (2003), p. 253.
26 The Secret Drafts of the Balfour Declaration, available at: http://web.nli.org.il/sites/NLI/English/library/reading_corner/Pages/balfour.aspx.
27 British Government, British Public Record Office, Cabinet No. 24/24 (August 1917).

Amery rejected Montagu with scorn, but nevertheless adjusted the draft by adding what would become the second of the Declaration's two stipulations, that 'nothing shall be done which may prejudice... the rights and political status enjoyed in any other country by such Jews who are fully contented with their existing nationality.'

The other stipulation was the result of concern that the exercise of Jewish rights in Palestine might jeopardise those of others. With Jews comprising only 10% of the population of Palestine, the principle of self-determination was clearly not being applied to the Arab community. A correspondent of Sykes, Anthony Pascal Albina, a Catholic merchant from Jerusalem, wrote:

[H]ow can the allies conciliate their engagement of freeing small nationalities, by imposing upon the Palestinian Arabs, who are the original settlers of the country, the rule of a foreign and hated race, a motley crowd of Poles, Russians, Rumanians, Spaniards, Yemenites, etc., who can claim absolutely no right over the country, except that of sentiment and the fact that their forefathers inhabited it over 2,000 years ago? The introduction into Palestine of Jewish rule, or even Jewish predominance, will mean the spoliation of the Arab inhabitants of their hereditary rights and the upsetting of the principles of nationalities... Politically, a Jewish state in Palestine will mean a permanent danger to a lasting peace in the Near East.[28]

As Ronald Storrs, the Military Governor of Jerusalem after the British conquest, later recalled:

The Declaration... took no account whatever of the feelings or desires of the actual inhabitants of Palestine. In its drafting, Arabs observed the main... portion to be reserved for the Jewish people, while the other races and creeds were not so much as named, either as Arabs, Moslems or Christians, but were lumped together under the negative and humiliating definition of 'Non-Jewish Communities' and relegated to subordinate provisos.[29]

---

28 Ronald Sanders, *The High Walls of Jerusalem* (New York: Holt, Rinehart and Winston, 1983), p. 586.
29 Ronald Storrs, *Lawrence of Arabia: Zionism and Palestine* (New York: Penguin Books, 1940), p. 51.

Gertrude Bell, a colleague of T E Lawrence, summed up her position in a letter, writing: 'I think we're planting the seeds for a century of unrest.'[30]

In an attempt to address this one-sidedness, Amery suggested that a second stipulation be added to the draft that read: '… it being clearly understood that nothing shall be done which may prejudice the civil and religious rights of existing non-Jewish communities in Palestine.' With this change the Declaration was complete. No significant further changes were made in the Milner-Amery draft of 4 October until the approval by the cabinet and the letter was sent to Lord Rothschild.

The implementation and after-life of the Balfour Declaration

Having explored both the text of the Balfour Declaration and its standing in international law, in this section I examine its implications, effects and legacies. The full text of the Declaration was incorporated into the Mandate document and even expanded to include the clause, 'Whereas recognition has thereby been given to the historical connection of the Jewish people with Palestine and to the grounds for reconstituting their national home in that country', which restored the language of the 'reconstitution' of the ancient Jewish national home. The Mandate lasted for 25 years, after which the State of Israel was established and the central idea of the Declaration was realised. But what came of the two stipulation clauses about the rights of minorities, both the non-Jews in Israel and the Jews in other countries?

The second stipulation, 'it being clearly understood that nothing shall be done which may prejudice… the rights and political status enjoyed by Jews in any other country', is generally seen as having been realised. The emancipation achieved by Jews living in France and elsewhere was not rescinded with the attainment of Jewish statehood.[31] But the reality is somewhat more complex. Just days before the General Assembly's adoption of resolution 181 which called for the partition

---

30 Gertrude Bell, *A Woman in Arabia: The Writings of the Queen of the Desert*, ed. Georgina Howell, (London: Penguin Classics 2015).

31 Interestingly, the legitimacy of Jewish life outside the borders of the ancestral homeland was questioned by many important Jewish thinkers of the Zionism movement. While one school of thought held that Zionism sought to save the *Jews* in immediate distress (and those whose condition was otherwise need not repatriate immediately, but could be nourished by the spiritual centre to be created in the homeland), another held that the mission of Zionism was to address the distress of *Judaism* by returning all the sons and daughters of the Jewish *nation* to the homeland for a transformation that would alter Judaism itself.

of Palestine into Jewish and Arab states, an Egyptian delegate, Heykal Pasha, addressed the Political Committee of the UN General Assembly:

> The United Nations... should not lose sight of the fact that the proposed solution might endanger a million Jews living in the Moslem countries. Partition of Palestine might create in those countries an anti-Semitism even more difficult to root out than the anti-Semitism which the Allies were trying to eradicate in Germany... If the United Nations decides to partition Palestine, it might be responsible for the massacre of a large number of Jews... A million Jews live in peace in Egypt [and other Muslim countries] and enjoy all rights of citizenship. They have no desire to emigrate to Palestine. However, if a Jewish State were established, nobody could prevent disorders. Riots would break out in Palestine, would spread through all the Arab states and might lead to a war between two races.[32]

From the Jewish side, Rabbi Stephen Wise, now president of the World Jewish Congress, appealed to US Secretary of State George Marshall:

> Between 800,000 and a million Jews in the Middle East and North Africa, exclusive of Palestine, are in 'the greatest danger of destruction' at the hands of Muslims being incited to holy war over the Partition of Palestine...[33]

Jewish life, limb and property were imperilled beyond the borders of Palestine/ Land of Israel in Algeria, Egypt, Iraq, Libya, Morocco, Syria, and Yemen. With the establishment of the State of Israel and the eruption of Israeli-Arab war in 1948 many Jews whose families had lived for generations in Arab lands found their future untenable and fled as refugees. Most were received by Israel; many by France and other countries.

While the existence of the State of Israel has not jeopardised the status of Jews living in most other countries and has not brought about serious challenges of dual-loyalty, Israel's *actions* have put some diaspora communities in difficult positions. After Israel's 1961 vote in the General Assembly to censure South Africa's

---

32 UN General Assembly, Second Session, Official Records, Ad Hoc Committee on the Palestinian Question, Summary Records of Meetings, Lake Success, NY, September 25 – November 15, 1947, p. 185. English version (from the French) by Ya'akov Meron, 'Why Jews Fled the Arab Countries', in *Middle East Quarterly* 2.3 (September 1995).
33 Bat Ye'or, *Islam and Dhimmitude: Where Civilizations Collide* (Madison: Fairleigh Dickinson University Press, 2002), pp. 175–6.

racial policies, the latter's Foreign Minister Eric Louw called upon South African Jews to criticise Israel and express solidarity with South Africa.[34] An intimidating private letter from Prime Minister Verwoerd to a Jewish citizen threatened anti-Semitic reactions.[35] Much more serious were the developments in Poland following the Six-Day War of June 1967. Israel's victory provided an opportunity to unleash anti-Semitism which continued Stalinist policies of the 1940s and early 1950s.[36] Just days after the war, Władysław Gomułka, the first secretary of the Polish United Workers Party stated of some Polish Jews that:

> [They] sympathized with the enemies of socialism, the 'Israeli aggressors', thereby forfeiting their claim to be loyal Polish citizens. These people were not just morally reprehensible; they also constituted a potential 'fifth column' in the country, which had to be eradicated...[37]

More generally, due to anti-Zionism and anti-Semitism fuelled by the Palestine-Israel conflict, it may be soberly assessed that the establishment of the State of Israel has negatively impacted the lives of some Jews remaining outside the national home. In fact, one can identify a new form of anti-Semitism distinct from its older siblings, which is a result of Zionism, the establishment of the State of Israel and the Palestine-Israel conflict.

The Israel-Arab – and in some cases Jewish-Muslim[38] – conflict has created a situation in which the old dangers to Jewish living around the world have been augmented by new threats. If in the past Jews contended with only anti-Semitism, now they are often the victims of anti-Zionism (at times combined with anti-Semitism). Examples of this would be the murder of three Jewish pupils and a teacher

---

34 Sasha Polakow-Suransky, *The Unspoken Alliance: Israel's Secret Relationship with Apartheid South Africa* (London: Random House, 2010), p. 31.
35 Gideon Shimoni, *Community and Conscience: The Jews in Apartheid South Africa* (Boston: Brandeis University Press, 2003), p. 50.
36 Włodzimierz Rozenbaum, 'The Anti-Zionist Campaign in Poland, June-December 1967', in *Canadian Slavonic Papers / Revue Canadienne des Slavistes* 20.2 (June 1978), pp. 218–236.
37 Simon Gansinger, 'Communists Against Jews: the Anti-Zionist Campaign in Poland in 1968', in *Fathom* (Autumn 2016), available at: http://fathomjournal.org/communists-against-jews-the-anti-zionist-campaign-in-poland-in-1968.
38 It is not my intention to assert that the essential nature of the conflict is religious (Jewish-Muslim) – quite the contrary is the case. Rather I seek to leave room for the outermost of the three circles in which the conflict takes place: (1) Israeli-Palestinian (including both Christians and Muslims); (2) Israeli-Arab; and (3) Israeli-Muslim which would, *inter alia*, include Iran.

in Toulouse, France in 2012 and the bombing of the offices of the Asociación Mutual Israelita Argentina in Buenos Aires in 1994, which injured hundreds and murdered 85 people. While this was not the case in these examples, some of the Jewish victims and targets of such violence may not even be engaged Zionists themselves. Ironically, the creation of the Jewish State, which was to have contributed to the security of the Jewish people, has sometimes jeopardised Jewish lives in the diaspora.

But perhaps more significant than the impact of stipulation number two is that of stipulation number one. One could say that the first stipulation is the unfinished business of the Balfour Declaration and, indeed, the State of Israel. The stipulation reads: 'nothing shall be done which may prejudice the civil and religious rights of existing non-Jewish communities in Palestine.' I will not address the political rights, which are absent and therefore lacking any guarantee. As Ronald Storrs observed: 'While their religions and civil rights were specifically to be safeguarded, of their political rights there was no mention whatever. Clearly, they had none.'[39] The dual promises to the Jewish and Arab peoples was concretised by the UN Partition Plan of November 1947 which called for the creation of two states in Palestine. The national rights of the Arabs were to have been realised in this Arab state. But what is the status of the Arab minority in the State of Israel? Israel's Proclamation of Independence, which references both the Balfour Declaration and the Mandate, acknowledges minority rights as follows:

> The State of Israel... will be based on freedom, justice and peace as envisaged by the prophets of Israel; it will ensure complete equality of social and political rights to all its inhabitants irrespective of religion, race or sex; it will guarantee freedom of religion, conscience, language, education and culture; it will safeguard the Holy Places of all religions.[40]

The Proclamation guaranteed freedom of language and other cultural expressions and accorded to the Arab minority 'complete equality of social and political rights', going beyond what Storrs had expected from the Proclamation.[41] Indeed, the Proclamation set the bar rather high regarding the status of the social, political and cultural rights of Arab citizens in Israel.

---

39 Sir Ronald Storrs, *Lawrence of Arabia: Zionism and Palestine* (London: Penguin, 1940), p. 66, available at: http://www.gwpda.org/memoir/Storrs/zionism/zionism.pdf.
40 See: https://www.knesset.gov.il/docs/eng/megilat_eng.htm.
41 It is, of course, possible that by 'political rights' Storrs was referring to what we might call 'national rights'.

Israel was defined in the Proclamation as a 'Jewish State'.[42] Since 1985, Israel has defined itself as a 'Jewish and democratic state'.[43] There has ensued a vigorous debate as to whether these two natures of the state were compatible and, whether non-Jews (to use the language of the Proclamation) could enjoy equal rights in a state defined as Jewish. A 2013 survey showed that: 'A sizeable majority of Jews (74.8%) believe that the State of Israel can be both Jewish and democratic. Only a third of Arab respondents share this view.'[44] The religious rights of non-Jewish Israelis are, to a great measure, upheld with minor short-fallings. Evaluation of this parameter ranges from noting the well-functioning state system of sharia courts serving the Muslim public in parallel to the Jewish rabbinic courts, to the current bill that would outlaw the muezzin's call to prayer at night.[45] A recent survey of challenges to Israeli democracy highlights several issues and lists three items in the section entitled 'Legislation Intended to Harm the Status or Rights of the Arab Minority in Israel'.[46] The main area of concern is a Proposed Basic Law entitled 'Israel – The Nation-State of the Jewish People'.[47] A Basic Law in Israel

---

42 The term 'Jewish State' (and 'Arab State') was already used by the UNGA Partition resolution of November 1947: 'Independent Arab and Jewish States... shall come into existence in Palestine' (Resolution 181 II). Future government of Palestine, Part 1.A.3, available at: https://unispal.un.org/DPA/DPR/unispal.nsf/0/7F0AF2BD897689B785256C33 0061D253.

43 The term democratic appears for the first time in Amendment 9 to Section 7A of Basic Law – The Knesset – 1958, which was adopted on 31 July 1985. Basic Law: The Knesset (Amendment No. 9), available at: https://www.knesset.gov.il/laws/special/eng/basic2_eng. htm.

44 Tamar Hermann et. al., *The Israeli Democracy Index* (Jerusalem: The Israel Democracy Institute, 2013), p. 8, available at: https://en.idi.org.il/media/5112/2013-democracy-index-main-findings.pdf. It is interesting to note that a 2017 follow-up survey showed that significantly more (32% vs. 23%) Israeli Jews sought to strengthen Israel's democratic character over its Jewish aspect. T. Hermann et. al., *The Israeli Democracy Index* (Jerusalem: The Israel Democracy Institute, 2017), p. 6, available at: https://en.idi.org.il/media/9837/israeli-democracy-index-2017-en-summary.pdf.

45 Though it should be noted that attempts to restrict the muezzin's call to prayer are not unique to Israel.

46 Debbie Gild-Hayo, 'Legislation Intended to Harm the Status or Rights of the Arab Minority in Israel', in *Overview of Anti-Democratic Legislation Advanced by the 20th Knesset*, Association for Civil Rights in Israel, pp. 10–13, available at: https://www. acri.org.il/en/wp-content/uploads/2018/02/December-Overview-of-Anti-Democratic-Legislation-2017.pdf. I have discussed some distressingly problematic aspects in 'Recent uses of Halakhic Discourse in Israel: Encouraging Racism and Violence', in Jesper Svartvik and Jakob Wirén, eds., *Religious Stereotyping and Interreligious Relations* (Basingstoke: Palgrave Macmillan, 2013), pp. 224–225.

47 The law in question was adopted by Israel's parliament on 19 July 2018.

has quasi-constitutional status. In addition to establishing Israel's national character as exclusively Jewish, the provisions of this bill stipulate that Hebrew would be the official language of the state and would lead to a lowered status for Arabic.[48] The others are bills concerning the disqualification or impeachment of members of the Knesset which are seen as targeting Arab delegates. To these may be added the change in the electoral threshold for a party's representatives to be elected to the Knesset. In March 2014, in advance of the elections for the current legislature, the vote percentage required to seat delegates was raised from 2 to 3.25 percent. As this was quite close to the anticipated support for several Arab parties, this was understood to be a move to diminish Arab representation.[49]

It is enough to look at the situation of the civil rights of the Arab minority in the State of Israel to see that the safeguards of this stipulation have not been fully realised. In this regard, Israel has not entirely lived up to the first stipulation of the Balfour Declaration nor to its own Proclamation of Independence. The language of the Declaration, which discusses the rights of Jewish and non-Jewish minorities, invites consideration of the situation from the perspective of majority-minority relations.[50]

Majority-minority relations in the Jewish tradition

I will conclude by examining what the Jewish tradition teaches in regard to majority-minority relations and what reality might look like according to this religious

---

48 There is disagreement regarding the current (since 1948) status of Arabic. For the maximalist view cf. Dafna Yitzhaki, *Minority Languages and Language Policy: The Case of Arabic in Israel*, Ph.D. Thesis, Bar-Ilan University, May 2008, p. 6fn. Aviad Bakshi presents a minimalist argument in *Is Arabic an Official Language in Israel?* (Jerusalem: The Institute for Zionist Strategies, 2011). English abstract available at: http://izs.org.il/2015/12/the-status-of-arabic-in-the-state-of-israel.

49 As a result of the change, several Arab parties (and one Jewish-Arab party) combined to form the Joint [Arab] List which was elected as the third largest party to the Knesset. Small Jewish parties were threatened by the change as well.

50 Majority-minority relations are a global issue taking different forms in different settings. With great regret, I conclude that the relations between Israel's Jewish majority and Palestinian Arab minority will be held hostage by the Israeli-Palestinian conflict until the conflict is successfully resolved. The civil rights of Palestinian Israelis, while improving slowly, are not likely to reach equality so long as Israelis perceive an existential threat from the Palestinian side. While disheartening, it may be instructive to contemplate, hypothetically, how much more difficult the civil rights struggle might have been in the US had Canada and Mexico both been populated by people of colour with a history of violence directed at the US.

imagination. The Jewish people is well schooled in the realities of minority life. From biblical times this has been the fate of the Jews: 'It is not because you are the most numerous of peoples that the Lord set His heart on you and chose you – indeed, you are the smallest of peoples' (Deuteronomy 7:7). The experience of the Jewish people for the last 2,000 years, until the creation of the modern State of Israel, has been that of a minority. But what does the Jewish tradition teach about the role and responsibilities of a majority towards the minority that lives amongst it, and what might that mean in the Israeli reality where Jews constitute the large majority?

Rabbi Samson Raphael Hirsch knew what it meant to be a minority. He was the rabbi of the secessionist Orthodox community in Frankfurt am Main – a community dominated by Reform Judaism in the 19th century. Commenting on the previous passage in Deuteronomy, 'For you are a people consecrated to the Lord your God: of all the peoples on earth the Lord your God chose you to be His treasured people' (v. 6), he wrote:

> 'God chose you' is an explanation of the preceding 'For you are a people consecrated to the Lord...' The whole purpose of your having been chosen was no other than to establish a national social life which would mould itself under the exclusive influence of God, i.e. which would conform with the dictates of His Torah.

On the dictates of the Torah with regard to the responsibilities of a majority to a minority population, Rabbi Hirsch explained in his commentary on Exodus 22:20–21 ('You shall not wrong a stranger or oppress him, for you were strangers in the land of Egypt') as follows:

> The great, meta-principle is oft-repeated in the Torah that it is not race, not descent, not birth nor country of origin, nor property, nor anything external or due to chance, but simply and purely the inner spiritual and moral worth of a human being, that gives him/her all the rights of a human being and of a citizen. This basic principle is further protected against infringement by the additional explanation, 'For you were *gerim* in the land of Egypt.' ... Your entire misfortune in Egypt was that you were 'foreigners' and 'aliens'. As such, according to the views of other nations, you had no right to be there, had no claim to property, to homeland, or to a dignified existence. It was permissible to do to you whatever they wished. As *gerim*, your rights were denied in Egypt. ... Therefore, beware, so runs the warning, from making

human rights in your own state conditional on anything other than on the basic humanity which every human being as such bears within him/her by virtue of being human. Any suppression of these human and civil rights opens the gate to the indiscriminate use of power and abuse of human beings, to the whole horror of Egyptian mishandling of human beings that was the root of abomination of Egypt.[51]

I have left the Hebrew term *ger* (plural: *gerim*) untranslated because it requires explanation. *Ger* does have the meaning of 'foreigner' or 'stranger'. But to leave it there is superficial. We must understand *ger* to mean the weak, vulnerable and disenfranchised in our society. Often these are the minorities. And I must clarify, I am not understanding *ger* to mean 'foreigner' or 'stranger' in the context of the Palestinian minority in the State of Israel. They are not strangers; they are native daughters and sons of the land. But they constitute a minority and as such are liable to be the weak, vulnerable and disenfranchised members of our society. In the Hebrew bible *gerim* are frequently linked to their peers in vulnerability – orphans and widows.

Multiple passages in the Torah make clear that *ger* can be understood in this way. Not only are we instructed to be sensitive and not oppress the *ger* but also other categories of vulnerable people in our community who are grouped together with the *ger* must receive compassionate treatment:

> You shall not wrong a stranger (*ger*) or oppress him, for you were strangers (*gerim*) in the land of Egypt. You shall not ill-treat any widow or orphan. If you do mistreat them, I will heed their outcry as soon as they cry out to Me, and My anger shall blaze forth… (Exodus 22:21–22).

> For the Lord… upholds the cause of the orphan and the widow, and befriends the stranger, providing him with food and clothing. You too must befriend the stranger, for you were strangers in the land of Egypt (Deuteronomy 10:17–19).

> Cursed be he who subverts the rights of the stranger, the orphan, and the widow… (Deuteronomy 27:19).[52]

---

51 Samson Raphael Hirsch, *The Pentateuch – translated and explained by Samson Raphael Hirsch*, transl. Isaac Levy (London 1956).
52 Cf. Deuteronomy 14:29, 16:14, 24:21, Isaiah 1:23 and Chap. 2 of Ruth.

Early rabbinic commentary on the verse elucidated by Rabbi Hirsch expands its
applicability to all of humankind. In the terse phrasing of the *Mekhilta de-Rabbi
Yishmael*, we read:

'You shall not ill-treat any widow or orphan' (Exodus 22:21).

This appears to include only the widow and the orphan; from where [may we
infer the extension of this law to] all other people?

The verse states, *Lo te 'anun* (לֹא תְעַנּוּן) – these are the words of Rabbi
Yishmael.[53]

Thus Rabbi Yishmael interprets the wording – or in this case spelling – as emphatic.
Or in the simpler formulation of the pre-eminent biblical commentator Rashi:
'The same applies to all people, but the Scripture speaks of the usual situation,
since they [widows and orphans] are weak and [they] are frequently oppressed.'[54]
As is widely mentioned, the Hebrew Bible regularly couples sensitivity to the
ger to the experience of Egyptian slavery, with the latter being the reason for the
former. The Talmud counts at least 36 such links.[55] For this Talmudic passage,
and much subsequent discussion, the term *ger* has been repurposed from meaning
vulnerable or stranger to denoting a convert to Judaism. This surprising metamor-
phosis has been well explained by Jill Jacobs:

For the rabbis, themselves living under foreign rule, it may have been
inconceivable to imagine a situation in which Jews constituted the majority
and non-Jews needed protection. Perhaps for this reason, the rabbis

---

53 *Mekhilta de-Rabbi Yishmael* is a Tannaitic source, i.e. dated before 220 CE. This close
reading of the verbal phrase, 'You shall not ill-treat' (*Lo te'anun*), points out the final
consonant, 'n', which might be considered superfluous. Rabbinic commitment to the Divine
purposefulness of each and every jot and tittle of scripture allows the suggestion that the
extra 'n' comes to provide emphasis. It was Rabbi Yishmael's determination that this
emphasis was meant to indicate an expansive interpretation including all of humanity. See
David Silverberg, *Parashat Mishpatim: 'You Shall Not Ill-Treat Any Widow or Orphan'*,
p.1, available at: https://www.mhcny.org/parasha/1136.pdf. Silverberg notes that the later
authority Maimonides did not concur with this interpretation.
54 *Ad* Exodus 22:21. Rashi, or Rabbi Shelomi Yitshaki, lived in the Rhineland between
1040–1105.
55 *Babylonian Talmud* Tractate Bava Metsia, p. 59b. Others include Exodus 23:9, Leviticus
19:34 and Deuteronomy 10:19. Barry L Schwartz calls this the argument from 'historical
empathy', available at: https://jps.org/for-you-were-strangers-in-the-land-of-egypt.

reconstructed the biblical mandate to protect the stranger as a warning not to discriminate against converts to Judaism.[56]

Unimaginable as it was to former generations, this revolution – from vulnerability to relative security; from powerlessness to power – has taken place and changed the reality of the Jewish people living in their ancestral homeland.

But inconceivable as such a transformation was, it was conceptually anticipated by the 11th-century Jewish philosopher Yehuda HaLevi in Spain. In his work, *The Book of Refutation and Proof in Support of the Abased Religion*, generally known as *The Kuzari*, he presents Judaism in dialogue with a pagan king. HaLevi extols Jewish morality (measured by his claim of closeness to God) as exhibited in a state of powerlessness:

> The Rabbi: I see thee reproaching us with our degradation and poverty, but the best of other religions boast of both. Do they not glorify him who said: 'He who smites thee on the right cheek, turn to him the left also;' and 'he who takes away thy coat, let him have thy shirt also.' He, and his friends and followers, after hundreds of years of contumely, flogging and slaying, attained their well-known success, and just in these things they glorify. This is also the history of the founder of Islam and his friends, who eventually prevailed, and became powerful. The nations boast of these, but not of these kings whose power and might are great, whose walls are strong, and whose chariots are terrible. Yet our relation to God is a closer one than if we had reached greatness already on earth.[57]

But the king protests that Jewish powerlessness is involuntary and that were the Jews empowered they would be no different from the gentiles:

> The Khazar King: This might be so, if your humility were voluntary; but it is involuntary, and if you had power you would slay.

And the Rabbi replies, admitting that Jewish powerlessness is not a strived-for virtue but rather a condition imposed from the outside:

---

56 'Ger'/Immigrant in 'Welcoming the Stranger', available at: http://www.on1foot.org/node/1204.
57 Medieval Sourcebook: Judah Ha-Levi: The Kuzari, part I, available at: http://www.fordham.edu/halsall/source/kuzari.asp, Paragraphs 113–115.

The Rabbi: Thou best touched our weak spot, O King of the Khazars.

The challenge of the Khazar King, known so well to HaLevi and expressed in his classic poetry with the words 'Zion lies beneath the fetter of Edom, and I am in Arab chains'[58] has been realised. With the establishment of a sovereign Jewish state the condition of powerlessness and vulnerability has been significantly eliminated.[59] Even more significantly, the empowered Jewish majority has, for the first time in over two millennia, a minority population living amongst it and dependent upon its policies and actions.

Since 1948, the scenario of the Declaration's first stipulation 'that nothing shall be done which may prejudice the civil and religious rights of existing non-Jewish communities in Palestine' has entered the crucible of historical trial. Not only the Declaration's proviso regarding the Arab minority, but also the weight of the Jewish tradition demand that great measures be taken to assure that the rights of the non-Jewish citizenry be respected to the highest degree possible.

The nation state with a minority of another national-ethnic-religious group provides an excellent application for John Rawls's theory of justice. His notion of decision and policy making from beyond an imagined 'veil of ignorance' in which even the situation of the less advantaged group is acceptable is a standard to which an empowered majority should aspire. For a people such as the Jews, who have known the realities of the disadvantaged position very well and for a very long time, it could be imagined that sensitivity and compassion towards the less-advantaged might come naturally. This idea is not exclusive to Rawls and dates from much earlier than the 1970s; indeed, it is found already in the Jewish tradition in one of its most fundamental texts. The basic principle of human rights, that all people are equal, is captured by the famous teaching of Rabbi Hillel of the 1st century BCE:

What is hateful to you, do not do to your fellow. This is the entire Torah; the rest is commentary. [60]

---

58 *My Heart is in the East and I am in the Uttermost West.* See: http://www.jewishvirtuallibrary.org/quot-my-heart-is-in-the-east-quot-yehuda-halevi.
59 Discussion of the persistent Jewish-Israeli sense of collective vulnerability is important and interesting but beyond the scope of the present essay.
60 Babylonian Talmud, Shabbat 31a. Jesus, of course, echoes this in the following century. The 'Golden Rule' is found across world religions. See: https://www.scarboromissions.ca/product/golden-rule-across-the-worlds-religions.

Bibliography

Amery, Leopold S, *My Political Life: War and peace, 1914–1929* (London: Hutchinson, 1953).

Baker, R S and W E Dodd, eds., *The Public Papers of Woodrow Wilson, War and Peace*, vol. I (New York: Harper, 1927).

Bakshi, Aviad, *Is Arabic an Official Language in Israel?* (Jerusalem: The Institute for Zionist Strategies, 2011).

Bell, Gertrude, *A Woman in Arabia: The Writings of the Queen of the Desert*, ed. Georgina Howell (London: Penguin Classics 2015).

Campus, Rita, 'The comparison between Zionists and Catholics in the pages of "Israel" during the 1920s', in Luciano Martini, ed., *Giorgio La Pira e la vocazione di Israele* 26.

Cohen, Raymond, 'Was Theology to Blame? The Holy See and Israel's Stony Path to Normalization', in Emma O'Donnell Polyakov, ed., *Antisemitism, Islamophobia, and Interreligious Hermeneutics: Ways of Seeing the Religious Other* (Leiden: Brill/Rodopi, Forthcoming).

Gansinger, Simon, 'Communists Against Jews: the Anti-Zionist Campaign in Poland in 1968', in *Fathom* (Autumn 2016), available at: http://fathomjournal.org/communists-against-jews-the-anti-zionist-campaign-in-poland-in-1968.

Gild-Hayo, Debbie, 'Legislation Intended to Harm the Status or Rights of the Arab Minority in Israel', in *Overview of Anti-Democratic Legislation Advanced by the 20th Knesset*, Association for Civil Rights in Israel.

Hermann, Tamar, et. al., *The Israeli Democracy Index* (Jerusalem: The Israel Democracy Institute, 2013).

Hermann, Tamar, et. al., *The Israeli Democracy Index* (Jerusalem: The Israel Democracy Institute, 2017).

Hirsch, Samson Raphael, *The Pentateuch – translated and explained by Samson Raphael Hirsch*, transl. Isaac Levy (London 1956).

The Koren Siddur, transl. Jonathan Sacks (Jerusalem: Koren, 2009).

Koestler, Arthur, *Promise and Fulfilment: Palestine 1917–1949* (New York: Macmillan, 1949), available at: https://archive.org/stream/promiseandfulfil006754mbp/promiseandfulfil006754mbp_djvu.txt.

Kramer, Martin, 'The Forgotten Truth about the Balfour Declaration', in *Mosaic Magazine*, 5 June 2017, available at: https://mosaicmagazine.com/essay/2017/06/the-forgotten-truth-about-the-balfour-declaration.

The Letters and Papers of Chaim Weizmann: Volume I, Series B, August 1898-July 1931, ed. Barnet Litvinoff (New Jersey: Transaction, 1983).

Mansfield, Peter, 'Lawrence and his Legacy', in *The British Empire Magazine* 76, available at: https://www.britishempire.co.uk/maproom/lawrenceandhislegacy.htm.

Meron, Ya'akov, 'Why Jews Fled the Arab Countries', in *Middle East Quarterly* 2.3 (September 1995).

Minerbi, Sergio, *The Vatican and Zionism: Conflict in the Holy Land, 1895–1925* (New York: Oxford University Press, 1990).

Ministere des Affaires Etrangeres, ed., *Documents diplomatiques français: 1921 (Annexes 10 janvier 1920–31 décembre 1921)* (Oxford: Peter Lang, 2005).

Nashashibi, Sharif, 'Balfour: Britain's original sin', in *Aljazeera*, 4 November 2014, available at: https://www.aljazeera.com/indepth/opinion/2014/11/balfour-britain-original-sin-201411472940231416.html.

Navon, Emmanuel, 'La France vue d'Israël: illusions perdues', in *Outre-Terre* 2.3 (2003).

Polakow-Suransky, Sasha, *The Unspoken Alliance: Israel's Secret Relationship with Apartheid South Africa* (London: Random House, 2010).

Quigley, Carroll, *The Anglo-American Establishment* (New York: Books in Focus, 1981).

Rozenbaum, Wlodzimierz, 'The Anti-Zionist Campaign in Poland, June-December 1967', in *Canadian Slavonic Papers / Revue Canadienne des Slavistes* 20.2 (June 1978), pp. 218–236.

Rubinstein, William D, 'The Secret of Leopold Amery', in *Historical Research* 73.181 (2000), pp. 175–196.

Sanders, Ronald, *The High Walls of Jerusalem* (New York: Holt, Rinehart and Winston, 1983).

Shimoni, Gideon, *Community and Conscience: The Jews in Apartheid South Africa* (Boston: Brandeis University Press, 2003).

Silverberg, David, *Parashat Mishpatim: 'You Shall Not Ill-Treat Any Widow or Orphan'*, available at: https://www.mhcny.org/parasha/1136.pdf.

Storrs, Ronald, *Lawrence of Arabia: Zionism and Palestine* (New York: Penguin Books, 1940).

Toynbee, Arnold J, 'The Present Situation in Palestine', in *International Affairs* 10.1 (1931), pp. 38–68.

Yarden, Ophir, 'Recent uses of Halakhic Discourse in Israel: Encouraging Racism and Violence', in Jesper Svartvik and Jakob Wirén, eds., *Religious Stereotyping and Interreligious Relations* (Basingstoke: Palgrave Macmillan, 2013).

Ye'or, Bat, *Islam and Dhimmitude: Where Civilizations Collide* (Madison: Fairleigh Dickinson University Press, 2002).

Yitzhaki, Dafna, *Minority Languages and Language Policy: The Case of Arabic in Israel*, Ph.D. Thesis, Bar-Ilan University, May 2008.

5

Diplomacy and the Religious Imagination

John Casson

Egypt has produced an unbroken story of religious imagination shaping state and society for at least 5,000 years. To this day, to explore the complexity of imaginations which shape our world, a good place to start is asking anyone on the Cairo microbus, 'Are you first a Muslim, a Christian, an African, an Arab or an Egyptian?' In my experience, if pressed, Egyptians usually opt in the end for an Egyptian national identity over a religious or wider cultural or geographical norm. But the question often vexes them, forcing a choice that does not reflect their identity and experience.

Egyptians of course are not alone in navigating the world with multiple identities, some of which are overtly religious and others not explicitly so. This fact underlines the importance of Mona Siddiqui's plea (Chapter Two) that we move beyond misrepresentative distinctions like 'religious' and 'secular'. From the perspective of my home in Cairo, the idea of a 'religious imagination' – presumably opposed to a 'normal', secular one – seems, frankly, quaint and outmoded.

Taking my profession of diplomacy as the starting point, I want to argue for a more comprehensive understanding of the tapestry of human imaginations which shape our world. To do this, I am going to explore what diplomacy and religion have to do with one another, reflecting on two decades as a British diplomat. I will make three points in particular:

1. Religion and diplomacy are in each other's space whether they like it or not, and this demands a deeper engagement between the practices and practitioners of each.

2. In reality, we find that this deeper engagement encounters obstacles and is typically limited for reasons and in ways I will elaborate on later.

3. Finally, by way of the confessions of a British diplomat, I indicate some areas where I believe we face a crisis of the diplomatic imagination and where we might look more to faith.

The diplomatic imagination

Before we get on to religion, let me start with political and diplomatic imaginations. It's popular to think of politics and diplomacy as profoundly cynical and Machiavellian enterprises. But diplomacy is in fact rooted in two fundamental moral imperatives.

First, by their nature, human beings are distinctive as animals that form moral communities of identity and loyalty. Benedict Anderson showed us how we exist of necessity in 'imagined communities' of nation, tribe, empire or even what Daesh (ISIS) called their Caliphate.[1] Each of these is a moral project (even the latter, which consciously sees itself enjoining the right and forbidding the wrong). These moral communities set human communities apart in allowing us to show loyalty, trust and altruism to those beyond our immediate genetic family or our social group of direct personal relationships. When they take the form of nations, binding their citizens in shared interests and loyalties, our imagined moral communities are a necessary condition for the profession of diplomacy, in which diplomats serve 'national interests' conceived of as altruistic loyalty to our national moral community. However, as Jonathan Sacks explores in his book, *Not in God's Name*, these moral communities are not only the basis for the human virtues of altruism, trust and sacrifice, but they also create a fundamental human problem at their boundaries, where others are by necessity excluded and competing moral communities are encountered.[2] Nations, tribes and Caliphates compete, producing violence, justifying it as altruistic, and feeding what Sacks calls a 'pathological dualism' between 'us' and 'them'.

The second moral imperative for diplomacy is thus the need to imagine ways to restrain this violence between human groups. As Sacks points out, this requires a human imagination not just of identity but also of universality, not just of loyalty but also of justice. This too is necessary for diplomacy and we find the diplomatic imagination of inter-group obligations in everything from international law, to

---

1 B Anderson, *Imagined Communities* (New York: Verso, 1991).
2 J Sacks, *Not in God's Name* (London: Hodder and Stoughton, 2016).

universal rights, balance of power theory and the sovereign rights of nations. So I see the core task of diplomacy not as holding cocktail parties, but as managing the boundary between national interests and global common goods, a boundary which is at the heart of the issues thrown up by globalisation – from Brexit, to the Balkans, to arguing about when to lift the travel ban on Sharm El Sheikh.

Diplomacy and religion

A moral imagination of identity and universality is integral, not incidental, to diplomacy. Of course, this is at the very heart of the religious imagination too. In most times and most places of human existence, the principal moral and imaginative resources for both group loyalty and universal morality have been religious. Diplomats need to stop treating faith as an exotic holdover or just a source of irrational disruptions. Polemicists can either simply condemn religion *per se* as the source of violence or defend it as inherently peaceable and a bastion against violence and immorality. But we have no choice but to engage with religion in its complexity, as an inextricable element of the tragedies and glories of the human imaginations that shape our world. Moreover, we need to have the humility and imagination ourselves to appreciate that faith is the most profound intellectual, social and personal resource which human history has produced for the task which over-matches us all: mediating compassion and justice in a globalised world of change, conflict, and power imbalances.

Egypt offers no shortage of examples of how religion is integral to the competing imaginations that shape the issues preoccupying diplomats and politicians. The 2013 struggle between the Muslim Brotherhood and its opponents was argued out in terms of the primacy of loyalty to religious or national identity. Even among those who accept, as most Egyptians do, that religion should remain at the core of national identity and social norms, the question of who should interpret that religion and how is profoundly contested. Terrorist attacks on Coptic Christians and the varied responses to them reflect competing imaginations of politics, morality and nation, seen through a religious lens. For me as a diplomatic practitioner, there is little point in an academic debate about whether religion as a general category should or should not shape Egypt as it does. Religion and diplomacy have no choice but to engage. We are in each other's space. Our imaginations overlap and contend, influence and interfere with each other.

Here I part company with those who wish that politicians would stay out of the defining debate preoccupying Sunni Islam. That choice simply does not exist. If Daesh considers the nation state an idolatrous construct to be destroyed and considers those who disagree non-believers who can be slain, then Daesh is intruding into the political space whether we like it or not. Diplomats and western politicians are by definition Westphalians, living out a belief in the nation state and liberal notions of universal rights upheld by the state. We need to be sophisticated and smart about the modest and sometimes counter-productive impact we as outsiders can have on intra-Islamic arguments. But we are participants in the debate and we have a huge stake in its outcome. Our human communities and the interactions at their boundaries are all shaped by imaginations which are at once political and religious, all of them implying theological assumptions about humanity and history. These imaginations contend, interact and overlap, and the specific shape of that re-imagining matters.

Uncritical endorsements of religion are as unhelpful as its condemnation. I very much share the critique of a lazy association of religion and violence and of those who essentialise and demonise faith as inherently violent, irrational or intolerant. But if we are too quick to defend faith from being demonised, there is a risk in turn of reducing and essentialising secularism and the criticism of religion in general – and indeed of essentialising religions as purely peaceable. If we are too quick to absolve religion and demonise secularism, we will obscure the true challenge we face as much as if we demonise faith. It is not enough to assert that religion is welcome or unwelcome. We need to go deeper and work harder by attempting to answer such questions as: *Which* religious imagination matters? Just as with any political imagination, the specific ideas, pathologies and mobilisations make all the difference. And while diplomats cannot resolve the theological debates for religion, the outcomes of the debate matter to us existentially and shape the outcomes we are working for.

Obstacles and limitations in engagement between diplomacy and religion

What I have set out so far points to *why* I think there is an imperative for greater religious literacy among diplomats, and greater engagement with religion, beyond the superficial scripts of empathy and protocol we so often fall back on. As we turn to the *how*, let me explore some reasons why this engagement turns out to be difficult and limited in practice. Again, I want to start not with the religious imagination, but with some inherent characteristics of the diplomatic imagination.

First of all, in the West at least, our government systems depend on an imagination pertaining to secular nationalism. Our institutions function because of shared loyalty to the nation state as a moral unit of solidarity and altruism, and to an effective ideology of utilitarianism and human rights of all citizens, in which the underlying philosophical and theological foundations are left largely unspoken. The civil service ethic which governs the conduct of officials such as myself, requires us to some extent to keep our personal beliefs tacit and to suppress religious identities should they come into conflict with the shared institutional imagination and identity. As a result there is hesitation amongst diplomats and officials about bringing the language of religion centre stage, even as an object of analysis, lest it create unease about potential heresies and competing allegiances that deviate from civil service 'neutrality'.

Second, when diplomats engage with diplomats of other countries, whatever the terms of the national discourse in the countries each represents, diplomacy between competing imaginations requires creating and accepting a neutral space for discussion. To take one example, Iranian diplomats and American diplomats at home may be committed to profoundly conflicting theo-political imaginations, but their negotiations on nuclear technological controls and economic sanctions have to be based on a shared imagination of great power pragmatism, with theological assertion kept to the opening statements before the cameras. Unless religious imaginations are suppressed or kept tacit the whole board tips over.

In other words, the disengagement of religion from diplomacy is not primarily due to religious illiteracy on the part of diplomats (although often it facilitates that). It reflects a category clash, which reveals the limitations of the diplomatic imagination, unable for political and philosophical reasons to address fully the theological implications of the issues it is concerned with, or the role of faith as a motivation, or the religious content of the imaginations that determine the diplomatic ethics of loyalty and universality. As a result, engagement between diplomacy and religion is typically limited in one of three ways:

First, we compartmentalise religion, permitting it to be a legitimate factor only in the categories of private motivation or of personal status laws that govern faith and family. In the West, the secularisation of the public sphere was hard won and became the basis for our modern democracy, dignity and development. But it can mean that when religion, despite our best efforts, resurfaces in the public realm we are baffled and perplexed. We diplomats need a deeper awareness that the insistence on the retreat of explicit religious identity motivation and authority from the public realm is producing a religious counter-reaction that shapes political imaginations around the world. Secular values are not always and everywhere experienced as liberty, empowerment and development. And we need to recognise that by compartmentalising faith, we are denying ourselves vital religious resources of social mobilisation and imagination on some of the defining issues in the public realm – from education and equality, to population and violence.

Second, we instrumentalise religion. Again, to take an example close to home for me, Cairo's Al-Azhar University as the oldest and most prestigious seat of Islamic scholarship in the Sunni world faces pressure from many directions to win the intellectual battle against extremism, and to condemn and denounce ideas and actions which pervert 'true religion'. But as a 1,000-year-old educational institution, Al-Azhar exists for many purposes and cannot be reduced to a political mouthpiece of our counter-terrorism efforts. Indeed, if we co-opt Al-Azhar too successfully, we undermine the very legitimacy that we wish to call to our aid in the battle against extremist imaginations. Diplomats need to let faith be faith, awkward though that may be. This is the principle behind the new UK-Al-Azhar PhD scholarship programme. We ask nothing of emerging Azhari leaders than that they use the resources we offer to become the very best Islamic scholars they can be.

It is worth pausing here to ask why the most common area of productive and sophisticated engagement between religion and diplomacy is conflict resolution? I would suggest in this area there is the most straightforward alignment between the peace-making mission of diplomats and the reconciliation mission of religious leaders, so the instrumentalisation problem does not arise sharply.

Thirdly, we institutionalise religion. Diplomats understandably seek out representatives of religion who are most recognisably like us. Where engagement with religion happens it is commonly in conference rooms with the internationally savvy representatives of the religious hierarchy. I once asked one of the leaders of the 2007 Common Word initiative between Christian and Muslim leaders how he proposed to make sure the laudable sentiments of the declaration entered the hearts and minds of a billion and more Muslims worldwide. His answer – that those Muslims' beliefs were shaped by 150 leaders all of whom were in his phone address book – sounds naïve in the light of the events since. But we display the same natural instinct everywhere – from the 2002 Alexandria Declaration on the Israeli-Palestinian conflict, to the focus on religious leaders' statements after every terrorist outrage; a necessary but insufficient response. Diplomats need to realise that the answer to a crisis of religious authority in a networked world is not just to cling ever more stoutly to those religious hierarchies whose authority is no longer accepted. We should not mistake talking to religious leaders for engagement with the currents of faith that are shaping our word. We need to go deeper and work harder.

Aspirations and confessions of a diplomat

If these are our limitations, what should our aspirations be?

Let's acknowledge that diplomacy and religion need each other, and that diplomats must make their contribution with a deeper understanding of both religion and faith. Diplomats must enhance their comprehension of religion – in Egypt, for example, we desperately need to get beyond the sterile debate between those who see the Muslim Brotherhood as a victimised Islamic equivalent of the Christian Democrats, and those who see them as indistinguishable from Daesh. Diplomats must also build deeper modes of engagement with religion and cultivate true partnerships between the two. We need to create a neutral space for engagement – neither on diplomacy's nor religion's terms alone. We need more explicit language in diplomatic circles about the varied roles of faith in the world we aim to influence, and about the theological assumptions that shape our own imagination. And we need to draw on the resources of faith to refresh our imaginations for a twenty-first century world where we resolve the competing demands of the local and the universal – for example re-imagining the obligation to the alien in an economy of global information, transportation and consumption.

While I am being aspirational, let me close by offering a more personal hope for a new contribution from religion too, rooted in the testimony of my experience as a diplomat. Discussions like this in foreign policy typically consider religion a problem for us policymakers to resolve with more religious literacy and more engagement to help save religion from itself. But I would like to remind those who serve as representatives of religion that we diplomats need you and the resources of faith and theology you can draw on for our wider diplomatic task. In my experience, diplomacy is a demanding business, and the resources available are thin for the task. We in the Middle East especially face a crisis of diplomatic imagination as to what kind of future co-existence between loyalty and co-operation we can build. We operate on the boundary of competing imaginations, colliding with each other, and trying to re-imagine a future for the world as it is, not as we or our inherited imaginations would like it to be. This is demanding intellectually. A diplomat needs to sustain a hopeful imagination that is neither cynical nor naïve. We need to be able to draw on an ethical imagination of the other, without eliminating our professional ethic of commitment to our own nation and moral community. We need a language to confront and go beyond the dualisms of 'us' and 'them', friend and foe.

Diplomacy is also demanding in terms of character, especially in leadership positions. It demands virtue, and wisdom of the heart and soul as well as of the head. That means mindful awareness of the self, the others and the world. It demands resources of compassion and empathy. It requires an inner place to root forgiveness and an irenic spirit which does not remember wrongs, especially in times when we may find ourselves demonised and lied about. It requires self-control, patience and perseverance. I would go as far as to say that you cannot be a good diplomat without paying attention to your inner life. Of course, different individuals will do this differently and many without any explicit faith or religious practice. But at the very least I think we can all recognise that the resources of faith have an enormous amount to offer for this task.

I end by appealing to religious leaders and scholars of religion to develop their political and diplomatic literacy as we diplomats develop our religious literacy. Diplomats need religious resources of theological imagination and faith which go beyond stale religious nationalism, oppositional or identity politics. We need you in ways both prophetic and practical to take up the task of supporting us as we strive to re-imagine the globalised world. Without religious imaginations we will not in the end be able to sustain globalisation.

Bibliography

Anderson, B, *Imagined Communities* (New York: Verso, 1991).
Sacks, J, *Not in God's Name* (London: Hodder and Stoughton, 2016).

6

The Musical Imagination in Religious Worship[1]

Mena Mark Hanna

Music has been our chosen means of communication with God since the earliest days of prayer: the first musical notations were to Sumerian gods; the Egyptians attributed the origin of music to the god Thoth; and, likewise for the Greeks, music was divine – it was invented to accompany the birth of Zeus. The anthropologist Roy Rappaport reasons that musical 'performance is the sine qua non of ritual, for if there is no performance there is no ritual'.[2] For our religious praise, musical performance cannot be uncoupled from rite, regardless of how one prays or who one prays to. At the heart of deep religious rumination or ecstatic congregational outpouring is, and always has been, music.

Music is also at the source of everything that defines us as human beings – how

---

1 This chapter is derived from the programme notes and pre-concert lecture for the Religious Imaginations and Global Transitions Conference on 14 June 2017 at Holy Trinity Sloane Square, London. The concert programme was as follows: *Coptic Paschal Psalm Cantillation* (traditional) performed by Mena Mark Hanna, cantor; *Missa Rigensis* by Uģis Prauliņš (1957–) performed by Holy Trinity Choir; Oliver Lallemant, conductor; *Wadi-n-Natrun* for solo cello by Mena Mark Hanna (1984–) performed by Rohan de Saram, cello; *The Threefold Priestly Blessing* by Zavel Zilberts (1881–1949) performed by Paul Heller, cantor; Peter Foggitt, organ; *Psalms* by Salamone Rossi (ca. 1570–1630) performed by Holy Trinity Choir; Oliver Lallemant, conductor; *Deux Melodies Hebraïques* for cello and piano by Maurice Ravel (1875–1937), arranged by Orfeo Mandozzi (1968) performed by Rohan de Saram, cello; Peter Foggitt, piano.
2 Roy Rappaport, *Ecology, Meaning, and Religion* (Richmond, CA: North Atlantic Books, 1979), pp. 176–177.

we relate to each other and how we struggle to comprehend the universe around us. The Greek mathematician Pythagoras, somewhat a cult figure, supposedly discovered that musical notes could translate into mathematical equations, the basis of what became known as the *Music of the Spheres* – the belief in a universe ordered by the same numerical proportions that govern music. Plato found music's effect on human emotion so powerful that it had the potential to subvert the rule of law and governance; he suggested banishing musical poetry from the ideal city of the Republic. And Aristotle described music as a pillar of society, including music in one of the four branches of education (along with reading and writing, gymnastics, and drawing). Unlike reading and writing, which have a practical or utilitarian usefulness, music is valuable because it leads to leisure. Proper leisure cultivates the mind and opens one's thoughts to deep intellectual exploration and curiosity; leisure can lead to the improvement of moral character. At least since the time of Aristotle, the conviction has existed that music makes us happier – yet it can dangerously destabilise human emotion; it can also make us think deeper – and may connect us to the natural universe, perhaps improve our moral character.

Still, the question arises: why is music a central aspect of human praise? I think the answer lies in three innate characteristics of the musical imagination in religion: first, music can be an encounter between language and voice, an encounter that has practical applications for religious worship; second, certain religious musical performances combine the roles of listener, performer and composer – for religious participant-performers, music is mysterious, ineffable and experiential; and third, religious music often blends the sacred with the mundane, bringing lowly human expression to the heights of heaven.

For the first characteristic, that of the encounter between language and voice, take the book of Psalms, attributed to David, as early evidence of religious creativity and inspiration, where songs and poems appeared as praise, reflections, and (sometimes) as utterances of frustration. The Qur'an refers to Psalms as inspired gifts from above.[3] Their centrality in the Abrahamic faiths is a result of their original function: David performed these psalms for himself and for whomever would listen; they are at once both private and publicly confessional. David, like Augustine in his autobiographical *Confessions*, describes his suffering and seeks divine guidance in Psalms. His Psalms are also vehicles of aural praise, and there are multiple examples of musical performance in David's Psalms.[4]

---

3 Sura 4, ayah 163; Sura 17, ayah 55 (Dawood).
4 Psalm 95, for example, 'O come, let us sing unto the Lord: let us make a joyful noise to the rock of our salvation.'

In both Jewish and Christian liturgical traditions, Psalms are used as they were originally intended: as a fusion of language and voice. This encounter, which Roland Barthes described as 'the grain of the voice',[5] is a space that sidesteps linguistic law and convention, because both music and language germinate within the human voice simultaneously. Each voice is unique and cannot be exactly replicated, an originality that luthiers and organologists have strived to emulate since time immemorial. In the Abrahamic traditions, the singing of psalms, the cantillation of scripture, Qur'anic chant, and the performance of liturgy all occur within this space.

A modern example is Uģis Prauliņš's *Missa Rigensis* (2003), written for a vast acoustic area meant to amplify the power of the human voice; the piece was premiered at Riga's cavernous medieval cathedral. Though Prauliņš has formal training in composition, his background is far more varied than the standard, thoroughly academicised contemporary composer of Western art music.[6] The *Missa Rigensis* stands out in its neo-Renaissance and neo-Baroque flairs, with the canonical 'Kyrie' and thick textural polyphony of the 'Credo'. Moreover, Prauliņš reinterprets the most common of Western liturgical texts, the Latin ordinary mass, and enlivens those words with a dazzling array of folk melodies, minimalist drones, and stylised speech. This is all done without the aid of an organ; Prauliņš is keen to preserve vocal utterance in its most natural form. To put it in another way: the *Missa Rigensis* has as its central attribute a celebration of 'the grain of the voice'.

For the second characteristic – the ambiguity of the roles of listener, performer and composer in religious music – I turn my attention to the towering musical cynosure in Western Christendom, J S Bach. Bach's music, even his secular and purely instrumental works, cannot be separated from his obsessive adoration of the Lutheran God. We know very little about Bach's life: what we do know is that he grew up in a society still reeling from the trauma of the Thirty Years' War and that his education was steeped in reactionary Protestant dogma. A cherished belief of the time, *Historia nihil repraesentat quod Christianus* (History is nothing but the demonstration of Christian truth), was enshrined in Johannes Buno's popular late 17th-century textbook *Historia Universalis*.[7] Bach's music lived through the

---

5 Roland Barthes, 'The Grain of the Voice', in *Image Music Text* (London: Fontana Press, 1977), pp. 179–189.
6 Prauliņš has arranged pop songs, performed in rock bands, and written several successful 'crossover' pieces.
7 Jan Chiapusso, 'Bach's Attitude Towards History', in *The Musical Quarterly* 39.3 (1953), p. 398.

church, through the organ, through the tradition of choir and composed liturgical worship. It is a zenith of musical complexity in the Western liturgical canon and his sacred music is pure: that is to say, it is strictly, unabashedly and avowedly religious, meant to be performed in the church by the ordained bodies of religious music in the Lutheran tradition – the choir led by the organist and Kapellmeister. And the listener? Maybe Bach meant God to be his listener. Or maybe Bach saw his music as an artistic manifestation of God's voice and, therefore, the congregation is meant to be the listener.

In Bach's great sacred oratorios, such as the *Matthäus-Passion* and *Johannes-Passion* or the *Weihnachts-Oratorium*, we have a Protestant Baroque manifestation of the medieval liturgical drama. In these massive, weighty works, we find text directly lifted from the gospels and interpolated with original text,[8] with various characters sung by soloists in recitative: the evangelists, Jesus, Judas, Peter, Pontius Pilate, Pilate's wife, etc. Christ's words, *vox Christi*, receive special compositional consideration and are generally accompanied by the power of the full orchestra. Likewise, the role of the choir receives a similar kind of compositional attention; the choir typically sings Lutheran chorales harmonised in four-part setting by Bach.[9]

These chorales raise the choir to a level of omniscient observer within the drama, sometimes using scripture to reflect upon the events taking place within the drama or rehashing fundamental theological doctrine, serving a function that is not dramatically dissimilar to that of the chorus in Classical Greek drama. These chorale harmonisations, based on Lutheran hymns, were known by Bach's contemporary congregation. There is some evidence that in some instances the chorales could have even been sung by the congregation in lieu of or in addition to a professional choir. Though the case of whether or not the congregation joined

---

8 We are certain that the original text for the *Matthäus-Passion* was by Christian Friedrich Henrici (more commonly known by his pen name Picander). Likewise, Picander has been suggested as Bach's likely collaborator for the *Weihnachts-Oratorium*, though whether or not he was the sole author of the text has been debated. See Walter Blankenburg, 'Die Bachforschung seit etwa 1965: Ergebnisse, Probleme, Aufgaben', in *Acta Musicologica* 50.1/2 (1978), p. 131. The origin of the libretto for the *Johannes-Passion* is less certain, although part of the non-biblical text was lifted variously from Barthold Heinrich Brockes's *Der für Sünde der Welt Gemarterte und Sterbende Jesus*, Christian Weiss's *Der weinende Jesus*, and Christian Heinrich Postel's *Johannes-Passion*. See: Blankenburg, 'Die Bachforschung seit etwa 1965: Ergebnisse, Probleme, Aufgaben', p. 119.

9 Bach's chorale harmonisations haunt the dreams of young music students. Almost all methods of teaching theory and harmony feature the Bach chorales as exemplars of compositional style.

in Bach's chorales in his Passions or Oratorios remains a hotly-debated issue,[10] the congregants' mere knowledge of and familiarity with these tunes already blurs a distinction between performer and listener. At the very least, one could assume, there was some humming along in the congregation. Moreover, lest we not forget, Bach himself performed his music, conducted his music, improvised upon his music and typified the performer/artist/congregant of the German Lutheran 18th century.

In Bach's time, religious music was written in a prescribed set of formal and compositional precepts, and there was little, if any, co-mingling of music of non-religious sources in religious ceremony.[11] But explicit co-mingling *did* happen – and still does – all the time. For this third characteristic of the musical imagination in religion, the mixture of sacred and mundane, a striking example exists in Islamic tradition. Islamic writings on music can largely be split into two categories: *sama'* (Arabic for 'to hear', or texts that discuss the theological and legal permissibility of music and dance) and *ghina'* (Arabic for 'to sing', or the body of work associated with music-making, musical play and performance – largely a secular body). Although the authorities on *sama'* mostly banned music that would fall under the rubric of *ghina'*, there are sometimes overlaps between the two categories, noted by musicologist Amnon Shiloah:

> It is interesting to note in this respect that the exclusive assimilation of
> the concept *ghina'* with a kind of urbanized art music and music making
> has occasionally led religious authorities to combine Koran cantillation,

---

10 The debate about vocal scoring in Bach's chorales have implications on today's historically informed performance practice of Bach's works and got off to a rumbling start with Joshua Rifkin's paper at the American Musicological Society meeting in Boston, November 1981. Rifkin suggests that Bach's choirs were much smaller than subsequent choral performances in the 19th and 20th centuries, and argues that Bach provided singers with parts for use by one single performer only. This has since be known as the 'one voice per part' theory. See: Joshua Rifkin, 'Bach's Chorus: A Preliminary Report', in *The Musical Times* 123.1677 (1982), pp. 747–751, pp. 753–754.

11 Bach's Lutheran chorales do have melodic origins in German (and sometimes even French!) religious and non-religious popular and folk songs, although the development of German music is so fundamentally intertwined with sacred rite that it is likely that Bach was not cognisant of these folk sources, and even if he were, it would likely not have occurred to him as a kind of sacred/mundane binary. Bach only wrote a few original chorale melodies, and his chorale harmonisations enjoyed such a fixed status in the German imagination, that it has been suggested that traditional chorales can be considered a substitute for national folk songs. See: Glenn Stanley, 'Bach's "Erbe": The Chorale in the German Oratorio of the Early Nineteenth Century', in *19th-Century Music* 11.2 (1987), pp. 123–34.

the singing of unaccompanied hymns, old Bedouin songs and the simple functional folk tunes marking events in the life of individual and community in the category of permissible forms of *sama'*.[12]

Music is never expressly discussed in the Qur'an, nor is there a central ecclesiastical authority within Islam; this may explain the reserved attitude that certain religious authorities in Islam may have toward an overt use of music in religious rite. Nevertheless, a clash of colloquial, local, or 'urbanised' music with sacred text or within the context of sacred rite is far more commonplace in the Islamic world than Western prejudices would have one believe. The loosening strictures on musical performance within Islamic rite, and, consequently, an increased union of the sacred and the mundane reached an interdisciplinary apotheosis with the rise and widening influence of the mystic and poet Mevlana Jalal al-din Rumi. This type of worship, associated with the Mevlevi Order of Sufi Islam, includes non-vocal elements such as an exhaustive dance (a practice known as 'whirling') and a large professional orchestra as part of the spiritual rite. The performances represent a peak in sophistication and spectacle. Scholars associated with the Mevlevi order, such as the Syrian mystic Abd al-Ghani al-Nabulusi and his disciple Muhammad al-Dikdikji, are among the most important Islamic philosophers on music, the tenets of its performance, and its function in worship. These scholars defend the use of musical instruments in religious worship and see music in all of its humanity and sensuality as a means of attaining religious ecstasy.

This mixture of sacred and mundane is not unique to Islamic tradition. The parody mass of the European Renaissance, a form in which composers based the musical themes of their masses on secular song, was one of the most popular means of liturgical setting.[13] Franco-Flemish composer Josquin des Prez, for example, wrote two settings of the mass ordinary based on the famous French secular song, *l'Homme Armé*.[14] The parody mass caused outrage at the Council of Trent, which famously sought to cleanse the Roman church of its 'lascivious and impure

---

12 Amnon Shiloah, 'Music and Religion in Islam', in *Acta Musicologica* 69.2 (1997), p. 143.
13 This manner of composition still lives on, exemplified by Prauliņš's *Missa Rigensis* described earlier.
14 A few hypotheses have been raised as to the origin and purpose of this popular folk tune during the Franco-Flemish Renaissance. As the text of the song does refer to an armed man who should be feared, and the song appeared around the time of the sack of Constantinople, is the song a rally for a new crusade against the Ottomans? Did the tune emanate from the popular pub, the *Maison l'homme armé*, a favourite haunt of composers Dufay, le Breton, and Ockeghem? Or was it simply a 'song of entertainment or farce'? See: Judith Cohen, 'Munus ab ignoto', in *Studia Musicologica Academiae Scientiarum Hungaricae* 22.1/4 (1980), pp. 188–89.

element'. Perhaps the outrage was justified: imagine the late Sir Peter Maxwell Davies composing a polyphonic Latin mass musically based on Taylor Swift's hit single, *Shake It Off*, and you have a close contemporary approximation to what Josquin and countless Renaissance composers did with their parody masses.[15]

It seems jarring! What motivated both renaissance composers and Islamic scholars to permit the use of secular musical elements in religious worship? Why does sacred music insist on blurring distinctions of performative roles, especially when ecclesiastical orders are mostly marked by stark hierarchy? It may seem strange in a lecture on the musical imagination in religious worship, but I think the words of a secular humanist, Aldous Huxley, seem most appropriate in helping to explain music's central tug toward the mystical:

> From pure sensation to the intuition of beauty, from pleasure and pain to love and the mystical ecstasy and death – all the things that are fundamental, all the things that, to the human spirit, are most profoundly significant, can only be experienced, not expressed. The rest is always and everywhere silence. After silence that which comes nearest to expressing the inexpressible is music.[16]

Huxley's words have a specific meaning for the religious listener. Music is not just emotionally immediate, it is intrinsically mysterious, taking place through time and space and being aural rather than visible. This impermanence and ineffability lends itself to religious worship, regardless of the supposed sanctity of the musical source or to whom a religious performance was intended. One cannot, for example, pray through painting; human prayer, even to a God of a timeless eternity, must take place in human time and must be experienced. And music comes closest to giving voice to those experiences which are innately human – and in their humanity, divine.

Across the Abrahamic traditions, and particularly in the setting and performance of Psalms, we experience some of this common divinity, and hear these three characteristics of religious music. We hear how global religious music can be. A Renaissance Italian Jewish composer, Salomone Rossi, wrote music that

---

15 The example is a little extreme, but the Council of Trent, which at its core was a counter-Reformation measure, was quite explicit in its denunciation of the parody mass. 15th-century composers who used the parody mass and had cherished the just-burgeoning ideals of European humanism, were interested in such popular songs solely from the perspective of compositional structure.

16 Aldous Huxley, 'The Rest is Silence', in *Music at Night and Other Essays* (New York: Doubleday Doran & Company, 1931), p. 17.

on the surface was nearly indistinguishable to that of his Christian counterparts, using the same musical signs and signifiers, harmonies and counterpoints, forms and structures. As a modern composer, Prauliņš uses the folk music of his native Latvia to localise and vernacularise the Latin mass, which was the dominant form of music composition for four hundred years. An ancient Coptic Christian Psalm cantillation, a 20th-century Jewish blessing, and a Muslim call to prayer demonstrate that these three manners of spiritual communication of the Abrahamic faiths occupy similar functions and constructions: built on a melodic backbone and ornamented with inimitable filigree – even the ornamental style and notational modes of these three types of cantillations can be hard to distinguish. In such works we hear, in all its glory, humanity's struggle to communicate with God through the musical imagination. But when we succeed and when we do communicate with God, we communicate through each other.

Bibliography

Barthes, Roland, 'The Grain of the Voice', in *Image Music Text* (London: Fontana Press, 1977), pp. 179–189.

Blankenburg, Walter, 'Die Bachforschung seit etwa 1965: Ergebnisse, Probleme, Aufgaben', in *Acta Musicologica* 50.1/2 (1978), pp. 93–154.

Chiapusso, Jan, 'Bach's Attitude Towards History', in *The Musical Quarterly* 39.3 (1953), pp. 396–414.

Cohen, Judith, 'Munus ab ignoto', in *Studia Musicologica Academiae Scientiarum Hungaricae* 22.1/4 (1980), pp. 187–204.

The Koran, ed. and transl. N J Dawood (London: Penguin, 2003).

Fellerer, K G, 'Church Music and the Council of Trent', in *The Musical Quarterly* 39.4 (1953), pp. 576–594.

Huxley, Aldous, 'The Rest is Silence', in *Music at Night and Other Essays* (New York: Doubleday Doran & Company, 1931), pp. 17–20.

Rappaport, Roy, *Ecology, Meaning, and Religion* (Richmond, CA: North Atlantic Books, 1979).

Rifkin, Joshua, 'Bach's Chorus: A Preliminary Report', in *The Musical Times* 123.1677 (1982), pp. 747–754.

Shiloah, Amnon, 'Music and Religion in Islam', in *Acta Musicologica* 69.2 (1997), pp. 143–155.

Stanley, Glenn, 'Bach's "Erbe": The Chorale in the German Oratorio of the Early Nineteenth Century', in *19th-Century Music* 11.2 (1987), pp. 121–149.

CROSSING
RELIGIOUS
IMAGINATIONS

7

Muhammad abu Zahra's Muslim Theology of Religions

Mohammed Gamal Abdelnour

'His publishers call him Imam, ranking him with the great figures of Islamic scholarship of the past, such as Abu Haneefah, Malik, Al-Shafie and Ibn Taimiyah. Indeed, he has a great affinity with all these, as we will presently explain. If we consider this title on the basis of its linguistic meaning, which is a leader who shows the way, then he certainly was an Imam. And if we take it to mean a scholar of broad and varied knowledge, then he was certainly an Imam.'

Excerpt from an article in *Arab News*[1]

Muhammad abu Zahra was born on March 29, 1898, in the Nile Delta of Egypt. Following a traditional *kuttāb* education,[2] 'he completed his secondary education at al-Ahmadi mosque in Tanta. In 1916, he entered the School of Shari'ah at al-Azhar in Cairo where he graduated in 1925. From 1932 to 1945, he held an appointment at the college of Usul al-Din, first as a teacher of rhetoric, then

---

1 See: http://www.arabnews.com/node/216148.
2 *Kuttāb*: the term goes back at least to the 10th century. It is an Arabic word meaning 'elementary schools'. Though it was primarily used for teaching children in reading, writing, grammar and Islamic studies such as *qirā'āt* (Qur'anic styles of recitation), other practical and theoretical subjects were also often taught. Until the 20th century, *katātīb* were the only means of mass education in much of the Islamic world. See: M Arsimov and C E Bosworth, *The Age of Achievement*, vol. 4 (Delhi: Banarsidass, 1999), pp. 4–33.

as a teacher of the history of religions, denominations, and sects.'[3] At al-Azhar today, abu Zahra is looked at as a polymath who has written over a dozen books on different areas, ranging from international relations in Islam to Islamic legal theories.[4] Of particular relevance to the Muslim Theology of Religions, he wrote two significant books:

Lectures in Comparative Religion, delivered in 1940 and published in 1965, and *Lectures on Christianity*, which were held and appeared in 1942. Abu Zahra's audience for his two books on Christianity and on ancient religions is clearly made up of students from al-Azhar. Therefore, his two books reflect a pattern of subconscious mimetic appropriation.[5]

In the areas of Islamic Theology as well as Islamic Law, abu Zahra's views are of capital importance to the modern study of Islam. This importance owes a lot to him being a 'critical insider' in the full sense of the two words. Thanks to an insider criticality, his views travelled far and wide across the Muslim world. In 2001, a British non-profit educational foundation was established and named after him (Abu Zahra Foundation),[6] aiming to revive this sense of criticality in the minds of Muslims living in the West. Abu Zahra died in 1974.

Abu Zahra's name is closely linked to the critique of the traditional theory of abrogation (*naskh*).[7] Although the theory of *naskh* has been central to the entire genre of Islamic studies, over the past century the theory has largely been critiqued. While abu Zahra's position on *naskh* has been examined extensively, the impact of such a position on his Muslim Theology of Religions has not been investigated yet, i.e. the salvation question.[8] This essay investigates two aspects of abu Zahra's Theology of Religions: *epistemology* and *soteriology*. To clarify,

---

3 J Waardenburg, *Muslim Perceptions of Other Religions: A Historical Survey* (Oxford: Oxford University Press, 1999), p. 244.

4 J Brown, *Misquoting Muhammad: The Challenges and Choices of Interpreting the Prophet's Legacy* (London: Oneworld Publications, 2014), p. 156.

5 Waardenburg, *Muslim Perceptions,* p. 244.

6 See: http://www.abuzahra.org/about-us/.

7 *Naskh* is 'making a revealed text supersede another. The grounds on which abrogation can be made are many; one of which is the chronologically later provenance of the repealing text (reflecting a change of mind or position adopted in the earlier text); another reason for abrogation is when one text itself commands the abandonment of a matter specified in another text'. See: W Hallaq, *An Introduction to Islamic Law* (Cambridge, Cambridge University Press, 2009), p. 171.

8 It is worth mentioning that abu Zahra did not solely reject *naskh* in order to provide the scriptural and theological ground for the potential salvation of non-Muslims, but rather his critique of *naskh* serves other purposes as well. Indeed, this shows the centrality of *naskh* in the Islamic traditions.

the epistemological question is concerned with evaluating the phenomenon of religions in terms of their efficacy of leading a valid path to salvation, whilst the soteriological question asks whether religions other than one's own have a chance of salvation in the Hereafter regardless of being salvifically effective or not. The chapter does not engage with *naskh* in the *Sunnah* (prophet Muhammad's legacy); it only engages with it vis-a-vis the Qur'an. It is, too, beyond the scope of this study to examine the theory of *naskh* in itself, but only to provide a context to abu Zahra's Muslim Theology of Religions.

The 'epistemology' question (*Naskh* Theory)

While *naskh* is accentuated by the majority of classical Muslim *ulema* and largely seen as a matter of 'doctrine', modern Islamicist scholars tend to question this outlook, seeing *naskh* primarily as an 'exegetical device' rather than a matter of 'doctrine'. A concrete example of this modern phenomenon is John Burton, who maintains that:

> The theory of *naskh* was an invention of *Fiqh* scholars and that a careful examination of the Qur'an itself produces no evidence that *naskh* of the sort of *Fiqh* scholars had in mind is envisioned in or exemplified by the Qur'an. The theory of *naskh* was developed as an exegetical device for dealing with apparent contradictions within the corpus of sacred texts; it allowed chronology to intervene as a means of eliminating real contradictions.[9]

Ahmad Hassan traces the theory back to the end of the first century of the *Hijrah* (the Prophet Muhammad's migration from Mecca 622 CE to Medina). He states: 'the idea of abrogation in the Qur'anic verses must have appeared towards the end of the first century of the *Hijrah*, because it existed in the early schools of law.'[10] However, it actually originates from the time of the companions of Muhammad.[11] Upon hearing the central Qur'anic verse on *naskh*; verse number 106, Sura 2, which reads:

---

9 B Weiss, 'The Sources of Islamic Law: Islamic Theories of Abrogation by John Burton', in *The American Oriental Society* 113.2 (1993), p. 304.
10 A Hassan, *The Theory of Naskh*, vol. 4 (Islamabad: International Islamic University, 1965), p. 184.
11 F Esack, *Qur'an Liberation & Pluralism: An Islamic Perspective of Interreligious Solidarity Against Oppression* (Oxford: Oxford University Press, 1997), p. 58.

مَا نَنْسَخْ مِنْ آيَةٍ أَوْ نُنْسِهَا نَأْتِ بِخَيْرٍ مِنْهَا أَوْ مِثْلِهَا أَلَمْ تَعْلَمْ أَنَّ اللهَ عَلَى كُلِّ شَيْءٍ قَدِيرٌ

and translates to: 'Any revelation We cause to be superseded or forgotten, We replace with something better or similar. Do you (Prophet) not know that God has power over everything,'[12] the companion Umar said: 'Ubbay is the best one to recite the Qur'an among us and Ali is our best judge, and we ignore what Ubbay says in that he does not leave anything he hears from the Messenger of God though God High Exalted has said: (for whatever order We *repeal or allow to be forgotten...* etc).'[13] What can be inferred from Umar's statement is that *naskh* has been discussed among the companions of the Prophet, and since Ubbay was against it, it can also be inferred that the theory was not unanimously accepted.

One question that needs to be asked, however, is whether this *hadīth* can stand as a proof for the rejectionists of *naskh*? It is highly unlikely that it can be used as such, since Ubbay was not against the theory per se, but apparently was against relinquishing something he knows for certain, i.e. having heard it himself directly from the Prophet, to something that has been transmitted to him through a third person, which may be less authentic. Therefore, for Ubbay, it is not a question of questioning *naskh* itself, but one of authentication. Yet Ubbay's position is still of relevance to abu Zahra in the sense that Ubbay must have interpreted this Qur'anic verse differently. That is to say, Ubbay does not seem to think that *naskh* can be deduced from such a verse and does not also seem to think it a matter of doctrine.

By way of investigating the central Qur'anic verse that seems to be highly endorsing *naskh*, a tripartite typology is offered.[14] This typology comprises the following elements: *sibāq* (prior-text), *lihāq* (post-text), *and siyāq* (context). *Sibāq* is what comes immediately before the examined text in terms of the Qur'anic ordering of verses; *lihāq* is what comes after it; and *siyāq* is basically the context wherein the prior-text, text and post-text meet. Indeed, any interpretation of a

---

12 M A S Abdel Haleem, *The Qur'an: A new Translation* (Oxford: Oxford University Press, 2010), p. 13.

13 Al-Bukhari, *Mokhtasar Sahih al-Bukhari*, transl. Dina Zidan and Ahmad Zidan (Cairo: Islamic INC. Publishing & Distribution, 1999), p. 928.

14 Although this tripartite typology is not literally developed by the classical Muslim scholars, implications of it can be found in the early *tafsīr* writings such as *Tafsir al-Tabari* (d. 310/923). See: Abdel-Hakeem al-Qasim, *Dilalat al-siyaq al-Qur'ani wa atharutha fi al-tafsir*, vol. 1 (Riyadh: Dar al-Tadmuriyyah, 2012).

Qur'anic text/verse that does not consider the prior-text as well as the post-text is believed not to adequately grasp the text.[15] In the pages that follow, this tripartite typology is applied to the Qur'anic verse at hand.

Discussing the verse quoted above, abu Zahra argues that most of the Qur'anic exegetes interpret the verse out of context. This mis-contextualisation occurs in taking the word آيَة in this verse to mean a literal Qur'anic verse (a piece of Qur'anic revelation), while, according to the Arabic lexical dictionaries,[16] the word آيَة is a homonym that has various connotations.[17] With that being said, interpreting the word آيَة here as a Qur'anic verse is not necessarily the only feasible option. Furthermore, such an interpretation is not espoused by neither the prior-text, nor the post-text, and therefore is not conductive toward delivering the message of the text adequately.

Two types of prior-texts can be introduced here.[18] First, 'textual prior-text'; second: 'historical prior-text'. The 'textual prior-text', in this context, is the verse that immediately precedes the examined Qur'anic verse, as opposed to the 'historical prior-text', which refers to an incidence/occasion that has happened in correspondence with the revelation. Regarding the 'textual prior-text', the Qur'anic verse that precedes ours, reads:

مَّا يَوَدُّ ٱلَّذِينَ كَفَرُواْ مِنْ أَهْلِ ٱلْكِتَبِ وَلَا ٱلْمُشْرِكِينَ أَن يُنَزَّلَ عَلَيْكُم مِّنْ خَيْرٍ مِّن رَّبِّكُمْ وَٱللَّهُ يَخْتَصُّ بِرَحْمَتِهِ مَن يَشَاءُ وَٱللَّهُ ذُو ٱلْفَضْلِ ٱلْعَظِيمِ

which translates as: 'neither those People of the Book who disbelieve nor the idolaters would like anything good to be sent down to you from your Lord, but God chooses for His grace whoever He will: His bounty has no limits.'[19] This verse has nothing to do with the theory of abrogation in the traditional sense of

15 M Abu Zahra, *Usul al-Fiqh* (Cairo: Dar al-Fikr al-Arabi, 1958), p. 184–197.

16 See: J M Cowan, *Arabic-English Dictionary* (New York: Spoken Languages Services, 1976), p. 36.

17 Although the primary meaning of the word *āyah* is divine sign/sign of God, the word holds nine other possible meanings: 1) proof/evidence; 2) miracle/portent; 3) exemplar/symbol; 4) revelation/message; 5) teachings/instructions; 6) Qur'anic verses; 7) lesson; 8) glory/wonder; 9) spell. See: M Badawi and M A S Abdel Haleem, *Arabic-English Dictionary of Qur'anic Usage* (Leiden & Boston: Brill, 2008), pp. 68–96.

18 See: M A S Abdel Haleem, 'The Role of Context in Interpreting and Translating the Qur'an', in *Journal of Qur'anic Studies* 20 (2018), pp. 47–66.

19 Abdel Haleem, *The Qur'an*, p. 13.

the term. Therefore, interpreting the next verse in terms of abrogating certain Qur'anic verses is tantamount to taking the verse out of its context.[20]

What about the historical prior-text? The verse above corresponds with an occasion that happened in the time of Prophet Muhammad; an occasion that verse 153, Sura 4, talks about, which reads:

يَسْأَلُكَ أَهْلُ الْكِتَابِ أَن تُنَزِّلَ عَلَيْهِمْ كِتَابًا مِّنَ السَّمَاء فَقَدْ سَأَلُواْ مُوسَى أَكْبَرَ مِن ذَلِكَ فَقَالُواْ أَرِنَا اللَّه جَهْرَةً

translated as: 'The People of the Book demand that you (Prophet) make a book *physically* come down to them from heaven, but they demanded even more than that of Moses when they said, (Show us God face to face).'[21] Linking the two verses together, the Qur'an tells the Prophet in Sura 2 that the unbelievers of Mecca were demanding a *physical* miracle, rather than an incorporeal one, i.e. the Qur'an. That is to say that the verses of Sura 2 were highly likely revealed as a response to the Meccan's demand; a response that lays down the foundations of Allah's law of miracles, stating that: 'any physical miracle We cause to be superseded or forgotten, We replace with a better or similar [i.e. non-physical] miracle' (the Qur'an).[22] Based on the above, interpreting the word آيَة here as a Qur'anic verse is highly remote, for the word *āyah* is not necessarily a Qur'anic verse but highly likely a physical miracle, if we consider the context. In fact, this is the capacity in which the Qur'an, more often than not, uses the term *āyah*.[23] As a corollary to this, neither the 'textual prior-text' or the 'historical prior-text' endorse the *naskh* interpretation, unless taken out of the 'prior-text' context, whether historical or textual.

The post-text, in this case, is verse number 108, which reads:

أَمْ تُرِيدُونَ أَن تَسْأَلُواْ رَسُولَكُمْ كَمَا سُئِلَ مُوسَى مِن قَبْلُ

translated as: 'Do you wish to demand of your messenger something similar to what was demanded of Moses?'[24] The question that then arises is: what was demanded of Moses other than physical miracles? The Qur'an talks about the

20 Abu Zahra, *Usul*, pp. 184–197.
21 Abdel Haleem, *The Qur'an*, p. 64.
22 Abdel Haleem, *The Qur'an*, p. 13.
23 See for instance: verse number 50, Sura 2, discussing the physical miracles of Jesus Christ.
24 Abdel Haleem, *The Qur'an*, p. 13.

Jews asking Moses all the time for physical miracles.[25] Historically speaking, this has also been demanded of Muhammad by the unbelievers of Quraysh. Why should an exegete then ignore the textual and historical prior-text and the textual and historical post-text for a literal reading? Indeed, ignoring the prior-text and the post-text, argues abu Zahra, seems to have diverted the majority of Qur'anic exegetes from a logical interpretation based on the context of the verse.[26]

Abu Zahra constantly reminds his readers that a Qur'an exegete is not to resort to the theory of *naskh* as long as there is another way with which the apparently contradictory Qur'anic verses can be reconciled. And since all verses as such can be reconciled without resorting to *naskh*, abu Zahra rejects the practice entirely, stating that the reliance on *naskh* has caused many controversies between Qur'anic exegetes. In this respect, Kamali writes:

The conventional theory of *naskh* has not been free of distortion and forced logic, yet the scholastic works of the *madhāhib* took for granted the conceptual validity and occurrence of abrogation in the Qur'an and *Sunnah*. The inherent tension that is visited here has perhaps been manifested in the *ulema*'s disagreement over the actual incidents of *naskh* in the Qur'an, and the distinction that is drawn between *naskh*, and specification of the general (*takhsīs al-'āmm*). Some of the instances of *naskh* were accordingly seen to be amounting to no more than *takhsīs*. The scope of disagreement over the occurrence of *naskh* was initially very wide and claims of several hundred instances of *naskh* in the Qur'an were gradually scrutinized and reduced by Jalāl al-Dīn al-Suyūtī, for example to about 30 cases, and then to only five by Shāh Walī Allāh Dihlawī. One of the early fourth century commentators of the Qur'an, Abū Muslim al-Isfāhnī, even claimed that abrogation had no place in the Qur'an whatsoever, stating that all the alleged cases of *naskh* were in effect instances of *takhsīs*... the basic tension between the classical theory of *naskh* and the timeless validity of the Qur'an prompted Imām al-Shāfi'ī into advancing the view that *naskh* was a form of explanation (*bayān*), rather than annulment, of one ruling by another.[27]

---

25 The al-Baqarah Sura reflects this.
26 M Abu Zahra, *Usul*, pp. 184–197.
27 M H Kamuli, 'Methodological Issues in Islamic Jurisprudence', in *Arab Law Quarterly* 11.1 (1996), pp. 13–14.

How Does abu Zahra's Take on Naskh Influence His Muslim Theology of Religions?

Abu Zahra's lack of subscription to the theory of *naskh* meant, *inter alia*, that he had to offer different readings of certain other Qur'anic verses, amongst which are those verses that talk about the fate of non-Islamic religions. In his, *Zahrat al-Tafasir* (literally translates as: *The Flowers of Exegeses*), abu Zahra deals elaborately with the central Qur'anic verse that discusses non-Islamic religions. This is verse number 62 in Sura 2, arguably the most pluralistic of Qur'anic verses. The verse reads:

إِنَّ الَّذِينَ آمَنُوا وَالَّذِينَ هَادُوا وَالنَّصَارَى وَالصَّابِئِينَ مَنْ آمَنَ بِاللَّهِ وَالْيَوْمِ الْآخِرِ

وَعَمِلَ صَالِحاً فَلَهُمْ أَجْرُهُمْ عِنْدَ رَبِّهِمْ وَلَا خَوْفٌ عَلَيْهِمْ وَلَا هُمْ يَحْزَنُونَ

and translates as: 'The (Muslim) believers, the Jews, the Christians, and the Sabians – all those who believe in God and the Last Day and doing good – will have their rewards with their Lord. No fear for them, nor will they grieve.'[28] Looking into the Qur'an commentaries shows that the vast majority of Qur'an exegetes explicate this verse in one of two ways: 1) subscribing to abrogation by stating that this verse is abrogated by verse number 85, Sura 3, which reads: 'Whoever seeks a way other than Islam, it will never be accepted from them, and in the Hereafter, they will be among the losers;'[29] or 2) specifying the generality of the verse, saying, for instance, that the acknowledged Christians, Jews, etc. here are only those who adhered to these religions before the advent of Prophet Muhammed, but when Muhammad came, they followed his message.[30]

Under the title, 'People are all Alike in the Sight of God if they Believe', abu Zahra explicates the verse at hand, looking at it as a statement from God to all humans, stating that 'belief' is accepted from *all* faith-groups and religious denominations as long as they believe in God, the Day of Judgement and perform good deeds.[31] This is the prime vehicle to salvation, abu Zahra says. Immersing himself in the discussion on a deeper level, abu Zahra examines these religions one by one. Starting with Islam, abu Zahra states that whoever follows Prophet Muhammad and aides his belief with the performance of good deeds that please

---

28 Abdel Haleem, *The Qur'an*, p. 9.
29 Khattab, *The Clear Qur'an: A Thematic English Translation* (Canada: Siraj Publications, 2016), p. 95.
30 See full discussion on the exegeses of this verse in: J D McAuliffe, *Qur'anic Christians: An Analysis of Classical and Modern Exegesis* (Cambridge: Cambridge University Press, 1991), pp. 93–128.
31 M Abu Zahra, *Zahrat al-Tafasir* (Cairo, Dar al-Fikr al-Arabi, 1987), p. 254.

God and benefits His creatures, is to appear under the category of those who need have no fear, and who will be spared from grief in this life and in the Hereafter.[32]

The same principal applies to non-Islamic religions. If Christians, Jews, Sabians, or any other faith group, believe in 'God, and that He begot no one nor was He begotten', and who believe in all his messengers and in the Hereafter, there will be no fear for them nor will they grieve.[33] However, abu Zahra offers a more detailed analysis when it comes to the Christians, arguing that there are two major disagreements between Christianity and Islam. The first one is to do with God and the second is to do with Prophet Muhammad. On the disagreement about God, abu Zahra explains:[34]

> Some Christians say that the Qur'an itself assures them that there will be
> no fear for them nor will they grieve; a statement that gives recognition to
> Christianity as a valid path to salvation on its own merits. We say: the Qur'an
> gives them that recognition on the condition that they believe in the oneness
> of God, He begot no one nor was He begotten, and that no one is comparable
> to Him. Do the Christians of today believe in these principals?! They rather
> say that God is a third of three, while God in the Qur'an says: Those who say
> 'God is one in a trinity' have certainly fallen into disbelief. They maintain,
> from the time of the Nicaean Council until this day, that Jesus Christ is divine,
> while the Qur'an says: Those who say 'God is the Messiah, son of Mary' have
> certainly fallen into disbelief.[35]

As for the second disagreement, in his discussion of verse number 20, Sura 3, abu Zahra denies the salvation of anyone who denies the prophethood of Prophet Muhammad. By way of reconciling the two discussions, abu Zahra seems to be arguing for the salvation of whoever acknowledges Muhammad as a Prophet even if they remain true to their religious tradition without converting to Islam. Hence abu Zahra, on the one hand, accepts that there is salvation outside of Islam (differing from the Exclusivists who see Islam as the only valid path to salvation), but on the other hand holds that one has to be a monotheist and acknowledge the message of Muhammad in order to gain salvation. Whether or not Christians are trinitarians in the way most Muslims understand trinity is a question to be studied in its

---

32 Abu Zahra, *Zahrat*, p. 254.
33 Abu Zahra, *Zahrat*, p. 254.
34 Unless otherwise stated, the translation is mine.
35 Abu Zahra, *Zahrat*, p. 256.

own merits, but of relevance here is that abu Zahra features as a 'Theo-centric theologian', which is a transformative shift in the Muslim Theology of Religions, for all Qur'an exegetes require not just believing in God as well as acknowledging Prophet Muhammad's prophethood, but conversion to Islam. Although abu Zahra is not the first to have such a position on non-Islamic religions,[36] his position is remarkable in that he solidifies it on the basis of his position on abrogation, which gives some *epistemic* recognition to non-Islamic religions, making the message of Islam more of a *confirmatory nature* to the previous monotheistic messages rather than one of *abrogatory nature*.

Furthermore, the verse which is used by the majority of commentators to abrogate the verse central to this essay, is used by abu Zahra in quite a different manner, that is, for confirming his Theo-centrism.[37] This is verse number 85, Sura 3, which reads:

وَمَنْ يَبْتَغِ غَيْرَ الْإِسْلَامِ دِينًا فَلَنْ يُقْبَلَ مِنْهُ وَهُوَ فِي الْآخِرَةِ مِنَ الْخَاسِرِينَ

and which translates as: 'Whoever seeks a way other than Islam, it will never be accepted from them, and in the Hereafter, they will be among the losers.'[38] While most of the Qur'an exegetes take the word 'Islam' here to be *technical* Islam, abu Zahra considers it a *linguistic* term. That is to say that the word Islam in this verse does not mean the Religion Islam, but *islam* as a word that implies surrendering to God and submitting to Him alone. To abu Zahra, the term *islam* can be replaced with 'purity/sincerity'.[39]

To conclude, abu Zahra gives epistemic recognition and salvation efficacy to any religion that is of monotheistic nature, believes in *all* prophets of God and encourages good deeds. These are the three prime requisites for an individual to lead a valid path to salvation. In the pages that follow, the fate of those who do not tread the path to salvation will be examined.

---

36 The Reformist School of Muhammad Abduh has a quite similar view.

37 'Theo-centrism' is not to be confused with 'pluralism'. Although there is some significant overlap, theo-centrism revolves around God while pluralism revolves, in very generic terms, around the concept of the 'Real'. See: http://www.ips.org.pk/theocentrism-and-pluralism-are-they-poles-apart/.

38 Khattab, *A Thematic English Translation*, p. 95.

39 Abu Zahra, *Zahrat*, p. 1302.

The 'soteriology' question
Do non-Islamic religions have a chance of salvation in the Hereafter?

Whereas the previous discussion was primarily *epistemological*, what is to come is substantially *soteriological*. The soteriological question here is: what is the fate of those non-Muslims who fail to meet the three requirements of salvation? More generally, what about those individuals who greatly contribute to the enhancement of people's lives? Would they simply be thrown into perdition as a result of their failure to embrace Islam? While modern Muslim scholars disagree on this question, the traditional position holds that such scholars, scientists and God-conscious people are entitled to a secular reward, e.g. being wealthy, healthy, praised in public, etc., but they are not entitled to a reward in the Hereafter. This is simply because in Islam a good deed will rewarded under two conditions of correct conduct and sincerity: 1) the deed must be conducted in compatibility with God's laws which have been revealed to Prophet Muhammad; 2) the intention has to be worshiping God and getting closer to Him through the performance of a good deed.[40] Based on these two conditions, such a category of people are entitled only to a secular reward in the Here, but not in the After. This is the traditional view.

The proceedings of a roundtable discussion, published in al-Azhar mosque magazine in 1955, shows that although many modern Muslim scholars were in line with the traditional position, a few were an exception. Abu Zahra participated in the roundtable and discussed this thorny question, concluding that anyone who meets the requirements of salvation in the Here will be saved in the After even if he does not convert to Islam. As for those who fail to meet any of these requisites, abu Zahra makes it 'clear that the deeds of non-Muslims, performed for the sake of humanity, are religiously meritorious in themselves, at least in circumstances in which the non-Muslim is not culpable for not adhering to Islam'.[41]

Accordingly, abu Zahra affirms that God's consciousness is the kernel and cornerstone of salvation. From verse number 115, Sura 3, which reads:

وَمَا يَفْعَلُوا مِنْ خَيْرٍ فَلَنْ يُكْفَرُوهُ وَاللهُ عَلِيمٌ بِالْمُتَّقِينَ

and translates as: 'And they will not be denied (the reward) for whatever good deeds they do: God knows exactly who is conscious of Him,'[42] abu Zahra borrows

---

40 M H Khalil, *Between Heaven and Hell: Islam, Salvation, and the Fate of Others* (Oxford: Oxford University Press, 2013), p. 46.
41 Khalil, *Heaven and Hell*, p. 46.
42 Abdel Haleem, *The Qur'an*, p. 43.

the foundation of his theocentric position and makes a more obvious stance.[43] It should be noted that this is abu Zahra's position on a verse that is interpreted by the majority of Muslim scholars to be entitling good non-Muslims to secular rewards only.

Conclusion

In this investigation, two aims were sought after. First, to introduce abu Zahra's position on the theory of *naskh* to the English reader, providing a hermeneutical tool that, more adequately, situates his position in the field of textual hermeneutics; a tool that I identify as 'the tripartite typology', and which comprises the three notions of *sibāq* (prior-text), *lihāq* (post-text), and *siyāq* (context). The second and prime aim of this essay was to show how abu Zahra's position on *naskh* influences his Muslim Theology of Religions *epistemologically* and *soteriologically*.

The most obvious finding to emerge from this paper is that abu Zahra can be possibly classified as a theocentric theologian whose theology of religions starts from God and revolves around Him rather than being centred on the Prophet. Abu Zahra's position is unique in the sense that although he is not an exclusivist in terms of salvation, he also is not a pluralist. That is to say that he is against loosening the religious differences and blurring the boundaries between the different faiths. The emphasis he places on the question of the Trinity makes this crystal clear.

One of the more significant findings to emerge from this chapter is that an exegete is not to explicate a Qur'anic verse in a vacuum. That is to say that the hermeneutical tool applied in the course of reading abu Zahra shows how considering the *sibāq*, *lihāq*, and *siyāq* can definitely play a significant role in grasping the Qur'anic message.

Bibliography
Books

Abdel Haleem, M A S, *The Qur'an: A new Translation* (Oxford: Oxford World's Classics, 2010).
Abu Zahra, M, *Usul al-Fiqh* (Cairo: Dar al-Fikr al-Arabi, 1958).
Abu Zahra, M, *Zahrat al-Tafasir* (Cairo: Dar al-Fikr al-Arabi, 1987).

---

43 Abu Zahra, *Zahrat*, p. 1371.

Al-Bukhari, *Mokhtasar Sahih al-Bukhari: Text and Translation*, transl. Dina Zidan and Ahmad Zidan (Cairo: Islamic INC. Publishing & Distribution, 1999).

Al-Qasim, A, *Dilalat al-siyaq al-Qur'ani wa atharutha fi al-tafsir*, vol. 1 (Riyadh: Dar al-Tadmuriyyah, 2012).

Arkoun, M, *Rethinking Islam, Common Questions and Uncommon Answers*, ed. and transl. Robert Lee (Colorado: Westview Press, 1994).

Arsimov, M S, and Bosworth, C E, *The Age of Achievement*, vol. 4 (Delhi: Banarsidass, 1999).

Badawi, E, and Abdel Haleem, M, *Arabic-English Dictionary of Qur'anic Usage* (Leiden & Boston: Brill, 2008).

Brown, J, *Misquoting Muhammad: The Challenges and Choices of Interpreting the Prophet's Legacy* (London: Oneworld Publications, 2014).

Cowan, J M, *Arabic-English Dictionary* (New York: Spoken Languages Services, 1976).

Esack, F, *Qur'an Liberation & Pluralism: An Islamic Perspective of Interreligious Solidarity Against Oppression* (Oxford: Oneworld Publications, 1997).

Goldziher, I, *Introduction to Islamic Theology and Law*, transl. Andras and Ruth Hamori (Princeton: Princeton University Press, 1981).

Hallaq, W, *An Introduction to Islamic Law* (Cambridge: Cambridge University Press, 2009).

Hassan, A, *The Theory of Naskh*, vol. 4 (Islamabad: International Islamic University, 1965).

Jackson, S, *On the Boundaries of Theological Tolerance in Islam* (Oxford: Oxford University Press, 2002).

Kärkkäinen, V, *An Introduction to the Theology of Religions: Biblical, Historical and Contemporary Perspectives* (Downers Grove: Intervarsity Press, 2003).

Khalil, M H, *Between Heaven and Hell: Islam, Salvation, and the Fate of Others* (Oxford: Oxford University Press, 2013).

Khattab, M, *The Clear Qur'an: A Thematic English Translation* (Canada: Siraj Publications, 2016).

Lamptey, J, *Towards a Muslima Theology of Religious Pluralism: The Qur'an, Feminist Theology and Religious Diversity* (Georgetown: PhD thesis at the University of Georgetown, 2011).

McAuliffe, J D, *Qur'anic Christians: An Analysis of Classical and Modern Exegesis* (Cambridge: Cambridge University Press, 1991).

Waardenburg, J, *Muslim Perceptions of Other Religions: A Historical Survey* (Oxford: Oxford University Press, 1999).

Articles

Abdel Haleem, M A S, 'The Role of Context in Interpreting and Translating the Qur'an', in *Journal of Qur'anic Studies* 20 (Edinburgh: Edinburgh University Press, 2018), pp. 44–66.

Barzegar, A, 'The Persistence of Heresy: Paul of Tarsus, ibn Saba, and Historical Narrative in Sunni Identity Formation', in *Cultural Memory and Islam* 58.2/3 (2011), pp. 202–231.

Kamali, M H, 'Methodological Issues in Islamic Jurisprudence', in *Arab Law Quarterly* 11.1 (1996), pp. 3–33.

Weiss, B, 'The Sources of Islamic Law: Islamic Theories of Abrogation by John Burton', in *Journal of the American Oriental Society* 113.2 (1993), pp. 304–306.

Online Sources

Abu Zahra, M, *Abu Zahra Foundation* website, available at: http://www. abuzahra.org/about-us/.

Morados, M, 'Theocentrism and Pluralism: Are they Poles Apart?', available at: http://www.ips.org.pk/theocentrism-and-pluralism-are-they-poles-apart/.

Salahi, A, 'Scholar of renown: Muhammad Abu Zahrah', in *Arab News*, available at: http://www.arabnews.com/node/216148.

8

The Field of Interfaith in the Middle East[1]

John Fahy

Introduction

In May 2017, President Donald Trump met with Pope Francis at the Vatican. Amidst pressing issues such as migration and climate change, it was reported that their brief conversation revolved around 'the promotion of peace in the world through political negotiation and interreligious dialogue'.[2] This could very well broadly describe Trump's first foreign trip as president, which also included stops in Saudi Arabia, Israel and the West Bank. That an American president would choose a whirlwind Abrahamic tour as his first engagement beyond home soil speaks both to the importance of religion in international affairs, and the increasingly prominent role of 'interfaith' dialogue in diplomatic relations.

It is possible to identify what could be described as 'interfaith' in the history of any of the major world religions. Popular examples include the Buddhist emperor Ashoka's rule in India, and *La Convivencia* in medieval Spain where Muslims, Christians and Jews, we are often told, lived peacefully side by side.[3] However, interfaith as we know it today – a fragmented field encompassing local, national

1 This essay was made possible by NPRP grant #7–585–6–020 from the Qatar National Research Fund (a member of Qatar Foundation). The statements made herein are solely the responsibility of the author.
2 See: https://press.vatican.va/content/salastampa/en/bollettino/pubblico/2017/05/24/170524a.html.
3 M Cohen, *Under Crescent and Cross: The Jews in the Middle Ages* (New Jersey: Princeton University Press, 1994).

and global initiatives – is a distinctly modern phenomenon that can be traced back to particular 19th- and 20th-century discourses and developments in the West.[4] While in its formative years the field of interfaith responded to, and was shaped by, predominantly Christian and secular agendas, it has more recently emerged as central to broader discourses that cohere around the problem of religious difference in a globalising world. Often spurred on by crisis events such as the Holocaust or the Cold War, interfaith gained unprecedented prominence in the wake of 9/11, particularly in Western liberal democracies, where as part of broader multiculturalist frameworks, interfaith initiatives were employed as strategies to promote social cohesion and combat the threat of radicalisation.[5] In 1980 there were 24 interfaith councils across the US, compared with 500 in 2006. In the UK there were 27 in 1987, compared with over 200 in 2007.[6] As a field of practice, or some would suggest, a movement, interfaith has garnered interest from all major religious traditions, including Islam, and can today be found all over the world, including in the Middle East.

Although Muslims have often been wary of interfaith dialogue (as indeed have all religious traditions), events of the late 20th and early 21st centuries have made interfaith engagement a political necessity. Muslims in the West have found interfaith dialogue an important means of combatting Islamophobia. In the wider Muslim world, countries such as Kazakhstan, Indonesia, Morocco, Turkey and Libya have all invested in interfaith initiatives. Muslim intellectual activists such as Anwar Ibrahim in Malaysia and former president of Iran Mohammad Khatami have long since championed interfaith and intercultural dialogue, often in response to Samuel Huntington's 'clash of civilisations' thesis.[7] The Middle East is today home to several high-profile organisations, including Jordan's Royal Institute for Inter-Faith Studies (founded in 1994) and Qatar's Doha International Center for Interfaith Dialogue (founded in 2008), among others. Governments in the region have also financed several initiatives in the West, such as the Saudi-funded King Abdullah bin Abdulaziz International Centre for Interreligious and

---

4 K Marshall, *Interfaith Journeys: An Exploration of History, Ideas and Future Directions* (Washington DC: World Faiths Development Dialogue, 2017), p. 9. On the history of Catholic interfaith developments in the 20th century, see Borelli, J, 'The Origins and Early Development of Interreligious Relations during the Century of the Church (1910–2010)', in *US Catholic Historian* 28.2 (2010), pp. 81–105.
5 A Halafoff, *The Multifaith Movement: Global Risks and Cosmopolitan Solutions* (New York: Springer, 2013).
6 Halafoff, *The Multifaith Movement: Global Risks and Cosmopolitan Solutions*, p. 72.
7 Samuel P Huntington, *The Clash of Civilizations and the Remaking of World Order* (London: Penguin Books, 1997).

Intercultural Dialogue in Vienna. Members of the Saudi royal family have also donated generously to a range of initiatives; in addition to dedicated centres in universities such as Harvard and Cambridge, for example, Prince Alwaleed bin Talal has funded the Center for Muslim-Christian Understanding in Georgetown University in Washington DC.[8]

As the region's interfaith initiatives have become increasingly prominent in recent years, they have drawn both acclaim and criticism. While they are often commended, for example, in US state department reports on religious freedom,[9] there remains much cynicism about the intentions of the region's governments who invest in the field of interfaith dialogue. It has often been pointed out that theirs is a political rather than a theological agenda. Islamic actors, we are told, 'initiate interfaith dialogue to signal their moderate stance to powerful others who are concerned with Islamic radicalisation and violence.'[10] They are sometimes presented as sycophantically scrambling to be part of the solution, and therefore not part of the problem, in the West's war on terror. Interfaith dialogue, it appears, has been embraced as a particularly effective means of making clear their allegiance to a cosmopolitan ethic that coheres around the values of tolerance, moderation and coexistence. While it is undoubtedly true that the field of interfaith in the Middle East should be understood in terms of its political rather than simply its theological agenda, and that state-involvement raises a particular set of questions, in looking back to the deeper history of the interfaith movement in the West, this chapter brings attention to the fact that this is not something new, nor is it unique to either the Middle East region or to Islam. It is just a different kind of political project, borne of a different kind of politics.

The history of interfaith

The 1893 Parliament of World's Religions in Chicago is often referred to as the beginning of the interfaith movement. The parliament was deliberately organised to coincide with the World's Fair and was in part conceived as a response to

---

8 Although the scope of this paper is confined for the most part to state-funded and transnational interfaith initiatives that have been established in the region, there are plenty of local grassroots initiatives that are often overlooked. See M Abu-Nimer, A Khoury and E Welty, *Unity in Diversity: Interfaith Dialogue in the Middle East* (Washington DC: US Institute of Peace Press, 2007).
9 See: https://www.state.gov/j/drl/irf/.
10 Turan Kayaoglu, 'Explaining Interfaith Dialogue in the Muslim World', in *Politics and Religion* 8.2 (2015), p. 236.

growing xenophobia in North America that resulted from increased immigration. It brought together representatives from the world's major religious traditions, including a range of Christian denominations, along with Hindus, Jains, Buddhists and some smaller new religious movements. Muslims, however, were noticeably underrepresented; the only Muslim to talk at the parliament was Mohammed Alexander Russell Webb, an American who had converted to Islam while stationed in the Philippines.[11] His talk, which referred to polygamy and the universality of Islam, was greeted with cries of 'shame' from the audience, and did little to foster mutual understanding, let alone good will.

Although the parliament was a landmark interfaith event, it was not so much an egalitarian platform, but rather, in the words of historian Marcus Braybrooke, a 'Christian assembly to which guests of other faiths were invited'.[12] From the almost 200 papers presented 78% were delivered by Christians.[13] In his record of the parliament, chairman John Henry Barrows revealingly noted that the event '…is clarifying many minds in regard to the nature of non-Christian faiths; it is deepening the general Christian interest in non-Christian nations; and it will bring before millions in Oriental lands the more truthful and beautiful aspects of Christianity'.[14] Despite this, there were many within the Christian fold that were firmly against it. The Archbishop of Canterbury and Pope Leo VIII opposed the gathering.[15]

Perhaps unsurprisingly the Christian leaning remained pervasive for much of the 20th century. The first interfaith organisation that can be traced to the parliament is what is today known as the International Association for Religious Freedom (IARF). When it first convened in Boston in 1900, it did so under the name of the 'International Council of Unitarian and other Liberal Religious Thinkers and Workers'. By 1910, its name had changed to 'The International Congress of Free Christians and other Religious Liberals' and in 1932 it had become 'The International Association for Liberal Christianity and Religious Freedom'.

---

11 M Braybrooke, *Pilgrimage of Hope: One Hundred Years of Global Interfaith Dialogue* (New York: Crossroad Publishing Company, 1992), p. 34.

12 Braybrooke, *Pilgrimage of Hope: One Hundred Years of Global Interfaith Dialogue*, p. 35.

13 Braybrooke, *Pilgrimage of Hope: One Hundred Years of Global Interfaith Dialogue*, p. 26.

14 Braybrooke, *Pilgrimage of Hope: One Hundred Years of Global Interfaith Dialogue*, p. 15.

15 K Marshall, *Interfaith Journeys: An Exploration of History, Ideas and Future Directions* (Washing DC: World Faiths Development Dialogue, 2017), pp. 11.

It only became the IARF in 1969.[16] Then there was the World Congress of Faiths, a deliberate imitation, albeit on nowhere near the same scale, of the Parliament of World's Religions, which first met in London in 1936.

Amidst a flourishing of social movements and an unprecedented boom of faith-based NGOs in the second half of the 20th century, the interfaith movement too enjoyed a period of growth. The 'Temple of Understanding', referred to by the press at the time as 'the spiritual United Nations', was established in 1960 and a decade later what is today known as 'Religions for Peace' was established. Another important milestone in the history of interfaith relations also occurred during these years. The Second Vatican Council and, in particular, 'Nostra Aetate' signalled a turning point in the Catholic Church's relationship with non-Christians. While it is probably best known for its historic revision of the church's position on the 2000-year-old charge of deicide against the Jews, it also profoundly recalibrated its relationship with other religious traditions, including Islam. To support Vatican II, the 'Pontifical Council for Interreligious Dialogue' was set up in 1964. The Vatican also established a special commission for relations with Muslims in 1974, while the World Council of Churches set up something similar in 1971. With respect to the Catholic Church, however, the focus was until recently predominantly on Christian-Jewish relations post-World War II.

While the interfaith movement had another period of growth in the late 20th century (with the establishment of the 'United Religions Initiative' and the 'World Faiths Development Dialogue', for example), as is the case with the broader resurgence of religion in international relations, 9/11 marks a particularly important watershed in the proliferation of interfaith initiatives around the globe. Since 9/11, the interfaith movement has been making waves at the highest political levels. The United Nations adopted a resolution in 2004 on the 'Promotion of Interreligious Dialogue'.[17] This resolution was a response to previous resolutions on 'The Global Agenda for Dialogue among Civilisations' (2001), and 'The Promotion of Religious and Cultural Understanding, Harmony and Cooperation' (2005). Since 2011, the first week of February every year has been designated by the UN as 'World Interfaith Harmony Week'.

Today the global field of interfaith comprises tens of thousands of initiatives, from small local grassroots efforts to national-level conflict resolution to

---

16 Braybrooke, *Pilgrimage of Hope: One Hundred Years of Global Interfaith Dialogue*, p. 49.
17 See: http://www.un-documents.net/a59r23.htm.

transnational organisations that span the globe. Some initiatives are more overtly theological, focusing on dialogue or scriptural reasoning, with the goal of identifying and promoting a set of common values, or what has been termed a 'global ethic'.[18] Others bring together religious leaders and communities to identify common socio-political goals that transcend religious difference, such as climate change, social justice, nuclear disarmament and poverty alleviation.

For their part, Muslims were often wary of the idea of interfaith dialogue and when they did partake, they were guests rather than hosts. As religion in general, and Islam in particular, re-emerged in international relations in the late 20th century, the situation changed. Interfaith initiatives, often state-sponsored, began to emerge throughout the Middle East. The trend accelerated in the wake of 9/11 and other terrorist attacks, after which interfaith dialogue came to represent an important mode of engagement through which Muslims could take part in the global conversation about Islam and extremism. At the same time, in Western liberal democracies, governments turned to interfaith dialogue as a means of promoting social cohesion and combatting extremism. As is the case when looking back on the interfaith movement over the course of the 20th century, interfaith initiatives today could be described as attempts to mobilise theological, or broadly speaking, religious resources to address pressing social and political issues. The interfaith movement then, in both the West and the Middle East, should not be understood as simply a religious, but rather a socio-political phenomenon.

Interfaith in the Middle East

Unlike the interfaith movement in the West, which has had a century to mature, the field of interfaith in the Middle East emerged in the space of a generation – and a particularly turbulent generation at that, springing up in the wake of a series of events that brought Islam to the attention of the international community. From the 1979 Iranian Revolution to the Salman Rushdie Affair and 9/11, Muslims have found themselves increasingly called upon to explain, and in many cases, defend their religion. The relationship between Islam and the West has been shaped by a post-9/11 political discourse that prescribes particular roles for Muslims in conversations about religious extremism, often confining the moral imagination to narratives of 'good Muslims', 'bad Muslims' and the 'clash of the civilisations' (Mamdani 2005). As a consequence, Islamic civil-society and

---

18 See: H Küng, *A Global Ethic for Global Politics and Economics* (Oxford: Oxford University Press, 1998).

faith-based initiatives have tended to adopt an apologetic tone; one that interfaith initiatives would later inherit.

As in the West, the second half of the 20th century saw a boom in civil society, transnational and faith-based NGOs in the Middle East. It was initiatives such as The Organisation of the Islamic Cooperation (originally The Organisation of the Islamic Conference, or OIC), itself a reaction to the events of 1967, that led the way in forging a transnational Islamic consciousness. Working closely with the United Nations, the OIC embarked in 2005 on a 10-year programme of action that sought to promote tolerance, moderation and modernisation. This involved striving to 'protect and defend the true image of Islam, to combat defamation of Islam and encourage dialogue among civilisations and religions'.[19] These goals are pervasive among Islamic civil society organisations throughout the region, whose agenda could be broadly characterised as promoting a positive image of Islam, on one hand, and dispelling common misconceptions, on the other. Many of these organisations have come to embrace interfaith dialogue as a means of achieving these goals; indeed, some are founded on the notion that interfaith is the only means of achieving these goals.

In the Middle East today there are dozens of organisations and initiatives, both governmental and non-governmental, local and national, that engage to a greater or lesser extent with interfaith dialogue. Some organisations style themselves explicitly in terms of their interfaith agenda, such as the Jordanian Interfaith Coexistence Research Center (founded in 2003), whose goal is to 'develop and implement educational programmes geared towards developing the concepts of peacebuilding using the interfaith perspective of human dignity, equality, justice, and freedom'.[20] Other examples include the Lebanese Adyan Foundation (founded in 2006) that aims for 'social cohesion and spiritual solidarity between individuals and communities, through positive relations, objective understanding and shared commitment'.[21] Lebanon is also home to the Arab Group for Muslim-Christian Dialogue, which first met in 1995. For some organisations, interfaith serves broader goals. Dubai's Kalam Research & Media, a think tank founded in 2009, seeks to 'revive the theological and spiritual discourse in Islam through its network of scholars, professionals and institutional partners around the world'.[22] To do so, it 'engages with leading theologians from other religious traditions,

---

19 See: http://www.oic-oci.org/page/?p_id=53&p_ref=27&lan=en.
20 See: https://www.insightonconflict.org/conflicts/jordan/peacebuilding-organisations/jicrc/.
21 See: http://adyanfoundation.org/about/profile/.
22 See: http://www.kalamresearch.com/~kalamres/about-us.php.

especially Christianity and Judaism [to promote] global, regional, and local inter-faith initiatives'. Iraq's Al-Hakim Foundation (founded in 2004) similarly enlists interfaith in support of its broader educational and humanitarian mission.

Under the patronage of Prince El Hassan bin Talal, The Royal Institute for Inter-Faith Studies in Jordan sets a slightly different tone. Rather than setting out in particular to promote a certain image of Islam, it frames its mission in the more interfaith-friendly terminology of promoting 'common human and ethical values', 'eliminating mutual misconceptions about the "other" and ulti-mately expanding these shared commonalities in the hope of promoting peaceful coexistence'.[23] Jordan has long been a pioneer of interfaith in the region, and is home to several centres that are geared more or less explicitly towards inter-faith goals (it was Jordan's King Abdullah II who was behind the UN Interfaith Harmony Week). The Royal Institute for Inter-Faith Studies and the Jordanian Interfaith Coexistence Research Center, founded in 1994 and 2003, respectively, can be traced back to Huntington's 'clash of civilisations' in the first instance, and 9/11 and the 'war on terror', in the second. Then there is the Royal Aal al-Bayt Institute for Islamic Thought, with which King Abdullah II and Prince Ghazi worked to produce the 2004 Amman Message. The Amman Message was an attempt to bring together a couple of hundred of the most senior *ulama* (Islamic scholars) to agree on 'what Islam is and what it is not, and what actions represent it and what actions do not'.[24] In other words, its goal was to reaffirm Islamic unity and values such as tolerance and moderation, while delegitimising, in both political and theological terms, terrorists who claim to be representing Islam. The widely-endorsed Amman Message was the focus of a gathering the fol-lowing year entitled, 'The International Islamic Conference: True Islam and its Role in Modern Society'. It also inspired a further initiative in 2007, an open letter signed by 138 prominent Muslim scholars to Christian leaders around the world, 'A Common Word Between Us and You'. Although also prompted by the 2005 Danish cartoon scandal, and a response to Pope Benedict's controversial Regensburg address, during which he made reference to a Byzantine emperor's derogatory remarks about Islam, the Common Word initiative is the culmination of decades of interfaith engagement by the Jordanian royal family.[25] Its success

---

23 See: http://www.riifs.org/index.php/en/about-us.

24 See: http://ammanmessage.com/.

25 For more on the background to the 'Common Word' initiative, see: D Christiansen, 'The Context of the "Common Word"', in *The Review of Faith and International Affairs* 6.4 (2008), pp. 49–52. For more details on the Christian response, see: Y Haddad and J Smith, 'The Quest for "A Common Word": Initial Christian Responses to a Muslim Initiative',

in the field of interfaith is rooted in its ability to cast itself in the role not only of a broker of consensus amongst members of the *Ummah* (the Islamic community), but also as mediator in the global conversation between the West and 'moderate Islam'. In 2009, resolutions were passed in both the US House of Representatives and the Senate, citing the Amman Message and praising Jordan as an 'instrumental partner in the fight against Al-Qaeda' and King Abdullah II as a leading voice in 'trying to reaffirm the true path of Islam'.[26]

While Jordan then has been a key player, in recent years, not to be outdone, various Gulf states have emerged as prominent advocates of the interfaith agenda. Two initiatives in particular stand out. Firstly, the Saudi-funded intergovernmental organisation, the King Abdullah bin Abdulaziz International Center for Interreligious and Intercultural Dialogue (KAICIID), was founded in 2012. A collaboration between the governments of Austria, Spain, Saudi Arabia and the Vatican, KAICIID is based in Vienna. Its advisory board comprises religious leaders from a wide range of traditions (including non-Abrahamic representatives) and its work includes interfaith dialogue events, publications, training programmes and outreach around the world. The Doha International Center for Interfaith Dialogue (DICID) is another prominent initiative that has garnered for its host Qatar a particularly influential role in the field of faith-based diplomacy. DICID was established as a result of a recommendation by the Emir in 2007, but the idea was first floated in 2003, when Qatar hosted the 'Building Bridges' seminar.[27] Qatar has also played a central role in the US-Islamic World Forum since its inception in 2004.

While countries such as Jordan, and more recently Gulf states such as Saudi Arabia and Qatar, have become prominent advocates of interfaith dialogue, their efforts have often been met with cynicism, particularly on the international stage. Interfaith dialogue in the Middle East is often described by commentators and participants alike as nothing more than a PR exercise. Some observers point to the irony of a 'Wahhabi state' preaching to the world about tolerance and moderation. Amongst academics it has often been noted that Middle Eastern interfaith initiatives are political tools that do not serve Islam as much as they do the interests of the states who invest in them. Michaelle Browers, for example, argues that, 'The [Amman] Message works better as a justification of the war on terror and

---

in *Islam and Christian-Muslim Relations* 20.4 (2009), pp. 369–388.
26 Kayaoglu, 'Explaining Interfaith Dialogue in the Muslim World', in *Politics and Religion* 8.2 (2015), p. 254.
27 See: https://berkleycenter.georgetown.edu/projects/the-building-bridges-seminar.

an identification of which side the "good guys" are on than as a propagator of moderate Islamic values.'[28]

It should be noted that there have been some very legitimate critiques levelled at the region's initiatives. Amidst a slew of organisations and events that focus on Christian-Muslim dialogue geared towards addressing the global 'clash of civilisations', there is very little to speak of in terms of what we might call 'intrafaith' engagement. In other words, while interfaith dialogue has emerged as a response to one set of geopolitical circumstances, where it has garnered much prestige for its hosts, there seems to be comparatively little attention paid to the equally important Sunni-Shia question in the region. Human rights concerns have also arisen. That Saudi Arabia, for example, would fund a high profile intergovernmental interfaith initiative that it cannot host – largely because of the country's lack of religious freedom – is not insignificant.

What I want to highlight here, however, is that although interfaith is certainly mobilised for political ends in the Middle East, this is not something new, nor is it particular to the region. The interfaith movement, as we have seen, has grown for over a century in response to crisis events, and has always been embedded in broader political projects, be it protesting against nuclear disarmament, fighting for social justice or making religious freedom a global agenda. Furthermore, the distinctly liberal agenda that has characterised the interfaith movement in the West for the last one hundred or so years is also recognisable in the Middle East today – in its focus on tolerance, co-existence and moderation. The question then is not to what extent interfaith in the Middle East serves a political rather than a theological agenda, but how and for what ends religion is politicised, and interfaith instrumentalised, in different parts of the world.

Conclusion

When Donald Trump visited the Vatican to discuss peacebuilding and interfaith dialogue with the Pope, there was very little questioning of his motives. That politics and religion would come up when the president meets the head of the Catholic Church, of course, is hardly surprising. Trump's speech about Islam to a room full of Middle Eastern leaders, although not warmly received by all, was similarly not criticised for mixing religion and politics. It appeared to be a wholly appropriate step for the president to take, and maybe a necessary step, given his campaign

---

28 M Browers, 'Official Islam and the Limits of Communicative Action: The Paradox of the Amman Message', in *Third World Quarterly* 32.5 (2011), p. 954.

rhetoric and persistent attempts to impose a Muslim travel ban. In other words, 'faith-based diplomacy'[29] is an increasingly normal dimension of international relations. Why then when Middle Eastern actors invest in interfaith dialogue – and champion faith-based diplomacy – are they met with so much cynicism?

Just as interfaith has emerged as a means of promoting social inclusion in multiculturalist democracies in the West, it has also been embraced by Islamic actors, institutions and governments as a means of dispelling misconceptions about Islam, and delegitimising the extremist elements that claim to be acting on behalf of Muslims. However, in the context of the wider Muslim world, and in the Middle East in particular, interfaith is often perceived as an overtly political project, wherein various states compete to represent 'moderate Islam', and in doing so, vie for the affection of Western powers. To be clear, I am not disagreeing with this assessment. I do, however, take issue with the tacit implication that interfaith has ever been, or should ever be, a purely theological enterprise. While interfaith has undoubtedly become politicised in the region, rather than approach that fact with outright cynicism, we would do well not only to try to better understand the necessity of that political project, but also recognise the inherently political dimensions of the interfaith movement in the West.

Bibliography

Abu-Nimer, M, Khoury, A, and Welty, E, *Unity in Diversity: Interfaith Dialogue in the Middle East* (Washington DC: US Institute of Peace Press, 2007).

Borelli, J, 'The Origins and Early Development of Interreligious Relations during the Century of the Church (1910–2010)', in *US Catholic Historian* 28.2 (2010), pp. 81–105.

Braybrooke, M, *Pilgrimage of Hope: One Hundred Years of Global Interfaith Dialogue* (New York: Crossroad Publishing Company, 1992).

Browers, M, 'Official Islam and the Limits of Communicative Action: The Paradox of the Amman Message', in *Third World Quarterly* 32.5 (2011), pp. 943–958.

Christiansen, D, 'The Context of the "Common Word"', in *The Review of Faith and International Affairs* 6.4 (2008), pp. 49–52.

Cohen, M, *Under Crescent and Cross: The Jews in the Middle Ages* (New Jersey: Princeton University Press, 1994).

---

29 D Johnston, ed., *Faith-based diplomacy: Trumping realpolitik* (Oxford: Oxford University Press, 2003).

Johnston, D, ed., *Faith-based diplomacy: Trumping realpolitik* (Oxford: Oxford University Press, 2003).

Küng, H, *A Global Ethic for Global Politics and Economics* (Oxford: Oxford University Press, 1998).

Haddad, Y, and Smith, J, 'The Quest for "A Common Word": Initial Christian Responses to a Muslim Initiative', in *Islam and Christian–Muslim Relations* 20.4 (2009), pp. 369–388.

Halafoff, A, *The Multifaith Movement: Global Risks and Cosmopolitan Solutions* (New York: Springer, 2013).

Kayaoglu, Turan, 'Explaining Interfaith Dialogue in the Muslim World', in *Politics and Religion* 8.2 (2015), pp. 236–262.

Mamdani, M, *Good Muslim, Bad Muslim: America, the Cold War, and the Roots of Terror* (New York: Harmony, 2005).

Marshall, K, *Interfaith Journeys: An Exploration of History, Ideas and Future Directions* (Washington DC: World Faiths Development Dialogue, 2017).

RE-IMAGINING
BELIEF

9

Reimagining the Formative Moments of Islam: The Case of Pakistani Scholar, Javed Ahmad Ghamidi, and his New Narrative of Early Islam

Kamran Bashir

Early Islam – from the ministry of the Prophet Muhammad to the expansion of the faith under the Early Caliphate[1] – has never ceased to be invoked in new forms in the imaginations of Muslims from the classical to the modern times.[2] The period gained a renewed importance in the nineteenth and early twentieth centuries in the wake of colonial dominance over Muslim lands. Imaginings of early Islam as a way of conceiving 'authentic' and 'pure' religious worldviews have assumed even more significance with the rise of militant organisations and entities in the post-colonial period down to the present day. Such articulations only highlight the fact that Islam's early period, despite its supreme importance for understanding the character of Muslim faith, is open to historical interpretations in terms of identifying factors and reasons behind the acts of warfare conducted by the Prophet and his Companions in the first century of Islam. It is against this historical background that the current chapter examines the works and scholarly activism of an important Pakistani Muslim religious scholar, Javed

---

1 We can treat early Islam as the period starting from the *hijra* ('migration') of the Prophet from Mecca to Medina in 622 CE to the end of the Early Caliphate in 661 CE, which resulted in the expansion of Islam from Arabia into the larger Near East.
2 For modern conceptions of early Islam and the Prophet's life, see: Kecia Ali, *The Lives of Muhammad* (Cambridge MA: Harvard University Press, 2014).

Ahmad Ghamidi (b. 1951). I shall situate Ghamidi's work within the traditions of reform in Muslim societies – the traditions that took shape most conspicuously from the late nineteenth century onwards. The significance of studying Ghamidi's work stems from a number of factors. The foremost among them seems to be its capacity to reflect internal debates currently occurring in Muslim societies on the validity of militancy and terrorism. He has also attracted considerable attention in academic discourses centred on the study of modern Islam. This interest is often sparked by his seemingly new, even 'heretical', lines of Islamic thought.[3] His presence as a public intellectual is visible on local and international media in relation to debates on current affairs in Muslim contexts.[4] Moreover, in addition to his impact on segments of his native society, appeal to his thought is manifested in the favourable reception of his work in global Muslim communities living in Europe, North America, and Oceania.[5] I argue that despite the considerable reception of his

3 In particular, Ghamidi is gaining considerable attention in discourses on militant Islam, secularism, and modernism in Muslim contexts. For some key academic works on Ghamidi, see: Muhammad Qasim Zaman, 'Islamic modernism, Ethics and Shari'a in Pakistan', in Robert W Hefner, ed., *Shari'a Law and Modern Muslim Ethics* (Bloomington: Indiana University Press, 2016), pp. 177–202; Muhammad Khalid Masud, 'Rethinking Shari'a: Javed Ahmad Ghamidi on Hudud', in *Die Welt des Islams* 47 (2007), pp. 356–375; Sadaf Aziz, 'Making a Sovereign State: Javed Ghamidi and "Enlightened Moderation"', in *Modern Asian Studies* 45 (2011), pp. 597–629; Humeira Iqtidar, 'Redefining "tradition" in Political Thought', in *European Journal of Political Theory* 15.4 (2016), pp. 424–444; H Amin, 'Post-Islamist intellectual trends in Pakistan: Javed Ahmad Ghamidi and his Discourse on Islam and Democracy', in *Islamic Studies* 51 (2012), pp. 169–192; S Yasmin, 'Islam, Identity and Discourses in Pakistan', in S Akbarzadeh, ed., *The Handbook of Political Islam* (London: Routledge, 2012), pp. 167–179; Riffat Hassan, 'Islamic Modernist and Reformist Discourse in South Asia', in Shireen T Hunter, ed., *Reformist Voices of Islam: Mediating Islam and Modernity* (New York: M E Sharpe, 2009), pp. 159–186; Humeira Iqtidar, 'Introduction: Tolerance in Modern Islamic Thought', in *ReOrient* 2.1 (2016), pp. 5–11; Ebrahim Moosa, 'Muslim Political Theology: Defamation, Apostasy and Anathema', in *International Symposium-Cartoons & Minarets Reflections on Muslim-Western Encounters* (2012), available at: http://hdl.handle.net/10161/6068; Asif Iftikhar, '*Jihad* and the Establishment of Islamic Global Order: A Comparative Study of the Worldviews and Interpretative Approaches of Abu al-A'la Mawdudi and Javed Ahmad Ghamidi', Master's Thesis, McGill University, 2004.

4 Kamran Bashir, 'Media and the Globalization of a New Rhetoric Against Terrorism and Political Islam: Reading Javed Ahmad Ghamidi's Couner-Narrative Against "Traditionalist" Islam', in a paper presented at the Media in Muslim Contexts Conference, Institute for the Study of Muslim Civilisations, London, November 3–4, 2016.

5 Born in the province of Punjab in Pakistan, Ghamidi studied the traditional Islamic sciences under private tutors and also received a university degree in the humanities from Lahore. In early 1980s, he established an institute for research in the Islamic sciences, called Al-Mawrid Institute of Islamic Sciences, in Lahore. Promoting Ghamidi's work through his

imaginative work, traditionalist[6] critique of Ghamidi's oeuvre have successfully portrayed it as an inauthentic interpretation of Islam and its history.

Before we study in detail what Ghamidi has contributed to the Muslim and academic discourses on early Islam, a few salient features of his biography are in order. He grew up receiving training in the traditional Islamic sciences in addition to modern education that earned him a university degree in Western philosophy and English literature. In terms of his writings, two of his religious works are most prominent. In his Urdu work, *Mizan* ('scale'), Ghamidi seeks to develop principles for understanding Islam's foundational texts and their applications to different realms of human life in order to modify sharia ('Islamic law') for a modern Muslim believer.[7] His second work, *Al-Bayan* ('exposition'), is an Urdu Qur'anic commentary[8] which he views as an advanced development of the seminal hermeneutics proposed by his intellectual ancestor, Hamid al-Din Farahi (d. 1930)[9] in colonial India in the late nineteenth and early twentieth centuries, later developed by Farahi's student, Amin Ahsan Islahi (d. 1997).

Given the scope and focus of this essay, I will concentrate on Ghamidi's interpretive narrative of early Islam, that is, his interpretation of certain key events from the life of the Prophet Muhammad and the Early Caliphate, a seminal period which the Chicago historian, Fred Donner characterises as 'Islamic Origins'.[10]

---

lectures, the institute has now acquired a global presence as Al-Mawrid Global with local chapters in North America, Europe, and Oceania. For his anti-jihad stance, he received threats from militants, and for that reason he migrated to Kuala Lumpur in 2009. Thanks to his appeal in modern educated sectors in Pakistan and elsewhere, Ghamidi is now a well-known television personality in Pakistan and on Youtube and social media.

6 I have used the terms 'traditionalist' and 'modernist' here in the sense of the perception that the former tends to subscribe to Muslim intellectual tradition while interpreting and understanding Islam and that the latter is inclined to understand Islam by dismissing the centuries-long tradition. I disagree with this prevalent perception about different Muslim groups. For a work of seminal importance on these typologies of Muslim scholars and groups, see: William E Shepard, 'Islam and Ideology: Towards a Typology', in *International Journal of Middle East Studies* 19 (1987), pp. 307–336. For a South Asian and Middle Eastern context, see: Muhammad Qasim Zaman, *The Ulama in Contemporary Islam: Custodians of Change* (Princeton: Princeton University Press, 2002).

7 Javed Ahmad Ghamidi, *Mizan* (Lahore, 2010).

8 Javed Ahmad Ghamidi, *Al-Bayan* (Lahore, 2016).

9 Farahi was a well-known commentator on the Qur'an in British India, whose work emphasised the coherence of the Qur'an in a milieu influenced by ideas of European Orientalists and Christian missionaries who criticised the Muslim scripture for its disjointed structure.

10 Fred M Donner, *Narratives of Islamic Origins: The Beginnings of Islamic Historical Writing* (Princeton: Princeton University Press, 1998).

Ghamidi calls his understanding of the early period a *jawābī bayāniya* ('counter-narrative'), that is, a response to a purported 'traditional narrative'.[11] Both the traditional narrative (as explained below) and Ghamidi's account are, in fact, specific religious responses to the fundamental historical question of why the acts of warfare and violence seen in the career of the Prophet Muhammad and in the early expansion of Islamic empire were carried out. The key question is: were these militant and expansionist acts meant for a specific time and place, or was their character universal? In other words, was it considered a religious duty for Muslims to continue the process of expansion over non-Muslim lands for all times to come?

Before I analyse Ghamidi's interpretation, it is important to identify what he calls a traditional narrative. According to the traditional narrative, Donner explains:

> [T]he expansion of Islam was an expression of God's will for mankind, and was linked to the religious dedication of the first Muslims, who galvanised by the new faith, embarked on their march to establish the *universal sovereignty of Islam*[12] and the Islamic state (*as the custodian of monotheistic heritage*).[13] It was also due, in their view, to the fact that God favored the Muslims and had a hand in their victories on the battlefield.[14]

In addition to this basic interpretation of the events of early Islam, the traditional narrative acquired further strength when it was supported by the later juristic interpretive engagements with a central historical question, that is: whether the legitimacy and even requirement of expanding the empire are valid for all times to come or not? To Ghamidi, later Muslim jurists, despite having considerable diversity of opinion, imparted the impression in their juristic discourses that the perpetual expansion of the Islamic state is a valid and desirable, even mandatory, religious objective.[15] Reading Muslim juristic discourses with an essentialist

---

11 Ghamidi wrote a newspaper article in the *Daily Jang* (Lahore) in 2015 that triggered a widespread response, including considerable censure, from many of the traditionalist scholarly quarters. See: Javed Ahmad Ghamidi, *Islam aur Riyasat: Aek Jawabi Bayaniya* (Islam and the State: A Counter-Narrative), in *Daily Jang*, 22 January 2015. Later Ghamidi wrote responses to his critics.
12 Emphasis added by me.
13 Parentheses are my intervention in order to elaborate the traditional narrative.
14 See: Introduction in Fred M Donner, ed., *The Expansion of the Early Islamic State* (Burlington: Ashgate, 2008), p. 7.
15 For an analysis of classical Muslim juristic discourses on jihad and related topics, see:

lens to discern a uniform traditional narrative on the question of the expansion of Islamic state can be problematic.[16] However, Muslim legal discourses have catered to the political and religious needs of militant organisations by offering legal vocabularies and their interpretations, such as *dār al-Islām* ('land of Islam'), *dār al-ḥarb* ('land of war' or 'non-Muslim lands') and *jīhād wa qitāl* ('jihad as militant struggle').[17] Despite the widespread reception of this traditional narrative, it is also true that the answer to this historical question remained unsettled in Muslim thought over the course of many centuries.

It is against this supposed traditional narrative and the questions it tries to answer that Ghamidi formulates his counter-narrative. Interpreting the nature of Islamic origins is an unfinished project to Ghamidi. His narrative is based on his creative reading of both the Bible and the Qur'an.[18] The basic conclusion of his narrative is that the acts of warfare and violence described in scriptures were divinely prescribed for only a certain period of time and were not meant to be temporally and spatially universal as the alleged traditional narrative posits. Although we already have precedents in the thought of other modern scholars for this line of reasoning,[19] Ghamidi's method of arriving at this conclusion is different from others in many ways. The central pillar of his counter-narrative is the fundamental difference he draws between what God expected from the Prophet, and what He requires from an individual believer or a community of believers who follow Islam after the generation of the Prophet and his Companions. This difference

---

Majid Khadduri, *War and Peace in the Law of Islam* (Baltimore: John Hopkins University Press, 1955).

16 The extend of the influence of classical, medieval, and early modern juristic discourses on the conduct of pre-modern Muslim state is a debatable issue. For many historians, there have always been non-religious motives, parallel to religious reasons, existing in Muslim polities that shaped their militant ventures. For a broader overview of the topic, see: Sami Zubaida, *Beyond Islam: A New Understanding of the Middle* East (London: I B Tauris, 2011).

17 In Muslim legal discussions, *dār al-Islām* denotes the land governed by sharia; and *dār al-ḥarb* as non-Muslim lands which can be conquered for subsequent implementation of sharia. These ideas, with their long discursive history in legal discussions, gained a new relevance in colonial India during the nineteenth century in the context of the rise of political Islam.

18 These ideas have been presented in relevant sections of Ghamidi's works, *Mizan* and *Al-Bayan*. Relevant content is found in his public lectures under the title, *Khutubat-i Daylas* ('Dallas Lectures') that he gave in the United States in 2015. The lectures can be accessed on Youtube. See: https://www.youtube.com/watch?v=NKsXOjL0iKs&index=1&list=PLvDnnnk YLWQdAizKCB6-ziHlCoCHqXA67.

19 For instance, Sayyid Ahmad Khan (d. 1898) in colonial India, and the Chicago modernist scholar, Fazlur Rahman (d. 1988), both emphasised the local and universal elements of Islamic foundational texts.

suggests that there were certain acts which were permissible for the Prophet to perform under certain conditions but are otherwise illegitimate for believers to commit. Hence, the Prophet was allowed at a specific phase of his ministry to wage war with his opponents. This phase came not at the beginning of his mission which began in Mecca, but at the time when the message reached its culmination to the extent that religious truth, through divine help, had been made glaringly evident before the Prophet's audiences in Mecca and Medina.[20] After this phase in the Prophet's ministry, the next stage came in the form of divine punishment, a retribution that Ghamidi reads as analogous to the one awaiting the wicked at the Last Judgment (al-ākhira). Thus, Ghamidi interprets the Qur'anic verdicts (or injunctions) that allowed the Prophet to wage war as something similar to the divine verdict on the day of the Last Judgment.[21] This means that to God, the war against the Meccans and others who had refused to believe the Prophet, was an earthly recompense for their rejection of the Prophet's clear, divinely controlled message, and similarly the prescribed killings mentioned in the Qur'an were the punishment for their deeds in advance of the Last Judgment.

Ghamidi's interpretation of these acts of warfare and violence also rests on another central idea in his thought. Reading the Bible and the Qur'an, he infers that within the tradition of Abrahamic religions, there seems to be a clear difference between an ordinary Prophet (termed nabī) and what we can call a 'Messenger on Special Duty' (termed rasūl). While ordinary prophets come and go (and may be successful in convincing their nation, or may be killed), the case of rusul ('messengers on special duty') is altogether different. They come to establish the regime of God on this earth, and their failure brings with it divine wrath, as manifested in biblical and Qur'anic punishment stories. Ghamidi elaborates that this divine punishment is implemented in two ways: in the case of a rasūl's failure, a natural calamity ruins the land where he is deputed, such as in the cases of Biblical and Qur'anic prophets like Noah and Lot; in the second case, if a rasūl is somewhere successful in establishing a polity, such as in the cases of early Israelite history mentioned in the book of Deuteronomy, and in the case of the Prophet Muhammad's Medinan city-state, this punishment is inflicted not through any natural catastrophe but through the hands of the prophet and his associates, as the Qur'an says: 'Allah will punish them by your hands and will disgrace them and give you victory over them.'[22]

---

20 Ghamidi used the term itmām al-ḥujja ('consummation of argument/evidence') for this phase of the prophetic ministry.

21 For instance, Ghamidi reads the Qur'anic chapter, Surat al-Tawba (Qur'an 9) under this light.

22 The Qur'an (9:14).

Given the complexity of the events in the formative history of Islam, Ghamidi faces some enduring interpretive challenges while developing this narrative, challenges which academic historians are also grappling with. In the case of the prophetic acts of warfare in Mecca and Medina, Ghamidi explains them somewhat conveniently through a literary analysis of the Qur'an. However, he struggles with the challenge of explaining the historical reason for the later expansion of the Islamic state from Arabia into the Byzantine and Sassanian lands during the Early Caliphate. Regarding this challenge, Ghamidi seems to imply that since both the traditional narrative and the explanations of secular Islamic historians for this expansion all rest, in the wake of scanty contemporary evidence,[23] on historical speculation and conjecture, he too can resort to a manner of speculation based on available historical evidence and the larger study of Abrahamic religions.[24] To him, the main reason for this post-Prophetic expansion was to make Mecca a symbol of monotheism for its being the haven of the divine sanctuary, the Ka'ba. This expansion kept Mecca permanently safe from non-Muslim hands. Thus, at the sanction of the Prophet, the two neighbouring empires were brought under the control of the Islamic state, without forcing their populations towards conversion to Islam. Ghamidi positions himself differently from his contemporary traditionalist opponents by stressing that this expansion was never imagined by the Prophet and his Companions as something to be pursued by Muslims perpetually for all times to come.[25] Its divine and prophetic sanction was limited to those specific

---

23 There are few extant historical sources that are contemporary to the events during the Early Caliphate. Later historical sources do not write specifically on the consciousness (in terms of any universal ideology to expand or not) with which the Companions of the Prophet Muhammad were pursuing their expansionist efforts. The matter was left to later Muslim historians and jurists to interpret what was actually intended by these acts of extending the empire.

24 I am grateful for the insights from Asif Iftikhar (Institute of Islamic Studies, McGill University) on the implications of Ghamidi's thought for the interpretation of events during the Early Caliphate.

25 Contemporary Muslim scholars in the Deoband tradition of Muslim reform and learning in South Asia are among Ghamidi's main opponents. For an introduction to Deoband, see: Barbara Metcalf, *Islamic Revival in British India: Deoband, 1860–1900* (Princeton: Princeton University Press, 1982). Scholars from the seminary Dar al-'Ulum Karachi in Pakistan, which represents Deoband in the country, have vehemently opposed Ghamidi's new narrative of early Islam. See: Taqi 'Uthmani, *Islam aur Riyasat* (Islam and the State), in *Daily Jang*, 27 January 2015. For another traditionalist position dismissing Ghamidi's viewpoint, see: Abu al-Hasan Alawi, *Jawab-i Ghazal dar 'Islam aur Riyasat: Aek Jawabi Bayaniya'* (A Response to 'Islam and the State: A Counter-Narrative'), in *Muhaddith* 47.1 (2015), available at: http://magazine.mohaddis.com/shumara/303-jan-feb-2015/2899-jawab-ghazal-islam-ryasat-jawabi-bayania.

nearby lands, to whose rulers the Prophet had sent letters in order to invite them
to embrace strict monotheism. For Ghamidi, later juristic opinions on the universal validity of expansion were merely interpretive acts, and not factual history or
a religious doctrine. In his opinion, these juristic opinions were, in fact, weak,
unfounded interpretations of Islamic origins. He insists that his and similar interpretations of early Islam can make way for new religious counter-narratives in
answer to evidently hegemonic traditional narrative(s).[26] Ghamidi's narrative has
potentially far-reaching implications for the way traditionalist scholarship com-
prehends Islam. His differentiating between the mission of the Prophet in contrast
to that of later believers has a major impact on the understanding and application
of some of the key ideas in Muslim intellectual history. The basic corollary of his
narrative is that punishments for the acts of *shirk* ('polytheism'), *kufr* ('denial
of the Prophet Muhammad'), and *irtidād* ('apostasy'), the legal issues lying at
the heart of classical and modern Islam, were limited to the time of the Prophet,
instead of being legislated for all times and places.[27] In other words, his narrative,
with its resultant religious worldview, presents a *believer-centred outlook of religion* in the aftermath of the Prophet's demise. Thus, in his opinion, the believers
living in the twenty-first century no longer need to play a role that was meant for
the Prophet and his Companions only, a role that was supervised by God and not
by human leaders of medieval or modern times.

    As mentioned above, the very need to conceive such a narrative reflects the ten-
sions and challenges faced by modern Muslim communities in terms of militant
movements and the rise of political Islam. After studying Ghamidi's counter-narrative, we can now analyse it and his larger body of work in two possible ways
within the scope of this chapter: by comparing and contrasting his ideas with traditionalist or fundamentalist positions; and through measuring the prospects and
potentials for the reception of his imaginative narrative and overall work. In comparing and contrasting Muslim religious scholars, secular academic discourses
employ decades-old categories to conceptualise Muslim scholarship. These are
the categories that distinguish one scholar from the other. By the standards of
this discourse, Ghamidi is understood as a 'modernist' and a liberal scholar, one

---

26 Ghamidi does not intend to offer this historical explanation as a fixed religious doctrine.
He seeks to encourage a dialogue to reopen this discussion around the interpretation of
events in early Islamic history. Thus, for him, there can be further improved understanding
of that remote past.
27 Muslim legal discourses have been continuously occupied with the questions pertaining
to the nature of punishments for these acts. The source of these punishments is seen in the
acts of the Prophet Muhammad, as recorded in hadith literature.

who wants to free Islam of any jihadi spirit and thus align it with Western values of peace and pluralism. The academic discourse holds modernists responsible for belittling Muslim intellectual tradition. Ghamidi and other modernists are contrasted with opposing groups of 'traditionalists', who are seen as the self-declared custodians of Muslim tradition. However, dismissing such academic categorisations, Ghamidi abhors any depiction of himself and his methodology as 'modernist', and he is loath to be seen as someone standing outside his centuries-long intellectual heritage, aligned with Western norms or demands.[28] For Ghamidi, his investigation of intellectual issues is based not on some imagined idea of the uniformity of tradition, but on its vibrancy and its internal periodical tendency to review the whole Muslim intellectual tradition. In this vein, Ghamidi reads the works of earlier well-received medieval and early modern Muslim scholars such as al-Ghazali (d. 1111), Ibn Taymiyya (d. 1328), and the Delhi polymath Shah Wali Allah (d. 1762) as historical precedents that reflected the periodical review of the character of the intellectual heritage.[29] Al-Ghazali is usually seen emphasising the theological and mystical aspects of Islam and Ibn Taymiyya as a representative of a hadith-based understanding of Islam. By comparison, Wali Allah strikes a balance between theology, mysticism, and hadith.[30] To Ghamidi, these established

---

28 Ghamidi writes:

Although this (Islamic) civilisation has been declining for the last three centuries, its natural (or organic) evolution has stopped, the effects of the Muslims' lack of concern for Islamic practices are evident, there has been mixing of many non-Muslim elements in this civilisation as well due to the passing of time, and that it needs reform from many aspects, *it is still my civilisation despite all that* [emphasis mine]. I am ready to work for its regeneration all the time, but I cannot abandon this civilisation in order to embrace the Western civilisation.

See his collection of early essays, including his autobiographical literary pieces: Javed Ahmad Ghamidi, *Maqamat* (Stations) (Lahore, 2010), p. 70.

29 While investigating the true character and the actual worldview prescribed by Islam, all these established figures in Islamic scholarly history confronted criticism from Muslim scholarly quarters for their apparently 'new' thinking. Wali Allah, for instance, wrote a treatise, *Al-Insaf fi Bayan Sabab al-Ikhtilaf* (The Fair Exposition of the Reasons of Disagreements), taking stock of the Muslim disagreements and their nature on legal issues all along the Muslim scholarly tradition. Al-Ghazali penned *Faysal Al-Tafriqa bayn al-Islam wa-l-Zandaqa* (The Criterion of Distinction between Islam and Clandestine Unbelief) on the question of what is heretical and what is true Islam.

30 For an introduction to the tradition of revisiting earlier opinions and disagreements in Muslim intellectual history, see: Jonathan A S Brown, *Misquoting Muhammad: The Challenge and Choices of Interpreting the Prophet's Legacy* (London: Oneworld Publications, 2014). Also see: Ebrahim Moosa, Introduction to *Shah Wali Allah's Treatises on Juristic Disagreement and Taqlid*, transl. Marcia Hermansen (Louisville: Fons Vitae, 2010), pp. vii–xxi.

authorities tread the path of reinterpreting Islamic intellectual heritage in various ways. Thus, he considers his work similar in approach to the resources of Muslim tradition, including the traditional narrative of the early period. In short, in reimagining early Islam, he claims to follow the path of his intellectual predecessors. However, despite the rising appeal of his work in many parts of the world, he is still struggling to gain a widespread reception of his work.

A few historical factors come to our notice when we reflect upon the reasons for the limited popularity of his message compared to that of his traditionalist opponents. First, Ghamidi's intellectual forefather, Hamid al-Din Farahi, and the predecessors of Ghamidi's opponents all belonged to the colonial order of British India of the late nineteenth and early twentieth centuries. By the time South Asia became independent in 1947, the intellectual traditions in which Ghamidi's opponents were embedded had already become successful in establishing a considerable institutional and intellectual base.[31] In contrast, his intellectual progenitor, Farahi, viewed the situation as requiring a thorough stock-taking of Muslim intellectual heritage from the very beginning. In methodological terms, this was more analogous to a secular academic approach to the study of a religious tradition than a reformist operation to identify and combat a social situation that needed immediate reform – which is what his opponents felt. Ghamidi's evident lack of strong institutional roots had a direct bearing on the relatively weak reception of his work. This is the reason for the scattered nature of his readership and religious following.

Another factor behind Ghamidi's restricted reception is the prevailing perception about his work as a way to respond to and comply with Western criticism of Islam as a militant faith. In a nutshell, he is portrayed as someone who speaks the language of an alien tradition, that is, Western civilisation. Ghamidi's claim apparently seems to suggest that the medieval and early modern figures of Islam such as al-Ghazali, Ibn Taymiyya and Wali Allah encouraged a holistic analysis of the development of the traditional Islamic sciences and the identification of the underlying spirit and thrust of Islam. Ghamidi utilises this historical precedent to support his case for the need to review the whole intellectual tradition of his own times, including the interpretation of early Islam.[32] However, the major question

---

31 For instance, traditionalist Deobandi schools with their formal or informal affiliation with the central seminary in the town of Deoband in North India, Dar al-'Ulum, were existing in good numbers.

32 Other Muslim scholars, who are labelled as 'modernists', also substantiated their positions after this reviewing of the tradition. See: Sayyid Ahmad Khan, "'Ulum-i Jadida' (Modern Sciences), in Isma'il Panipati, ed., *Maqalat-i Sir Sayyid* (Essays by Sir Sayyid),

that arises is: if certain medieval and early modern thinkers were later successful in achieving a broad reception among Muslims, why could modern Muslim intellectuals such as Ghamidi not enjoy the same status as 'authentic' Muslim scholars, given their rigorous work. It seems that the later reception of al-Ghazali, Ibn Taymiyya, and Wali Allah is based on the perception of traditionalist scholars that these intellectual figures worked in largely indigenous Muslim milieus and thus, all their ideas, despite their innovative character at times, were rooted in Muslim tradition. By contrast, Ghamidi's novelty, perceived as a heresy by his opponents, is seen as a rational response to the criticism levelled by the West on Islam and its early history of expansion.[33] The phenomenon of seeing Ghamidi as a scholar who succumbs to an alien, and in many ways hostile, tradition is manifested in the joint criticism levelled at him in those Muslim intellectual quarters that are otherwise belligerent towards each other. In South Asia, religious groups such as Deobandis, Barelwis, Ahl-i Hadith ('the people of hadith')[34] and Sufis have all been participating in antagonistic debates, even going so far as to lable each other *kāfir* ('infidel') or *mulḥid* ('heretic'). However, in their intellectual combat with Ghamidi, they somehow emerge as united in viewing him as a heretic of a very different nature. In the view of Ghamidi's opponents, Deobandis and Salafis debate with each other using the shared paradigms of Muslim tradition; by contrast, Ghamidi is thought to reason from outside the tradition. This imagined situation is built on the idea of the 'otherness' of any opinion that is analogous to Western theories. However, Ghamidi's self-assessment is quite contrary to the widespread impression of him

---

vol. 7 (Lahore: Majlis Taraqqi Adab, 1991), pp. 211–212; Fazlur Rahman, *Islam and Modernity: Transformation of an Intellectual Tradition* (Chicago: Chicago Univeristy Press, 1982). In contrast to modernist scholars, writings of traditionalist scholars like Abu'l Hasan al-Nadwi (d. 1999) impress upon agreed-upon threads in Muslim intellectual tradition, including the one encouraging the expansion of Islam into non-Muslim lands. For an influential writing in this regard, see: Abu'l Hasan al-Nadwi, *Madha Khasara al-'Alam bi-Inhitaṭ al-Muslimin* (What did the World lose with the Decline of the Muslim World) (Cairo, not dated). Also see: Roxanne L Euben and Muhammad Qasim Zaman, eds., *Princeton Readings in Islamist Thought: Texts and Contexts from al-Banna to Bin Laden* (Princeton: Princeton University Press, 2009).

33 For a relatively recent polemical work dismissing Ghamidi's position, see: Muhammad Rafiq, *Fitna-yi Ghamidiyat ka 'Ilmi Mahasaba* (Academic Analysis of the Sedition of Ghamidi-ness) (Lahore, not dated).

34 These three schools of thought originated in colonial India in the nineteenth century. The Deobandi school places an emphasis on the tradition of Muslim legal thought in their decisions on new legal issues; the Barelwi school accentuates devotional piety towards the Prophet Muhammad; and the groups configured under the Ahl-i Hadith label stress prophetic traditions for seeking what is considered 'authentic' Islam. The last one is frequently grouped with the Wahhabi and Salafi traditions.

as a Western critic. Despite having studied Western thought, he views himself through and through a traditionalist, someone who is rooted in a religious tradition that is precious to him.

In short, in Ghamidi, we have an interesting case of how internal debates in the circles of modern Muslim scholarship are taking place around the notion of Islamic origins in which one group attempts to curb the reimagining of religious tradition by another group. Ghamidi's work (and his resultant activism) does offer a parallel choice and opportunity to break new grounds in interpreting the era of Islamic origins in the wake of hegemonic traditionalist understandings of the seminal period. However, his position is polemically and discursively weakened by his opponents who succeed in portraying him, on different media platforms, as someone who is impressed by the Western criticism of Islam and its history and who follows a path that they perceive as diverging from an imagined, unified intellectual heritage. On the contrary, Ghamidi views himself as a committed follower of the Muslim intellectual past, a tradition that encourages and allows revisiting older positions, as manifested in the works of al-Ghazali, Ibn Taymiyya, and Wali Allah. Modern Muslim religious scholarship, in the attempt to reimagine the narrative of Islamic faith, needs to go beyond the polemics between different groups and eschew judging each other based on hidden assumptions and unfounded perceptions.

Bibliography

Ahmad Khan, Sayyid, ''Ulum-i Jadida' (Modern Sciences), in Isma'il Panipati, ed., *Maqalat-i Sir Sayyid* (Essays by Sir Sayyid), vol. 7 (Lahore: Majlis Taraqqi Adab, 1991), pp. 211–212.

Alawi, Abu al-Hasan, *Jawab-i Ghazal dar 'Islam awr Riyasat: Aek Jawabi Bayaniya'* ('A Response to 'Islam and State: A Counter-Narrative'), in *Muhaddith* 47.1 (2015), available at: http://magazine.mohaddis.com/shumara/303-jan-feb-2015/2899-jawab-ghazal-islam-ryasat-jawabi-bayania.

Ali, Kecia, *The Lives of Muhammad* (Cambridge MA: Harvard University Press, 2014).

Amin, H, 'Post-Islamist intellectual trends in Pakistan: Javed Ahmad Ghamidi and his Discourse on Islam and Democracy', in *Islamic Studies* 51 (2012), pp. 169–192.

Aziz, Sadaf, 'Making a Sovereign State: Javed Ghamidi and "Enlightened Moderation"', in *Modern Asian Studies* 45 (2011), pp. 597–629.

Bashir, Kamran, 'Media and the Globalization of a New Rhetoric Against Terrorism and Political Islam: Reading Javed Ahmad Ghamidi's Counter-Narrative Against "Traditionalist" Islam', in a paper presented at the Media in Muslim Contexts Conference, Institute for the Study of Muslim Civilisations, London, November 3–4, 2016.

Brown, Jonathan A S, *Misquoting Muhammad: The Challenge and Choices of Interpreting the Prophet's Legacy* (London: Oneworld Publications, 2014).

Donner, Fred M, ed., *The Expansion of the Early Islamic State* (Burlington: Ashgate, 2008).

Donner, Fred M, *Narratives of Islamic Origins: The Beginnings of Islamic Historical Writing* (Princeton: Darwin Press, 1998).

Euben, Roxanne L, and Zaman, Muhammad Qasim Zaman, eds., *Princeton Readings in Islamist Thought: Texts and Contexts from al-Banna to Bin Laden* (Princeton: Manitoba Education and Advanced Learning, Alternate Formats Library, 2009).

Ghamidi, Javed Ahmad, *Al-Bayan* (Lahore: Al-Mawrid, 2016).

Ghamidi, Javed Ahmad, *Islam aur Riyasat: Aek Jawabi Bayaniya* (Islam and the State: A Counter-Narrative), in *Daily Jang*, 22 January 2015.

Ghamidi, Javed Ahmad, *Maqamat* (Stations) (Lahore, 2010).

Ghamidi, Javed Ahmad, *Mizan* (Lahore, 2010).

Hassan, Riffat, 'Islamic Modernist and Reformist Discourse in South Asia', in Hunter, Shireen T, ed., *Reformist Voices of Islam: Mediating Islam and Modernity* (New York: M E Sharpe, 2009), pp. 159–186.

Iftikhar, Asif, '*Jihad* and the Establishment of Islamic Global Order: A Comparative Study of the Worldviews and Interpretative Approaches of Abu al-A'la Mawdudi and Javed Ahmad Ghamidi', Master's Thesis, McGill University, 2004.

Iqtidar, Humeira, 'Introduction: Tolerance in Modern Islamic Thought', in *ReOrient* 2.1 (2016), pp. 5–11.

Iqtidar, Humeira, 'Redefining "tradition" in Political Thought', in *European Journal of Political Theory* 15.4 (2016), pp. 424–444.

Khadduri, Majid, *War and Peace in the Law of Islam* (Baltimore: John Hopkins University Press, 1955).

Masud, Muhammad Khalid, 'Rethinking Shari'a: Javed Ahmad Ghamidi on Hudud', in *Die Welt des Islams* 47 (2007), pp. 356–75.

Metcalf, Barbara, *Islamic Revival in British India: Deoband, 1860–1900* (Princeton: Princeton University Press, 1982).

Moosa, Ebrahim, 'Muslim Political Theology: Defamation, Apostasy and
    Anathema', in *International Symposium-Cartoons & Minarets Reflections
    on Muslim-Western Encounters* (2012), available at: http://hdl.handle.
    net/10161/6068.
Moosa, Ebrahim, Introduction to *Shah Wali Allah's Treatises on Juristic
    Disagreement and Taqlid*, transl. Marcia Hermansen (Louisville: Fons Vitae,
    2010), pp. vii–xxi.
al-Nadwi, Abu'l Hasan, *Madha Khasara al-'Alam bi-Inhitat al-Muslimin* (What
    did the World lose with the Decline of the Muslim World) (Cairo, not dated).
Rafiq, Muhammad, *Fitna-yi Ghamidiyat ka 'Ilmi Mahasaba* (Academic
    Analysis of the Sedition of Ghamidi-ness) (Lahore, not dated).
Rahman, Fazlur, *Islam and Modernity: Transformation of an Intellectual
    Tradition* (Chicago: University of Chicago Press, 1982).
Shepard, William E, 'Islam and Ideology: Towards a Typology', in *International
    Journal of Middle East Studies* 19 (1987), pp. 307–336.
Taqi 'Uthmani, *Islam awr Riyasat* (Islam and State), in *Daily Jang*, 27 January
    2015.
Yasmin, S, 'Islam, Identity and Discourses in Pakistan', in Akbarzadeh, S, ed.,
    The Handbook of Political Islam (London: Routledge, 2012), pp. 167–179.
Zaman, Muhammad Qasim, 'Islamic modernism, Ethics and Shari'a in
    Pakistan', in Robert W Hefner, ed., *Shari'a Law and Modern Muslim Ethics*
    (Bloomington: Indiana University Press, 2016), pp. 177–202.
Zaman, Muhammad Qasim, *The Ulama in Contemporary Islam: Custodians of
    Change* (Princeton: Princeton University Press, 2002).
Zubaida, Sami, *Beyond Islam: A New Understanding of the Middle* East
    (London: I B Tauris, 2011).

10

Lived Belief in Cross-Cultural Comparison

Abby Day

Introduction

This essay draws on fieldwork experiences in 2012 during research exploring 'Belief in Cultural Relations'. I will be discussing fieldwork in Egypt during the time of the early so-called Arab Spring, and comparing it to findings from research in England. I will be using an analytical, multi-dimensional framework that I developed to allow cross-cultural comparisons, particularly over such hotly-contested terms as 'belief', and consider the efficacy of its application. Seven dimensions of belief – content, source, practice, salience, function, and how it varies over time and place – are analysed.

Since the time of my Egyptian fieldwork, spring has turned to autumn, to winter and back several times. Discussions with many of my research participants changed my perception of what was initially presented in media as 'Arab Spring': there are multiple 'Arab' identities as well as interpretations of the revolutions that swept the region. My interlocutors preferred discussing 'transitions in the Arab world'. This phrasing, for me, is necessarily cautious and tentative. I am neither an Arab nor am I a scholar of the region or of Islam. The experience I report here and analyse is that of a guest – some might say interloper – in both a region and a discipline. From the conferences and seminars I attended in 2012 and 2013 I observed what appeared to be distinctly different disciplinary grabs for the 'Arab Spring': some scholars were studying religion from a social sciences perspective, others were geographers, as well as political scientists, anthropologists or Arabists. We were all trying to understand and make sense of events in different ways. I had been awarded research funding because of my extensive work on the concept of 'belief' – understood, I have argued, as a subset of religion and related not only to religious beliefs but to more socially embedded identities, with people 'believing in belonging', as I phrased it, to family, ethnic, moral and other important social identities.

Being amongst young people in Cairo and Qena, just one year after their revolution to oust the Mubarak regime, challenged my understanding of what the dominant paradigm described religion as, particularly for those educated within a 'western' model that conveniently separates religion from other social institutions, such as politics, or from other social structures, such as class, gender and identity. Discussions with my interlocuters[1] showed the shortfalls of these separations. It seemed ridiculous to discuss the political future of Egypt with a young Muslim as if politics and religion were separate. It did not make any sense to see a young woman's modest dress as unrelated to how she wanted to position herself as a modern, devout female. And how could anyone hope to understand the complex identities of a Coptic Christian who was religious, female, Egyptian, politically active and culturally sensitive to her hijab-wearing best friend seated next to her?

While intersectionality or interdisciplinarity sometimes seem like academic fictions that only continue the trope of separation, religion *is* political to many people; it *is* how some see themselves as men and women, and it *is* an ethnic identity.

Method

My days in Qena and Cairo were spent with small groups of young people who came to discuss their thoughts about their 'beliefs', and their hopes and fears, for the future. Back in the UK, fieldwork consisted of extensive email exchanges and Skype calls with those I had met in Egypt and through attendance at London and Oxford based conferences and symposia all focused on understanding the so-called Arab Spring. In March 2012, I designed and hosted a three-day conference at the University of Kent, inviting young people from the UK, Egypt and Tunisia to participate. When at first I confided in a Muslim colleague from Egypt that I was unsure about the conference's success, due to funding, travel and visa issues, he reassured me: 'you have to believe in it.'

---

1 Participants were self-selected after an invitation sent to a large network drawn from a variety of organisations. Due to subsequent events and the need for anonymity, I will use pseudonyms and mask the sites and organisations with whom I worked.

I will now turn to fieldwork descriptions and thematic analysis according to my multi-dimensional framework.

A drive through time

The road between Luxor and Qena appeared, on the map, to suggest a drive-time of half an hour to 45 minutes: just over thirty miles or fifty-two kilometres. Why we were allowing two hours confused me, until I saw the route – a narrow road with only occasional places where it was safe to overtake a slow-moving vehicle or donkey-led cart. On either side were verdant fields, and rudimentary houses, often guards standing with rifles outside more opulent residences, sometimes stalls selling fruits or vegetables, and always the flowing Nile. We were in a region known as Upper Egypt. The following is a direct excerpt from my fieldnotes:

As we're driving slowly through the checkpoint outside Luxor airport, police are idly snapping pieces of sugar cane from where they're loaded on the backs of trucks and chewing on them. Small children are striding importantly next to a man on a horse pulling more sugar cane. On the drive now as we're going through Upper Egypt either side of the road it looks like we have gone back hundreds of years. Most people are walking, riding horses or donkey carts, and men are riding on camels with baskets. There are a few bicycles and scooters and some trucks on the road, often with lots of people riding on top of them. All the women I see on this trip are head-to-toe in black, though their faces are uncovered. Younger women are also covered but wearing more colourful clothing. There's lots of straight road but it's interrupted frequently by narrowing with metal drums and boxes, apparently to force the traffic to slow as it enters more populated areas. There are no potholes or bumps, it's well-maintained. Although we are moving along a single carriageway people are driving as if there are four lanes, constantly passing each other at high speed, occasionally just honking to warn someone. Men are standing around in long robes with lots of scarves; I can see some are wearing jeans underneath. The houses look like they're all multi-occupancy. The landscape is mostly green. There's an occasional market at a crossroads, stacked high with oranges. There are lots of small children; I'm wondering why they're not in school. People are constantly whipping their donkeys.

Upper and Lower Egypt are sometimes referred to as The Two Lands, ancient kingdoms united in 3000 BCE. The distinction between upper and lower refers to the flow of the Nile from East Africa to the Mediterranean: Upper Egypt lies to the south of Lower Egypt.

One year before our visit, massive, violent protests erupted in Qena when it was announced that the new governor would be Emad Shehata Michael, a Coptic Christian; this would be the second time in a row a Christian had held the post in the predominantly Muslim region. Analysis and commentary featured the complex, historical reasons behind the outcry, not all of which were religious. Upper Egypt had been subject to centuries of conflict with long-standing family and ethnic divisions and feuds.[2] Upper Egypt had contemporary resonance for my research as it is one of the heartlands of the Society of Muslim Brothers, better known as the Muslim Brotherhood, where they were active for decades bringing medical and educational services to the largely rural population. This kind of involvement led to them becoming 'the most successful grassroots movement across the entire region', writes Magdi Abdelhadi, former BBC Arab Affairs correspondent:

> Their hospitals and other charity work have been a key component in their history to evolve as a movement from and to the people. This has often been criticised by their rivals as bribing the electorate. That may very well appear to be so at times of election. But their bond with their constituencies is not seasonal. Care for the poor and the weak is central to Islamic teaching, and they would not have enjoyed the support they do if they had not lived up to those ideals.[3]

We were not heading towards a meeting with the Brothers – at least not in any official sense, but to talk with young people in Qena. Some may have been members of the Muslim Brotherhood; we would not necessarily know, or ask. Their activities were open and almost taken for granted. These were the days when the organisation and its members were not afraid to reveal their identity; they had not yet been declared a terrorist organisation by the new, military-led government which overthrew the post-revolution Morsi-headed government only one year after it had been elected. I remembered the young man I had met in Cairo just before we left for Luxor. Tall, well-dressed, impeccably mannered, he shook my hand as I

2 See: http://english.ahram.org.eg/~/NewsContent/1/64/10319/Egypt/Politics-/Qena-protests-against-Christian-governor-escalate.aspx.
3 See: https://www.theguardian.com/commentisfree/2012/jun/25/muslim-brotherhood-egypt.

left our interview, saying: 'Please tell the British people they have nothing to fear from the Muslim Brotherhood.'[4]

One of the first issues I wanted to explore with the young people centred on what people meant by 'belief': Was this a tenet, such as a piece of doctrine? Or a sense of faith, such as implied by an earlier English formulation of 'belief' as 'beloved', or loyalty, to the 'fief'? Mindful of long-standing anthropological cautionary notes about the Euro-centric, Christian nature of the term, I was surprised by how apparently unproblematic it was to the young people with whom I talked. Had William Cantwell Smith, Rodney Needham and Malcom Ruel had their way, anthropology scholars would have dropped the term 'belief' forty years ago. A religious studies scholar, Smith (1967, 1977, 1978, 1979) discussed how the term 'belief' has its roots in Christianity. He discussed how 'belief' in Christianity changed over time from something denoting trust, reciprocity, fidelity and love to a more contingent, or propositional form. Needham (1972) provided an exhaustive account of how the term belief was used, and concluded it had a distinctly Christian lineage and orientation. Asad (1993) argued that the category of belief has been inextricably linked to specific historic creations of what it means to be Christian. That creation is produced by what Christian leaders authorise as legitimate practices and beliefs and what then becomes, like much of knowledge,[5] sedimented and reinforced, layer upon layer, in both public discourse and epistemological practices. Ruel followed that line of argument and proposed a difference between a propositional form of belief to one that expresses faith and trust.[6] Ruel identified four fallacies about belief: 1) that it is central to all religions, in the same way that it is central to Christianity; 2) that belief guides and therefore explains behaviour; 3) that belief is psychological; and 4) that it is the belief, not the object of belief, that is most important.[7] He offered a way of thinking about belief that profoundly influenced future scholars by suggesting a distinction between 'belief in' (trust in) and 'belief that' (propositional belief). Ruel concluded it is best to use the term 'belief' as we might use 'faith' if what we mean is 'trust'.[8]

---

4 His hope was fulfilled nearly four years later when, after an extensive review, the UK government decided in December 2015 not to declare them a terrorist organisation.

5 M Foucault, *The Archeology of Knowledge* (London: Tavistock, 1972).

6 See, for example: J Robbins, 'Continuity thinking and the problem of Christian culture', in *Current Anthropology* 48.1 (2007), pp. 5–17; J Robbins, 'What is a Christian? Notes toward an anthropology of Christianity', in *Religion* 33.3 (2012), pp. 191–199; M Ruel, 'Christians as believers', in John Davis, ed., *Religious Organization and Religious Experience*, Asa Monograph 21 (London: New York, 2008), pp. 9–32.

7 Ruel, 'Christians as believers', pp. 29–29.

8 Ruel, 'Christians as believers', p. 32.

Following Needham, Ruel and Smith, Asad argued that scholars such as Geertz (and, I suggest, therefore implicitly Weber) adopted meaning-centred, order-based, universalistic definitions of religion without showing how, and under what conditions, such meanings are constructed. Asad maintained that religion, and belief, were historically contingent and shaped by powerful leaders who authenticated and legitimised certain forms of belief and not others. Asad argued that, with the advance of Enlightenment and the rise of science, religious leaders in the seventeenth century shifted the emphasis of religious adherence to safeguard it from the emerging rationalist, scientific problematic. Belief became less of an observable practice and something more private where an 'emphasis on belief meant that hence forth religion could be conceived as a set of propositions to which believers gave assent'.[9] When Robbins (2007) reviewed Ruel, Smith and Asad, he agreed that it is a 'propositional' sense of 'believing that' which causes problems in cross-cultural comparisons and 'among those anthropologists and other comparativists who have carefully considered "believing" in the "believe that" sense, none see it as a cross-culturally valid concept, while some do see the "believe in" concept or something like it translating quite well'.[10]

My longitudinal involvement with young people in the UK helped me conclude that, rather than dispense with belief, it is more useful to develop a contextualised understanding of it and present it in more than just one mode. The narratives of the young people I studied did not correspond to 'belief systems' as described by, for example, Borhek and Curtis (1975) whose analysis focused on mainly cognitive and empirical measures of a belief system's levels of commitment and validity. What I observed was less of a system than a dynamic and often an emotionally-charged narrative. During my initial UK research (2011) and further longitudinal research (2013) when I returned to the cases I had originally studied, I did not find that young people were drifting through an amoral universe or unable to cope with life's challenges in the absence of grand meta-narratives. They were informed and sustained by the social relationships and contexts in which they felt they belonged. In contrast to, for example, Needham and Ruel, I argue that a rich interpretation of belief, combined with a multi-dimensional approach, allows its utility for cross-comparative purposes. The analytical model I derived inductively from those studies was the one I tentatively imposed on the Egyptian research to test its cross-cultural portability. Its purpose was to understand belief through dimensions, rather than definitions.

---

9 T Asad, *Genealogies of Religion: Discipline and Reasons of Power in Christianity and Islam* (Baltimore: Johns Hopkins University Press, 1993), pp. 40–41.
10 Robbins, 'Continuity thinking and the problem of Christian culture', p. 15.

Seven dimensions of belief[11]
Content

People's beliefs have content, which is expressed by different religions in different ways. In a Christian context, these are often described as 'creedal' because they form the words of the 'creeds' recited every Sunday as a list of the religion's tenets. 'The Word', believed to be emanating from God and Christ, is central to Christianity.[12] As discussed above, this is why Needham and other scholars have cautioned against generalising the importance of 'belief'. Most people, I found, 'believe' in their relationships with other people, specifically those with whom they have adherent, affective reciprocal relationships, most commonly partners, family and friends. Their beliefs were most often a way of expressing their relationship to something or someone else, and therefore closely linked to personal and group identity: an expression of 'what I make of me in relation to x'. They often did so using vivid examples with rich emotional content drawn from their own lives.

To begin conversations about what people believed, I started by asking: 'What do you believe in?' In Egypt, as in the UK, I received a good number of responses. The question served as a useful technique both to begin dialogue and to identify those people whose religious beliefs were triggered immediately. Some tended to answer the question straightaway, such as, in the UK, Joe, 14, who said he believed in 'all the Catholic beliefs' and attends church regularly. Jane, 61, a teacher said: 'I believe in God, one God, which I define as a spiritual being or a spiritual presence, no gender, all loving, all powerful, all mighty, creator.' For others, my opening question provoked complex responses: Terry, for example, a 49-year-old English agricultural worker, immediately put the question back to me: 'Are you asking do I believe in God – is that what you're aiming for?' Liz, 55, who runs her own home-based business, wanted to know whether she could talk about beliefs that were not necessarily religious: 'And I'll ask you – what do you mean? What do I believe in? Which area of life, or, death?' I generally answered such questions openly, by saying I did not know; belief was a widely misunderstood topic, both religious and non-religious: what did they think?

In Egypt, some people also asked me if I was thinking specifically about religion – 'or?' I said it was up to them. While a few answered in religious terms,

---

11 This section draws primarily on my initial PhD research (Day 2006), its subsequent expansion and publication (Day 2011;13) and my UK longitudinal study (Day x)
12 See: W Keane, *Christian Moderns* (Berkley and Los Angeles: University of California Press, 2007).

I was interested to hear that even those who were visibly religious – wearing a headscarf or a cross – answered with relational examples, such as 'good family relations'. During another group discussion, before I had a chance to ask them directly what they believed in, one young man referred to the situation in Libya, telling us he was not sure that the revolutionaries there 'believed' in the same ideals as the Egyptians. That comment gave me the opportunity to further ask: 'what is belief?' One young woman, incorporating the term in its faith-based mode, said, 'to have something you trust and that you don't need to have further conversation about or approval'. Another woman, echoing a similar sentiment, said 'you're certain about what you are seeing in reality and certain so you can act without considering'.

Sources

I was interested in where people thought their beliefs came from. A young woman in Egypt, for example, said, 'from family, from education, from the environment, from my personality'. This was typical of most people's responses both in Egypt and the UK. The examples they gave were of people with whom they have had or have a strong emotional relationship. Most people I talked with, in both the UK and Egypt, trace their beliefs to their family roots, followed by life experience, by which they usually mean the consequences of events. People describe their familial influences partly as what they have been told to do and partly by observing what people do, most markedly observing the ideal behaviour of, usually, a mother or a grandmother.

The other occasions when I observed a strong emotional response to questions about the origins of belief were when people were criticising other people's beliefs, or lack thereof. It was sometimes through a tension between their beliefs as somehow indigenous to their culture and in contrast to 'others' that the importance of cultural influence came through. A common theme that emerged from my interviews, irrespective of age, is how people usually place belief-formation as an activity which happened in the past and is now complete. While they may identify multiple sources and life experience as belief-builders, the structure is now, for them, a finished project. It may not be so, they sometimes point out, for others. The exception is when they consider other people whom they do not see as their equals. These 'others' are often responsible for infecting the beliefs of 'people we know'. In saying this, I do not want to fall into the trap of assuming that 'culture' is fixed and static, but I noticed that was how most of my interlocutors perceived it. This helped me think about how they performed acts of cultural maintenance, such as, in the British case, choosing the category of 'Christian' to self-identify on the national census. As David Oswell has said: 'Culture in all its flexibility allows us to think not just of the stuff that is carried, but also all that goes on in the carrying.'[13]

A minority of people attributed the source of their beliefs to 'God'. They believed that God was the source of their beliefs which became articulated on earth through the Bible and Jesus or, in the case of Muslims, through the Qur'an and Muhammad. These people, whom I will call theocentrics, differ from the other, anthropocentric people I interviewed in identifying the source of their belief as God. The discussion about resources and content was intertwined for the theocentrics to such extent that I concluded that for them content and source are indivisible.

Practice

Once I had identified with people what they believed in, including their moral beliefs, I would ask them how they put those beliefs into practice. This frequently stalled the interview. There did not seem to be to most of my informants a seamless transition from what they believed in and what they did in practice. For the most part, they had already covered the answer in responding to my first question, or in discussing their morals and values. Having already answered my question about what they believed in, they often appeared confused that I was, in effect, repeating it. Those who seemed to effortlessly separate the idea of belief from practice were my theocentric interlocutors. When I asked how they put their beliefs into practice, they said that they practised in their everyday lives, through their work, which they sometimes saw as a vocation, and through behaving in ways they described as kind, helpful and loving. Their separation of belief and practice may go some way in explaining why it is that theocentrics think people who do not believe in their religion would not carry out similar practices, such as being kind and loving.

When we discussed further ideas, particularly around questions about what made each person happy, what was important to them, and what they hoped for the future, the responses were similarly located in relational contexts. One young Egyptian woman, in her third year of law school, said, 'I want to make my father and mother happy, satisfied with me'. A third-year female Medical student echoed

---

13 D Oswell, 'Introduction: From the Beginning', in D Oswell, ed., *Culture and Society: An Introduction to Cultural Studies* (London: SAGE, 2006), p. 3.

the sentiment: 'By doing my best every day, to have friends and a family who like you, to have great teachers.' The practical, mundane nature of their concerns and experiences arose even amongst the most visibly religious. One young man, for example, identified himself as Salafi. He said one of the best features of post-revolution Egypt was that he could now travel on holiday with his wife between Qena and Hurghada without being pulled over by the police. The apparent congeniality between Muslims and Christians during the heady days of the revolution was something that arose repeatedly amongst those who had been there, in the front line as it were. Divisiveness amongst religions was a strategy of the Mubarak regime, I was often told; a technique of 'divide and conquer'. In her account of the revolution, Ahdaf Soueif (2012) described that during the Tahrir square occupations both Muslim and Christian prayers were said on Fridays and Sundays, and 'Amens' rang out across the square after the prayers. She describes how many of the young activists told her that violence against Coptic Christians was led by the police, not the revolutionaries. In one case, activists persuaded parents of young Christians who had been killed to demand autopsies: these revealed that they had been shot, with arms far beyond the reach of the revolutionaries. As Soueif described it, the spectre of inter-religious violence was a feature of the Mubarak regime.[14]

Salience

The degree to which certain beliefs mattered to people differs. The way people described what they believed in and how they had come to have those beliefs also indicated to me the degree to which they thought those beliefs important. Most people I interviewed in my British study (2011) only described themselves as Christian in a national, ethnic or political context, such as when responding to a religious question on the national census, or discussing wider issues of immigration: otherwise it seemed to be of passing importance, as if religion was a half-remembered thought, or residual belief which they had not reviewed recently but to which they still adhered in certain contexts. I described at length in 2011 how other people discussed with intensity and passion what their religion meant to them and how they could not imagine their lives without it. Those beliefs were spoken about with conviction and sometimes passion to indicate to me the high degree of salience they held for people. In Egypt, a young man said, 'belief in Islam means I am perfectly attached to Islam. I'm attached to it.'

The degree of salience was also reinforced by the interviewee's tendency to

---

14 See: A Soueif, *My City, Our Revolution* (London: Bloomsbury, 2012).

tell me detailed stories about real-life experiences which illustrated for them the importance of relationships. Several British young people told me about their important friends and what they did with their friends, as well as about ex-partners and how they felt threatened or rejected by them. In a similar way, older people told me about losing or gaining a partner and how that made them feel, and about their unresolved relationships with their children and parents. What appeared not so important to the majority of people I interviewed, irrespective of age, class and gender, was the metaphysical: what is the meaning of life? Why we are here? How did we get here? And where are we going? Most people, I conclude, are far more preoccupied with the mundane matters in their lives to give such ontological questions much thought.

Function

What does religion 'do' for people and society? Belief in the importance of adherent relationships obviously had a function in terms of identity. Although belief may function as a preserver of a form of social control, the nature of demarcating between 'them' and 'us' may function to strengthen 'our' sense of belonging to 'us' through both a process of affiliation and disaffiliation. Using the case of the UK census question on religion (2011), I argue that the majority of people who said they would have ticked 'Christian' did so mainly for three reasons: because they were affiliating to a family group; they were affiliating to an ethnic group or disaffiliating from an ethnic group; they were aspiring to belong to a group perceived as respectable.

Above all, the UK research participants impressed upon me their desire to have their beliefs understood and respected as *their* beliefs, not the beliefs of others imposed on them. This fervour did not, I maintain, arise from an ethical position wherein they respect the rights of all people to hold divergent beliefs: indeed, they were often critical and dismissive of other people's beliefs, while retaining the conviction that their own beliefs are to be respected. This is not, I suggest, a contradiction or hypocrisy. Belief, as I argued above, is to many people a statement about the self, a way of saying who we are: 'I believe, therefore I am.' Defending their own beliefs is an important way to enhance people's identities; opposing other people's beliefs functions in the same way to the same end.

During discussions with Egyptian and Tunisian young people it became clear quickly that religion had a political function in an open, coherent way that I did not usually encounter in the UK where the idea of a separation of church and state exists strongly in the public imagination. A young man in Egypt, for example, said strongly: 'there's no difference between religion and politics. Muhammad revealed what Allah said and he was also head of the community.' Another young man agreed: 'I don't like to separate religion from other aspects of life.' Involvement in political activism was, as it transpired during the latter days of the revolution, deeply risky. One young man said: 'I'm from Upper Egypt, I'm a member of the Muslim Brotherhood.[15] I've travelled before but now it is said I can't travel because I'm a member of the Muslim Brotherhood. I ask lots of questions, and people ask me lots of questions: they asked who paid for me, my roommates were afraid.' The following exchange shows the risks they felt they were taking:

Question: Do you feel Egypt is now different?
Man 1: Yes, it's different. The Muslim Brotherhood were separate, now we
    can speak a bit, now we are free to speak.
Man 2: Yes.
Man 3: We're still afraid; we still travel with knives in the car.
Man 4: Regarding the standard of living – nothing has changed yet, but
    freedom of speech, we were all deprived of it before.
Man 1: There's still some fear.

A Tunisian man at a conference I attended shortly after my Egypt visit said that during the Tunisian revolution there was fierce contestation for dominance between religious groups and political groups. He said that at one stage someone replaced on a building the Tunisian flag with a flag representing the Salafists: 'this caught attention!'

The desired outcome of political change differed amongst my research participants. A young Egyptian man told me that it was a misconception to say that people were campaigning for democracy or that the claim that 'people were revolting to establish democracy is not true, but dignity and a better life. Democracy is one political model. In Tahrir Square it was anarchy agreed amongst people'. Another man I talked to some months later discussed the then recent Egyptian referendum on changes to the constitution. He recounted an anecdote: a woman asked one of the people supervising the polling station which way she should vote. When he said he could not tell her, she said, 'well just tell me which one will bring down the price of tomatoes.' Hence, he described what people were worrying about: their everyday lives.

---

15 Note that this conversation occurred in 2012, before the Muslim Brotherhood was declared a terrorist organisation,

Following a similar line of reasoning, a Tunisian man told me he thought there was a division between those he described as the 'political elite' and young people, whom, he said, had less of an ideology than an ideal, epitomised by such revolutionary slogans as: 'employment, freedom and social dignity'. He further explained:

> The political elite said let's have elections, as if it's just about putting a paper in a box and going home. We see demonstrations of the most radical on each side, thousands of people who were demanding an Islamic state, a Salafi demonstration. Now, in two weeks there will be a demand for a civil state – demonstrations and counter demonstrations! So, there's disappointment amongst young people and we can't see a way out. Politicians are now just worried about the next elections. Youth are pushing politics on the street, not through parliament, because they weren't elected. So, it's a huge issue with the political elite, with dogma.

Whatever the political way forward might have been, one thing that seemed to unite young people I talked with from Egypt, Tunisia, Jordan and Libya was the firm conviction that theirs was a local issue and other players, from the Gulf States, United States or Europe, should not get involved.

Time and place

In Egypt, several young people drew my attention to the revolutionary actions of their parents in protests over the years: dissent was not invented in the so-called Arab Spring. Acknowledgement of parental influence was possibly one reason the protestors who lined the streets and Tahrir Square in the days of the 2011 chanted: 'We're your sons and daughters too – What we're doing is for you.' When we discussed their future, a common response both in Egypt and during discussions I later conducted with Egyptian young people, was rooted in the cultural and temporal specificity of the recent revolution. Their main questions consisted of: What is my contribution to civil society? How can I do it? How can I learn about other cultures? Most were aware that religion was taking a new, more assertive role in the public sphere. During discussions in London, an Egyptian man reflected on the religious inflection. The sudden visibility in the political arena of conservative Islam was a surprise to him and to others: 'Our Salafi friends were never involved in the public sphere. We didn't know the difference between the Muslim Brotherhood or Salafis or that there were six different forms of Salafism.'

Religion was perceived as both empowering and a threat, just as it is in Europe. Recent debates about whether Muslim women should be veiled in public can often mask underlying concerns relating to other political and national-identity issues.[16] One young Egyptian man told me that 'the cultural context I live in is the biggest influence in my life, and Islam more now than ever'. He said that the move towards increased religious involvement is generational: thirty years earlier 'you wouldn't see women in niqab but now people aren't against Islamists'.

Conclusion

As I researched belief in the UK, both at a fixed time (2011), longitudinally (2013), and then in Egypt and the UK during the time of rapid transitions in the Arab world, its contextual nature became clear. Beliefs vary over time and place, and some are as rooted in the past as they are in projections about the future. I argued that beliefs are fairly stable over time, with any changes being prompted by changes in social relationships rather than dogma or indoctrination.

A minority responded either immediately or very soon into the interview that they believed in God. They also tended to say at different times in the interview that their most important relationship was with God. The way they described their moral beliefs was often spoken in reference to what God would want. This never occurred with the anthropocentrics. The theocentric minority also described their relationship with God as the over-arching canopy which protected them and gave meaning to their lives. They, like the anthropocentric, had strong human relationships but they did not put those relationships at the centre of their beliefs. In summary, people with anthropocentric beliefs articulate their beliefs primarily in reference to their human relationships. Unless coaxed into seeing belief in non-religious terms, they may say that they believe in 'nothing', as if they do not regard their human-centred beliefs in the same category as religious beliefs. People with a theocentric belief system also discuss human relationships but cite God and their relationship to Him as what they believe in. Many of the people I interviewed in both the UK and Egypt did not talk about God or other divine beings. If they are asked a forced question about religion and answer 'Christian' or 'Muslim', they often do so because of family or ethnic reasons. While I

---

16 See, for example: H Henkel and T Sunier, 'Are Muslim Women in Europe Threatening the Secular Public Sphere?', in *Social Anthropology* 17 (2009), pp. 471–479; M Fernando, 'Exceptional Citizens: Secular Muslim Women and the Politics of Difference in France', in *Social Anthropology* 17 (2009), pp. 379–392.

was tempted to call those people 'humanists', I settled on 'anthropocentric'. This word, conveying the belief that human beings are 'centric' sufficed at this stage particularly because it suggests an orientation to a mode of belief rather than an adherence to a particular doctrine.

In March 2012, I designed and hosted a three-day conference at the University of Kent. Delegates and keynote speakers included post-graduate presenters drawn from my UK, Egyptian and Tunisian network, and several senior scholars of religion from the UK and the United States. Others were selected as audience-participants from a targeted open call. To further explore the effectiveness of my analytical model, sessions were created according to my framework's dimensions of content, sources, function, and salience. Introductory, mid-point and concluding presentations drew out implications of time and place. Papers included such topics as: human rights and the global economy; roots of religion and extremism; Christian prayer for human rights; and teaching Islam and Christianity.

How religion and belief is defined and lived will differ by time and place, and the model discussed above has served as a useful, multi-dimensional interpretive framework. It helps draw out not just the creedal, propositional forms of belief, but how it is lived,[17] experienced and negotiated on the ground.

Bibliography

Ammerman, N T, *Everyday Religion: Observing Modern Religious Lives* (Oxford and New York: Oxford University Press, 2007).

Asad, T, *Genealogies of Religion: Discipline and Reasons of Power in Christianity and Islam* (Baltimore: Johns Hopkins University Press, 1993).

Borhek, J T, and Curtis, R F, *A Sociology of Belief* (New York: John Wiley and Sons, 1975).

Day, A, *Believing in Belonging: Belief and Social Identity in the Modern World* (Oxford: Oxford University Press, 2011; 2013).

Day, A, 'Varieties of belief over time: reflections from a longitudinal study of youth and belief', in *Journal of Contemporary Religion* 28.2 (2013), pp. 277–293, available at: https://doi.org/10.1080/13537903.2013.783339.

Fernando, M, 'Exceptional Citizens: Secular Muslim Women and the Politics of Difference in France', in *Social Anthropology* 17 (2009), pp. 379–392.

Foucault, M, *The Archeology of Knowledge* (London: Tavistock, 1972).

---

17 See: M McGuire, *Lived Religion: Faith and Practice in Everyday Life* (Oxford: Oxford University Press, 2008).

Henkel, H, and Sunier, T, 'Are Muslim Women in Europe Threatening the Secular Public Sphere?', in *Social Anthropology* 17 (2009), pp. 471–479.

Keane, W, *Christian Moderns* (Berkley and Los Angeles: University of California Press, 2007).

McGuire, M, *Lived Religion: Faith and Practice in Everyday Life* (Oxford: Oxford University Press, 2008).

Needham, R, *Belief, Language and Experience* (Chicago: Chicago University Press, 1972).

Oswell, D, 'Introduction: From the Beginning', in D Oswell, ed., *Culture and Society: An Introduction to Cultural Studies* (London: SAGE, 2006), pp. 1–12.

Soueif, A, *My City, Our Revolution* (London: Bloomsbury, 2012).

Robbins, J, 'Continuity thinking and the problem of Christian culture', in *Current Anthropology* 48.1 (2007), pp. 5–17.

Robbins, J, 'What is a Christian? Notes toward an anthropology of Christianity', in *Religion* 33.3 (2012), pp. 191–199.

Ruel, M, 'Christians as believers', in John Davis, ed., *Religious Organization and Religious Experience*, Asa Monograph 21 (London: New York, 2008), pp. 9–32.

Smith, W C, *Belief and History* (Charlottesville: University of Virginia Press, 1977).

Smith, W C, *Faith and belief* (Princeton: Princeton University Press, 1979).

Smith, W C, *The Meaning and End of Religion* (London: Spck, 1978).

Smith, W C, *Problems of Religious Truth* (New York: Scribner's, 1967).

11

New Religious Movements as Resources in a Changing World

Eileen Barker

Karl Marx is known for arguing that the economic base of a society determines its general culture and ideas, and that religion is 'the opium of the masses'.[1] On the other hand, the German sociologist Max Weber argued that this was not necessarily so, most famously with his thesis that the Protestant ethic was largely responsible for the rise of modern capitalism.[2] This chapter starts from an assumption that, at any time, there are thousands of voices, ideas, and practices 'out there', although only a few will be chosen while the rest fall by the wayside, unheeded or soon to be forgotten. But there will always be some that are adopted, initially by only a small group of people who will experiment with this new (or renewed) resource, which may then be adopted or adapted by the wider society.

'Cults', 'sects' and new religious movements (NRMs)

There are over a thousand different religions active in the UK today, and many thousands more elsewhere throughout the world.[3] In the sociological literature, concepts such as 'cult' and 'sect' have technical meanings, but in popular parlance

1 Karl Marx, 'Contribution to the Critique of Hegel's Philosophy of the Right' (1843–4), in Thomas Bottomore, ed., *Karl Marx: Early Writings* (London: Watts, 1963), pp. 43–59.
2 Max Weber, *The Protestant Ethic and the Spirit of Capitalism* (1930) (London: Unwin, 1995).
3 The Inform website houses some information on over 5,000 religious organisations. See: www.Inform.ac.

they now tend to mean a religion or group of which the speaker disapproves. As a consequence, since the early 1970s, scholars have tended to prefer to talk about new religious movements (NRMs). There are problems with this concept too, but for present purposes, following the theologian Paul Tillich, religion is defined very broadly as a system of beliefs and practices that address questions of ultimate concern; and a new religious movement is one that consists primarily of a first-generation membership.[4] Although not perfect, this approach can help us to look for certain characteristics that new religions often, but by no means always, share. First, however, it needs to be stressed, that the one fact of which we can be sure concerning new religions is that we cannot generalise about them; they do differ in every conceivable way.

Nonetheless, the very fact that an NRM is defined as having first-generation membership means that its members are converts, and converts tend to be far more enthusiastic, even fanatic, than those born into their religion. Secondly, NRMs tend to appeal disproportionately to an atypical section of the population – in the past they have frequently appealed to the socially, economically and/or politically oppressed; the wave of new religions that became visible in the West in the 1960s and 1970s, however, appealed disproportionately to young, middle-class, white adults who were well-educated and came from what, according to several criteria, would be called 'good families'. Thirdly, founders of NRMs are often charismatic leaders who wield charismatic authority, are unbound by rules or tradition, and can change their minds at a moment's notice. Fourthly, the movement's *Weltanschauung* can be of a strictly dichotomous nature, with clear-cut boundaries between, for example, godly and satanic, good and bad, right and wrong, before and after, and, perhaps most significantly, them and us. Fifthly, NRMs are likely to be treated with suspicion, fear, discrimination and antagonism by the host society. This is hardly surprising as they are offering an alternative to those who may well have a vested interest in preserving the *status quo*. And, finally, new religions change far more radically and rapidly than older religions. Although some (such as the Amish or Hutterites) manage to maintain what sociologists might technically call sectarian characteristics into second and subsequent generations, most new religions that survive undergo 'denominationalisation', accommodating to, and being increasingly accommodated by, the wider society. While the religions cited in what follows are by no means all still first-generation movements, most of the practices and beliefs referred to are the result of their early days, before any accommodation to society had fully taken place.

---

4 Paul Tillich, *Dynamics of Faith* (New York: Harper and Row, 1957), pp. 1–4.

Politics

The third and fourth of these characteristics (charismatic authority and a dichotomous worldview) can enable a new religion to pursue, in a relatively single-minded way, a particular kind of political structure (although many will combine this with theocratic beliefs). This structure may be authoritarian (Jim Jones' People's Temple); democratic (the Findhorn community); bureaucratic (Scientology); patriarchal (the Plymouth Brethren); matriarchal (the Brahma Kumaris); or anarchistic (some 'virtual religions', such as Discordianism, to be found on the Internet).

It has been argued that early Christianity introduced the idea of the separation of Church and State (Matthew 22:21; Mark 12:17). Such separation was not, however, widely accepted within Christendom until the Reformation and when the Anabaptists in the early sixteenth century taught that the church should be composed of free, 'uncompelled' people, without the state coercing people's consciences. The early Anabaptists were, consequently, routinely drowned or burnt at the stake, but it was these ideas which would eventually play a significant role in the adoption of the First Amendment of the US Constitution in 1791,[5] which continues to be hotly defended by religions old and new in the United States (and elsewhere), but perhaps most notably by the Anabaptist-inspired Baptist Joint Committee for Religious Liberty, which today declares itself to be 'the only faith-based agency devoted solely to religious liberty and the institutional separation of church and state'.[6]

The law

NRMs have long tested the boundaries of legal definitions and challenged existing norms and protocols. Although they generally obey the law of the land, Jehovah's Witnesses have, since their inception, refused to put the law of man above the Law of God, and when the two conflict, they have been prepared to die rather than submit to the law of man. Around 10,000 Witnesses were incarcerated in Auschwitz and other concentration camps during the Second World War when, unlike Jews, homosexuals or gypsies, they could have been released had they sworn

---

5 'Congress shall make no law respecting an establishment of religion, or prohibiting the free exercise thereof; or abridging the freedom of speech, or of the press; or the right of the people peaceably to assemble, and to petition the Government for a redress of grievances.'
6 See: http://bjconline.org/; See also: James Dunn, 'Neutrality and the Establishment Clause', in P J Weber, ed., *Equal Separation: Understanding the Religion Clauses of the First Amendment* (Westport: Greenwood, 1990), pp. 55–72.

allegiance to the Nazi regime.[7] Though not with such dire results, US students could legally be expelled from their school if they refused to salute the American flag, until in 1943 the US Supreme Court ruled in a case brought by a Jehovah's Witness that it was unconstitutional to enforce activities such as the flag salute.[8] While there were several religions, notably the Society of Friends (the Quakers), who undoubtedly contributed to changes in the law regarding conscientious objection, Jehovah's Witnesses have played and continue to play a significant role in changing the law in numerous countries throughout the world.[9] At the time of writing, the Constitution of South Korea is being seriously challenged while 317 Witnesses are being held in prison,[10] and hundreds more have a criminal record for refusing to take part in military service.[11] Jehovah's Witnesses have also played an important role in securing the right to proselytise. Between 1938 and 1992 there were around 20,000 cases in Greece of Witnesses being accused of proselytism. One of these, Minos Kokkinakis, was exiled six times, arrested over sixty times and served about five years in prison. In a landmark judgement, the European Court of Human Rights (ECtHR) ruled in 1992 that Greece had violated Article 9 of the European Convention on Human Rights,[12] and was ordered to pay Kokkinakis three million drachmas (about 10,000 euros).[13] Indeed, Jehovah's Witnesses' contribution to changing and redefining the law by bringing cases before the ECtHR,[14] the US Supreme Court and many other Courts of Appeal has had a

---

7 Christine King, *The Nazi State and the Nazi New Religions* (Toronto: Edwin Mellen, 1982).
8 D R Manwaring, *Render Unto Caesar: The Flag-Salute Controversy* (Chicago: University of Chicago Press, 1962); Charles Russo, ed., *Encyclopedia of Education Law* (Los Angeles: Sage, 2008), pp. 642–644.
9 Amnesty International, *Conscientious Objection to Military Service* (London, 1991); Gerhard Besier and Katarzyna Stokosa, *Jehovah's Witnesses in Europe. Past and Present* (Newcastle: Cambridge Scholars, 2016); Gary Perkins, *Bible Student Conscientious Objectors in World War* (Charleston, SC: Hupomone Press, 2016).
10 See: https://www.jw.org/en/news/legal/by-region/world/jehovahs-witnesses-in-prison-2/.
11 See: https://www.jw.org/en/news/legal/by-region/south-korea/groundswell-recognition-right-to-conscientious-objection/.
12 *Freedom to manifest one's religion or beliefs shall be subject only to such limitations as are prescribed by law and are necessary in a democratic society in the interests of public safety, for the protection of public order, health or morals, or for the protection of the rights and freedoms of others.*
13 Besier and Stokosa, *Jehovah's Witnesses in Europe. Past and Present*, pp. 293–295; V Lykes and James T Richardson, 'The European Court of Human Rights, Minority Religions, and New Versus Original Member States', in James Richardson and François Bellanger, eds., *Legal Cases, New and Religious Movements, and Minority Faiths* (Aldershot: Ashgate, 2014), p. 177fn.
14 For details of NRM cases that have appeared before the ECtHR, see: Lykes and

significant effect not only on the community of Witnesses, but also on the rest of the social world – especially, though by no means only, in the realm of religious freedom.[15]

Other areas where new religions have fought to have the law changed or clarified include those of the definition of religion and of access to tax privileges. The Church of Scientology has long fought on these fronts in a number of countries. In 1969 it succeeded in becoming incorporated in South Australia and Victoria under the name of the 'Church of the New Faith', and eventually, having been refused tax-exemption at various levels on the grounds of not really being a religion, won acceptance as a *bona fide* religion by the High Court of Australia.[16] In the United States, Scientology had been recognised as a religion back in 1957, but in 1967 its tax-exempt status was revoked in California, where it was headquartered. Then in October 1993, ending one of the longest-running tax disputes in American history, the Inland Revenue Service agreed to grant tax exemption to the Church and more than 150 of its related corporations, which would, reportedly, save the organisation at least tens of millions of dollars a year.[17]

In England and Wales, it had long been assumed that 'the advancement of religion' was synonymous with the promotion of the Church of England. Gradually, however, the concept expanded to include other faiths and denominations with, in common law, religion coming to be defined as 'faith in a god and worship of that god'.[18] Then, partly, it might be argued, because of the sudden visibility of unpopular new religions or 'cults', the 2006 Charities Act (elaborated in 2011) stated that 'Public Benefit' needed to be demonstrated. This resulted in the Church of Jesus Christ of Latter-day Saints (known as the Mormon Church) losing an appeal at the ECtHR in 2014 to register its Temples, which are open only to Mormons. And while Scientology eventually found that, in certain circumstances, it might be accepted as a religion, it was unable to demonstrate its public benefit to the satisfaction of the Charity Commissioners. It was, however, by no means clear exactly where the law drew the line between benefits and dis-benefits and between

Richardson, 'The European Court of Human Rights, Minority Religions, and New Versus Original Member States', pp. 171–201.

15 James T Richardson, 'In Defense of Religious Rights: Jehovah's Witness Legal Cases around the World', in Stephen Hunt, ed., *Handbook of Contemporary Christianity: Movements, Institutions & Allegiance* (Leiden: Brill, 2016), pp. 285–307.

16 *Church of New Faith v Commissioner of Pay-Roll Tax* (1983).

17 See: http://www.nytimes.com/1993/10/14/us/scientologists-granted-tax-exemption-by-the-us.html.

18 Russell Sandberg, *Religion and Legal Pluralism* (Farnham: Ashgate, 2015), p. 27.

public and restricted access, and when the Plymouth Brethren Christian Church (popularly known as the Exclusive Brethren) applied to register one of its Trusts, this was denied on the basis of a number of complaints that claimed its practices were detrimental not only for many of its members but also for former members and the families of members who were completely cut off from their relatives. Furthermore, it was argued, the exclusiveness of the Church meant that it offered no public benefit. This test case became something of a *cause célèbre* with clergy, politicians and the media arguing forcefully on both 'sides'.[19] Eventually, in 2014, the Charity Commissioners decided to grant charitable status so long as the Trust amended its deeds, and then only on the understanding that the status was provisional and subject to withdrawal if further substantial complaints were received.[20]

Meanwhile, in 2013, the Supreme Court ruled not only that Scientology should be recognised as a religion but also that one of its London buildings could be described as a 'place of meeting for religious worship' and recorded as a place for the solemnisation of marriages. In their unanimous decision, the Supreme Court justices said that a 1970 ruling's definition of religious worship as involving 'reverence or veneration of God or of a supreme being'[21] was out of date and that religion should not be confined to religions which recognise a supreme deity: 'To do so would be a form of religious discrimination unacceptable in today's society.' Furthermore, recognising the Scientology building as a place of worship would mean that 'Buddhist temples do not need to be squeezed in by way of an unexplained exception'.[22]

Other movements that have tested the courts as to whether or not they can be regarded as 'religious' include a number of what have been termed 'invented religions'. These have been defined by Cusack (2010) as those which assert that their teachings are new not only because they cannot be traced to some divine revelation, but also because they are, explicitly, the product of human imagination.[23] At least two of these have challenged the application of laws referring to religious dress. The founder of the International Church of Jediism, which claims

---

19 See: https://www.thetimes.co.uk/article/brethren-in-the-spotlight-z7strgx8h88; https://lh4.googleusercontent.com/-YYdZenb394Y/VQlDqWfxoTI/AAAAAAAACN8/Qvos5H3wcwQ/s640/blogger-image--445961326.jpg.
20 See: https://www.gov.uk/government/uploads/system/uploads/attachment_data/file/500364/preston_down_trust.pdf.
21 *R v Registrar General ex parte Segerdal and another* (1970).
22 See video of Lord Toulson's judgement at: http://www.bbc.co.uk/news/uk-25331754.
23 See: https://www.theregister.co.uk/2001/10/09/jedi_knights_achieve_official_recognition/.

500,000 followers worldwide,[24] was told that wearing the hood of his religious robe flouted the rules of a large grocery chain in which he was shopping, leading him to announce he would be seeking legal advice. More successfully, Pastafarians, followers of the Church of the Flying Spaghetti Monster,[25] have persuaded (some) authorities to 'bend the rules' concerning official photographs for passports and driving licences by allowing them to wear colanders as their religious headgear.[26]

Returning, on a more sober note, to challenges and clarifications of legal approaches to tax law, although Jehovah's Witnesses had been officially registered in France since 1947, they were sent a tax bill for over $50 million in 1998, which would have annihilated the movement in France. This was justified by means of a new definition of contributions to Witness congregations as being equivalent to gifts made to individuals, and taxed at a high rate (60 percent). The Witnesses sought redress through the French court system, but to no avail.[27] They then appealed to the ECtHR, which, finally in 2011, ruled in their favour, stating that to force the dissolution of a religious group was a violation of Article 9, and that the Witnesses could not have foreseen the change in interpretation of the gift provisions of the tax code. The Court later administered considerable damage and cost awards to refund the money required to appeal the case, thereby sending a clear message to all Council of Europe nations that religious groups should be allowed to function. Two other, smaller religious organisations (the Aumists and the Evangelical Missionary Church) were also threatened by the new interpretation of French tax codes, and the ECtHR ruled in favour of them too, with large damage awards.

NRMs have also played a role in determining the precise application of the Free Exercise Clause of the US First Amendment (see note 5 above). A central issue is the extent to which the state can regulate the activities of religious organisations. Many, but not all, regulatory statutes provide exemptions from coverage

---

24 In the England and Wales 2001 Census, 390, 127 people stated their religion as Jedi, making it the fourth largest reported religion.

25 See: https://wrldrels.org/2016/10/08/church-of-the-flying-spaghetti-monster/.

26 See: http://www.dailymail.co.uk/news/article-2014553/Pastafarian-wins-right-wear-sieve-head-driving-licence-photo-does-belong-Church-Flying-Spaghetti-Monster.html/; http://www.independent.co.uk/news/people/news/pastafarian-lindsay-miller-allowed-to-wear-colander-on-head-in-driving-licence-photo-a6735351.html/; http://www.telegraph.co.uk/news/religion/11521455/Pastafarian-accuses-DVLA-of-discrimination-for-rejecting-photo-of-him-with-a-colander-on-his-head.html.

27 Lykes and Richardson, 'The European Court of Human Rights, Minority Religions, and New Versus Original Member States', p. 180.

for religious organisations. However, in the mid-1980s a case was brought by the US Department of Labor against the Alamo Foundation, claiming it had violated the minimum wage, overtime, and record-keeping provisions of the Fair Labor Standards Act (FLSA) by operating a variety of commercial businesses that were staffed by approximately 300 'associates', most of whom had been drug addicts, derelicts, or criminals before their rehabilitation. These associates received no wages, but were provided with food, clothing, shelter, and other benefits such as medical care. The Foundation claimed such activities were part of its religious mission, to 'establish, conduct and maintain an evangelistic church, and generally to do those things needful for the promotion of Christian faith, virtue and charity', and it was a violation of the Free Exercise Clause for the state to interfere and insist that 'volunteer associates' should be paid a minimum wage. The US Supreme Court concluded, however, that the associates' Free Exercise rights were not infringed as they were free to return their wages to the Foundation. Furthermore, since the Supreme Court's 1985 decision, Congress has refused to exempt the commercial activities of religious organisations from FLSA coverage, although retaining an exemption for employees engaged in non-commercial activities.[28]

Another aspect of the Free Exercise Clause was challenged when Jimmy Swaggart Ministries, an evangelical organisation, held numerous religious events throughout the United States, selling religious and other merchandise. In 1980, California's Board of Equalization informed the Ministries that its sales were not exempt from California's Sales and Use Tax. The Ministries objected, claiming the First Amendment exempted its products from the tax. Eventually the Supreme Court ruled that, for the First Amendment to be violated, the tax would have had to place a 'substantial burden on the observation of a central religious belief or practice' that would require a 'compelling governmental interest' to withstand the Ministries' challenge. Because the tax imposed was on items sold, not a general exercise of religious liberty, the Court held the Ministries were not exempt. As a result, state regulation of religious affairs was increased, giving religious organisations less independence from generally applicable laws.[29]

Yet another aspect of the legal implementation of the First Amendment was

---

28 US Supreme Court, *Tony and Susan Alamo Foundation v. Secretary of Labor* (1985). See: https://supreme.justia.com/cases/federal/us/471/290/; http://uscivilliberties.org/cases/4600-tony-and-susan-alamo-foundation-v-secretary-of-labor-471-us-290–1985.html.
29 *Jimmy Swaggart Ministries, appellant v. Board of Equalization of California* (1990). See: http://uscivilliberties.org/cases/3995-jimmy-swaggart-ministries-v-board-of-equalization-of-california-493-us-378–1990.html.

brought to the US Supreme Court by the International Society for Krishna Consciousness (ISKCON), when the California Supreme Court upheld a Los Angeles International Airport (LAX) ordinance barring devotees from soliciting donations inside airport terminals. After winning in the district court then losing in the circuit court, ISKCON finally lost its case in 1992 when the Supreme Court ruled 6 to 3 that the city's prohibition was constitutional because an airport terminal was not a 'public forum'.[30] In 2010, the Krishnas tried again, but on appeal the California Supreme Court again ruled that the LAX restriction on solicitation was constitutional, thereby narrowing ISKCON's legal options.[31]

On a somewhat different tack, Italian cases concerning the Children of God's practice of 'flirty fishing',[32] and the Romanian Movement for Spiritual Integration into the Absolute's (MISA's) use of adult movies as a way of spreading their ideas,[33] have contributed to redefining legal notions about prostitution and pornography.

Businesses

Although new religions tend to emphasise theological and/or spiritual beliefs, this does not mean they may not be concerned with matters of business, sometimes in surprisingly innovative ways.

The Perfectionist Oneida Community, founded in 1848 by John Humphrey Noyes in Oneida, NY is probably best known for its unconventional sexual practices and 'complex marriages'.[34] It is, however, also remarkable for establishing one of the earliest joint-stock companies, in which members became shareholders and which included a woman on its board of directors. The Community canned fruits and vegetables; made animal traps and chains; travelling bags; mop sticks; sewing silk; surgical instruments; and, most successfully, silverware. Indeed, although the community has long since died out, Oneida Ltd continues to thrive

---

30 See: http://www.nytimes.com/1992/06/27/us/the-supreme-court-justices-uphold-airports-right-to-ban-begging.html.
31 See: https://www.csmonitor.com/USA/Justice/2010/0325/Court-upholds-ban-on-Hare-Krishna-soliciting-in-LAX-airport.
32 See: http://www.cesnur.org/testi/TheFamily/italy.htm/.
33 See: http://www.cesnur.org/2016/daejin_mi_misa.pdf/.
34 Lawrence Foster, *Women, Family, and Utopia: Communal Experiments of the Shakers, the Oneida Community, and the Mormons* (New York: Syracuse University Press, 1991); George Wallingford Noyes (compiler) and Lawrence Foster, ed., *Free Love in Utopia: John Humphrey Noyes and the Origin of the Oneida Community* (Champaign: University of Illinois Press, 2001).

and be known throughout the world for its tableware and other products.[35] The
Amana Colonies in Iowa were early producers of household appliances including
refrigerators and freezers; they have also been credited with inventing the first
home microwave oven, the Amana Radarange.[36] The so-called Shakers movement, a mid-eighteenth century offshoot of the Quakers, although it currently has
only two surviving members, remains known for scores of inventions, such as as
the circular saw; the apple parer; the wheel-driven washing machine; the Shaker
Seed Company; its distinctive oval-shaped boxes and, above all, its simple, yet
elegant wooden furniture.[37] Another, later, religious community that contributed
to material culture was the Harmony Society which engaged in various constructions, including houses, churches and granaries, employing innovative techniques
such as the use of modular building.[38]

Turning to the late twentieth century, among NRMs that have played a role in
developments in computer programming was the 'suicide cult', Heaven's Gate.[39]
The Mormon Church, thanks to its practice of baptising the dead, has established
the world's largest genealogical library and become famous for its genealogical-
search software.[40] Amway is among a number of organisations that have been
dubbed cult-like with its promotion of pyramid selling.[41] Although it denies it is
a religion, Landmark Forum, an outcome of Erhard Seminar Training (*est*), falls
into the category of what have been termed 'self religions'[42] or 'world-affirming
religions'.[43] It and other movements of this kind have introduced special 'Human
Potential' techniques that are widely employed by large multi-national businesses

35 See: https://www.oneida.com/flatware/fine-flatware.html/; https://www.oneida.com/
aboutoneida/the-oneida-story/.
36 See: https://www.nps.gov/nr/travel/amana/amana.htm/; http://theconversation.com/hot-
food-fast-the-home-microwave-oven-turns-50–74249/; https://amana.com/catalog/category.
jsp?parentCategoryId=585&categoryId=1047/.
37 See: https://www.metmuseum.org/toah/hd/shak/hd_shak.htm/.
38 Paul Douglas, *Architecture, Artifacts, and Arts in the Harmony Society of George Rapp:
The Material Culture of a Nineteenth-Century American Utopian Community* (Lewiston:
Edwin Mellen, 2008).
39 See: https://motherboard.vice.com/en_us/article/pgapzy/heavens-gate-web-designers-
higher-source-suicide-cult/; http://onlinelibrary.wiley.com/doi/10.1111/j.1083–6101.1997.
tb00077.x/full/.
40 https://www.familysearch.org/locations/saltlakecity-library/.
41 https://www.cs.cmu.edu/~dst/Amway/AUS/cultism.htm/.
42 Paul Heelas, 'Californian Self Religions and Socializing the Subjective', in Eileen Barker,
ed., *New Religious Movements: A Perspective for Understanding Society* (Lewiston: Edwin
Mellen, 1982), pp. 69–85.
43 Roy Wallis, *The Elementary Forms of the New Religious Life* (London: Routledge and
Kegan Paul, 1984).

to 'develop' their work force. Transcendental Meditation is similarly taught in corporations, schools and prisons.[44] More recently, a number of Buddhist groups new to the West have been teaching 'mindfulness' to a wide range of individuals and institutions.[45] Likewise, numerous varieties of yogic practices are now encouraged in some Western schools and corporations.[46]

Healthy living and healing

Sometimes known for the introduction of Kellogg's cornflakes,[47] Seventh-Day Adventists, whose members are alleged to live up to ten years longer than most Americans,[48] has, since its inception, offered stress management classes,[49] warned against the harmful effects of tobacco and excess salt, and advocated a healthy vegetarian diet, breathing and other exercises, and adequate rest. Its sanitarians and hospitals are known throughout the world for their research into preventative medicine.[50] Mormonism is another religion that claims its members live longer than average due to its theologically-based rules on diet and fasting.[51]

When ISKCON first started attracting young hippies in the late 1960s, fears were expressed about health hazards for devotees, who were expected to restrain from meat, gambling, intoxicants and illicit drugs. Since then, the movement's vegetarian restaurants have become increasingly popular and have undoubtedly contributed to the radical change in attitudes about what constitutes a healthy diet.[52] Several other NRMs have introduced products that claim to have medicinal

44 See: https://www.meditationtrust.com/about-the-meditation-trust/.

45 See: http://blogs.lse.ac.uk/religionpublicsphere/2017/04/we-need-to-talk-about-mindfulness-the-changing-face-of-religion-and-the-secular-in-the-public-sphere/; https://www.huffingtonpost.com/sarah-rudell-beach-/is-mindfulness-a-religion_b_6136612.html/.

46 See: https://www.gomammoth.co.uk/corporate-fitness-classes/yoga/?gclid=EAIaIQobC hMIp6r7gsex2AIVqr_tCh34UwCrEAAYAiAAEgKIe_D_BwE/; https://www.yogajournal.com/teach/teaching-yoga-in-the-workplace/.

47 See: https://www.huffingtonpost.com/whitny-braun/seventhday-adventist-church-gave-you-cereal_b_9527964.html/.

48 See: http://www.bbc.co.uk/news/magazine-30351406/.

49 See: http://vienna23.adventistchurchconnect.org/article/96/the-ministries-of-our-church/health-ministries/god-s-7-step-plan-for-relieving-stress/.

50 Chris Rucker, *Seventh-Day Diet: A Practical Plan to Apply the Adventist Lifestyle to Live Longer, Healthier, and Slimmer in the 21st Century* (Nampa: Pacific Press, 2002).

51 See: https://www.lds.org/topics/fasting-and-fast-offerings?lang=eng/; https://www.washingtonpost.com/blogs/she-the-people/post/mormonism-good-for-the-body-as-well-as-the-soul/2012/06/20/gJQARk3IqV_blog.html?utm_term=.7dea6a962816/.

52 Benjamin Zeller, 'Food Practices, Culture and Social Dynamics in the Hare Krishna Movement', in Carole Cusack and Alex Norman, eds., *Handbook of New Religions and*

properties according to Ayurveda traditions; Sikh Dharma's Yogi Tea is but one example,[53] Unificationism's Ilhwa Ginseng products provide another.[54]

The Jehovah's Witnesses' controversial interpretation of the Bible forbidding blood transfusions (Genesis 9:4; Leviticus 17:14; Deuteronomy 12:23; Acts 15:29) has resulted in the death of several members, including children. This has, however, stimulated research into bloodless alternatives which are, reportedly, both safer and cheaper to administer.[55]

Welfare, good works and education

Many NRMs have made imaginative contributions to the well-being of non-members, although not all their acts of charity are appreciated – sometimes for good reason. Through its Narconon[56] and Criminon[57] programmes, Scientology offers help for, respectively, drug addiction and prisoners. The Family International's work in Africa's black townships provides food, literacy classes and help in combatting AIDs.[58] The Holy Order of MANS pioneered confidential shelters for victims of domestic violence; various iterations of their 'Raphael Houses' are now a fixture in most mid-size towns throughout the US.[59] The Jesus Fellowship provides lodging and employment for the homeless and unemployed and a drop-in centre for migrants and others in a converted Northampton cinema.[60] ISKCON's 'Food for Life' programme supplies hot meals for the homeless and victims in war zones and disaster areas.[61]

Unimpressed by state schools, NRMs commonly Home School or establish their own schools, often using innovative methods. One of the more influential educational systems, found in Waldorf schools (of which there are now over 900 worldwide), owes its origins to Anthroposophy.[62] Scientology promotes its 'Study

Cultural Production (Leiden: Brill, 2012), pp. 681–702; see also: http://www.iskcon.org/vegetarianism/.
53 See: http://www.yogitea.com/en/our-story/.
54 See: http://ilhwakoreanginseng.com/.
55 See: https://www.ncbi.nlm.nih.gov/pubmed/28150313/.
56 See: http://www.narconon.org/.
57 See: http://www.criminon.org/.
58 See: http://www.familyafrica.com/index.php/projects/.
59 See: http://www.raphaelhouse.org/.
60 See: http://jesus.org.uk/about-jesus-army/.
61 See: https://ffl.org/.
62 Liselotte Frisk, 'The Anthroposophical Movement and the Waldorf Educational System', in Carole Cusack and Alex Norman, eds., _Handbook of New Religions and Cultural_

Technology'.[63] Several NRMs have founded seminaries, colleges and universities where non-members are exposed to alternative world-views. Examples include the Unification Church;[64] Soka Gakkai;[65] Transcendental Meditation;[66] and some, such as Oral Roberts University, associated with Televangelism.[67]

The arts

A wide range of artists have been inspired by the teachings of NRMs such as Scientology; Theosophy; Swedenborgianism; Christian Science; Daesoon Jinri-hoe; MISA; and various spiritual and esoteric movements.[68] Traditional Korean and Chinese culture has been introduced to the West through, respectively, Unificationism's Little Angels Ballet;[69] and Falun Gong's Shen Yun.[70] Films 'with a message' include Unificationism's *Incheon*, starring Laurence Olivier,[71] numerous videos produced by the Church of Almighty God, praising God and condemning the Chinese government,[72] and The Family International's *Kiddy Viddies* and *Treasure Attic* series for children.[73]

There is a strong link between Rastafari and Reggae music, particularly as exemplified by Bob Marley, whose lyrics were rich in both biblical and political injunctions.[74] Rastafari have also made important contributions to the visual arts,

Production (Leiden: Brill, 2012), pp. 192–211. See also: http://www.waldorfanswers.org/ Waldorf.htm/.

63 See: http://www.able.org/appliedscholastics/.

64 See: https://uts.edu/index.php/; https://www.topuniversities.com/universities/sun-moon-university/; https://www.bridgew.edu/.

65 See: http://www.soka.edu/?gclid=EAIaIQobChMIi-Ttu5my2AIVrLDtCh1w6QLpEAAYA SAAEgJnmfD_BwE/; https://www.soka.ac.jp/en/

66 See: https://www.mum.edu/.

67 See: https://www.oru.edu/.

68 http://www.cesnur.org/religions_and_arts.htm/.

69 https://www.youtube.com/watch?v=RUYcjmC9rqQ/.

70 http://www.shenyun.com/learn/article/read/item/Pwua6-S5xXk/misconception-2-shen-yun-falun-gong-political.html/.

71 http://www.imdb.com/title/tt0084132/.

72 https://www.youtube.com/watch?v=MPN3kBnoWx4/; https://www.facebook.com/ ChristianOLFF/photos/a.904012683045318.1073741827.903969406382979/141665153844809 4/?type=3&theater/.

73 Gordon Shepherd and Gary Shepherd, *Talking with the Children of God: Prophecy and Transformation in a Radical Religious Group* (Urbana: University of Illinois Press, 2010), p. 120; see also: http://tvtropes.org/pmwiki/pmwiki.php/Series/TreasureAttic/; http://www. nubeat.org/vid7.html/.

74 Nathaniel Murrell and Justin Snider, 'Identity, Subversion, and Reconstruction 'Riddims': Reggae as Cultural Expressions of Rastafarian Theology', in Carole Cusack and Alex

poetry and documentary films.[75] So far as architecture is concerned, several NRMs have constructed complexes that have become places of 'religious tourism'. ISKCON's New Vrindavan in West Virginia is one example;[76] Swaminarayan Mandirs are another.[77] Also renowned for 'sculptural architecture' is Rudolf Steiner's Goetheanum.[78] Indeed, Steiner and Anthroposophy have been innovators *par excellence*, contributing to the worlds of politics, banking, diet, medicine, costume, poetry, literature, drama, painting, sculpture, dance (Eurythmy), and biodynamic agriculture.[79]

Among the literary genres to which NRMs have made a significant contribution is that of science fiction. L Ron Hubbard was a prolific sci-fi author, and some suggest that Scientology itself owes its origins to science fiction. The Church of All Worlds boasts that it 'may be the first religion to draw as much of its inspiration from the past, embracing science fiction as mythology with the same enthusiasm as we embrace the classical myths of ancient times'.[80]

The media

Several NRMs have developed newspapers and journals that are read far beyond their membership. *The Christian Science Monitor* and Unificationism's *Washington Times* are but two examples of papers covering international news. 'Freebies' include Jehovah's Witnesses' *Watchtower* and *Awake!* and the Worldwide Church of God's *Plain Truth,* which peaked at a worldwide circulation of 8.4 million in 1985.[81] Herbert W Armstrong's Radio Church of God (later the WCG, broadcasting as *The World Tomorrow*) started in the 1930s reaching millions of listeners; then, by the mid-1980s, under Armstrong's son, Garner Ted, a television

Norman, eds., *Handbook of New Religions and Cultural Production* (Leiden: Brill, 2012), pp. 495–518.

75 Darren Middleton, *Rastafari and the Arts* (New York: Routledge, 2015).

76 http://www.newvrindaban.com/.

77 Raymond Williams and Yogi Trivedi, eds., *Swaminarayan Hinduism: Tradition, Adaptation, Identity* (Oxford: Oxford University Press, 2016).

78 Carole Cusack and Alex Norman, eds., *Handbook of New Religions and Cultural Production* (Leiden: Brill, 2012), pp. 174–191.

79 Ibid., part three.

80 Oberon Zell, 'The Church of All Worlds', in Carole Cusack and Pavol Kosnáč, eds., *Fiction, Invention and Hyper-Reality: From Popular Culture to Religion* (Abingdon: Routledge, 2017), p. 266; Carole Cusack, *Invented Religions: Imagination, Fiction and Faith* (Farnham: Ashgate, 2010).

81 Stephen Flurry, *Raising the Ruins: The Fight to Revive the Legacy of Herbert W. Armstrong* (Philadelphia Church of God Inc, 2006), p. 2.

version, aired on 382 US stations with 36 outlets internationally, was dwarfing tel-evangelists such as Jim Bakker, Jerry Falwell, Oral Roberts, Robert Schuller and Jimmy Swaggart.[82] More recently, scores of new religions have made an impact through the Internet and social media. Among the more prominent of these are the 'invented religions', such as Discordianism.[83]

Environmentalism and ecology

There are literally hundreds of new spiritual and religious communities and groups that focus on human interaction with and dependency upon nature, Gaia and/or the environment.[84] The New Age Movement and most Pagan groups are obvious examples.[85] To a greater or lesser degree, movements such as the Find-horn Community;[86] the Church of All Worlds;[87] The Farm Ecovillage;[88] the Sri Aurobindo Ashram;[89] and Anthroposophy have been responsible for raising con-sciousness about ecological possibilities and disasters. The Holy Order of MANS was instrumental in organising a North American Conference on Religion and Ecology which catalysed ecology action-groups in many mainstream Christian denominations in the 1980s.[90]

Concluding remark

Much, much more could be written about the many ways in which NRMs have contributed to what Robbins and Bromley have referred to as a 'subterranean

---

82 Ibid.

83 David Robertson, 'Making the Donkey Visible: Discordianism in the Works of Robert Anton Wilson', in Carole Cusack and Alex Norman, eds., *Handbook of New Religions and Cultural Production* (Leiden: Brill, 2012), pp. 421–441.

84 James Lovelock, 'Gaia', in William Bloom, ed., *The New Age: An Anthology of Essential Writings* (London: Random Century, 1991); Miller, Timothy, *American Communes, 1860– 1960* (New York: Garland, 1990).

85 Graham Harvey, *Animism: Respecting the Living World* (London: Hurst, 2005).

86 See: https://www.findhorn.org/.

87 See: http://caw.org/content/.

88 See: http://www.thefarm.org/.

89 See: http://www.sriaurobindoashram.org/ashram/saa/index.php/.

90 Phillip C Lucas, 'From Holy Order of MANS to Christ the Savior Brotherhood: The Radical Transformation of an Esoteric Christian Order', in T Miller, ed., *America's Alternative Religions* (Albany: State University of New York, 1995), pp. 141–148.

cultural tradition'.[91] I have tried to indicate just a few of the many ways in which their social, political, economic, theological and cultural experiments can make a significant contribution to the wider society. For better or worse (probably for both), there can be little doubt that the imaginations of new religions provide a noteworthy resource in an ever-changing world.

Bibliography

Amnesty International, *Conscientious Objection to Military Service* (London, 1991).

Besier, Gerhard, and Stokosa, Katarzyna, *Jehovah's Witnesses in Europe. Past and Present* (Newcastle: Cambridge Scholars, 2016).

Cusack, Carole, *Invented Religions: Imagination, Fiction and Faith* (Farnham: Ashgate, 2010).

Cusack, Carole, 'Science Fiction as Scripture: Robert A. Heinlein's *Stranger in a Strange Land* and the Church of All Worlds', in *Literature & Aesthetics* 19 (2009), pp. 72–91.

Cusack, Carole, and Norman, Alex, eds., *Handbook of New Religions and Cultural Production* (Leiden: Brill, 2012).

Douglas, Paul, *Architecture, Artefacts, and Arts in the Harmony Society of George Rapp: The Material Culture of a Nineteenth-Century American Utopian Community*, (Lewiston: Edwin Mellen, 2008).

Dunn, James, 'Neutrality and the Establishment Clause', in J P Weber, ed., *Equal Separation: Understanding the Religion Clauses of the First Amendment* (Westport: Greenwood, 1990), pp. 55–72.

Flurry, Stephen, *Raising the Ruins: The Fight to Revive the Legacy of Herbert W. Armstrong* (Philadelphia Church of God Inc, 2006).

Foster, Lawrence, *Women, Family, and Utopia: Communal Experiments of the Shakers, the Oneida Community, and the Mormons* (New York: Syracuse University Press, 1991).

Frisk, Liselotte, 'The Anthroposophical Movement and the Waldorf Educational System', in Carole Cusack and Alex Norman, eds., *Handbook of New Religions and Cultural Production* (Leiden: Brill, 2012), pp. 192–211.

Harvey, Graham, *Animism: Respecting the Living World* (London: Hurst, 2005).

---

91 Thomas Robbins and David G Bromley, 'What have we Learned about New Religions? New Religious Movements as Experiments', in *Religious Studies Review* 19.2 (1993), p. 211.

Heelas, Paul, 'Californian Self Religions and Socializing the Subjective', in Eileen Barker, ed., *New Religious Movements: A Perspective for Understanding Society* (Lewiston: Edwin Mellen, 1982), pp. 69–85.

King, Christine, *The Nazi State and the Nazi New Religions* (Toronto: Edwin Mellen, 1982).

Lovelock, James, 'Gaia', in William Bloom, ed., *The New Age: An Anthology of Essential Writings* (London: Random Century, 1991).

Lucas, Phillip C, 'From Holy Order of MANS to Christ the Savior Brotherhood: The Radical Transformation of an Esoteric Christian Order', in T Miller, ed., *America's Alternative Religions* (Albany: State University of New York, 1995), pp. 141–148.

Lykes, V, and Richardson, James, 'The European Court of Human Rights, Minority Religions, and New Versus Original Member States', in James T Richardson and Bellanger, François, eds., *Legal Cases, New and Religious Movements, and Minority Faiths* (Aldershot: Ashgate, 2014), pp. 171–201.

Manwaring, D R, *Render Unto Caesar: The Flag-Salute Controversy* (Chicago: University of Chicago Press, 1962).

Marx, Karl, 'Contribution to the Critique of Hegel's Philosophy of the Right' (1843–4), in Thomas Bottomore, ed., *Karl Marx: Early Writings* (London: Watts, 1963), pp. 43–59.

Middleton, Darren, *Rastafari and the Arts* (New York: Routledge, 2015).

Miller, Timothy, *American Communes, 1860–1960* (New York: Garland, 1990).

Murrell, Nathaniel, and Snider, Justin, 'Identity, Subversion, and Reconstruction 'Riddims': Reggae as Cultural Expressions of Rastafarian Theology', in Carole Cusack and Alex Norman, eds., *Handbook of New Religions and Cultural Production* (Leiden: Brill, 2012), pp. 495–518.

Noyes, George Wallingford (compiler), Foster, Lawrence, ed., *Free Love in Utopia: John Humphrey Noyes and the Origin of the Oneida Community* (Champaign: University of Illinois Press, 2001).

Perkins, Gary, *Bible Student Conscientious Objectors in World War* (Charleston, SC: Hupomone Press, 2016).

Richardson, James T, 'In Defense of Religious Rights: Jehovah's Witness Legal Cases around the World', in Stephen Hunt, ed., *Handbook of Contemporary Christianity: Movements, Institutions & Allegiance* (Leiden: Brill, 2016), pp. 285–307.

Richardson, James T, 'Update on Jehovah's Witness cases before the European Court of Human Rights: implications of a surprising partnership', in *Religion, State and Society* 45.3–4 (2017), pp. 232–248.

Robertson, David, 'Making the Donkey Visible: Discordianism in the Works of Robert Anton Wilson', in Carole Cusack and Alex Norman, eds., *Handbook of New Religions and Cultural Production* (Leiden: Brill, 2012), pp. 421–441.

Robbins, Thomas, and Bromley, David, 'What have we Learned about New Religions? New Religious Movements as Experiments', in *Religious Studies Review* 19.2 (1993), pp. 209–216.

Rucker, Chris, *Seventh-Day Diet: A Practical Plan to Apply the Adventist Lifestyle to Live Longer, Healthier, and Slimmer in the 21st Century* (Nampa: Pacific Press, 2002).

Russo, Charles, ed., *Encyclopedia of Education Law* (Los Angeles: Sage, 2008).

Sandberg, Russell, *Religion and Legal Pluralism* (Farnham: Ashgate, 2015).

Shepherd, Gordon, and Shepherd, Gary, *Talking with the Children of God: Prophecy and Transformation in a Radical Religious Group* (Urbana: University of Illinois Press, 2010).

Tillich, Paul, *Dynamics of Faith* (New York: Harper and Row, 1957).

Wallis, Roy, *The Elementary Forms of the New Religious Life* (London: Routledge and Kegan Paul, 1984).

Weber, Max, *The Protestant Ethic and the Spirit of Capitalism* (1930) (London: Unwin, 1995).

Williams, Raymond, and Trivedi, Yogi, eds., *Swaminarayan Hinduism: Tradition, Adaptation, Identity* (Oxford: Oxford University Press, 2016).

Zell, Oberon, 'The Church of All Worlds', in Carole Cusack and Pavol Kosnáč, eds., *Fiction, Invention and Hyper-Reality: From Popular Culture to Religion* (Abingdon: Routledge, 2017), pp. 261–702.

Zeller, Benjamin, 'Food Practices, Culture and Social Dynamics in the Hare Krishna Movement', in Carole Cusack and Alex Norman, eds., *Handbook of New Religions and Cultural Production* (Leiden: Brill, 2012), pp. 681–702.

12

Human Rights as a Narrative of Faith

Jenna Reinbold

I have been intensely interested in the question of how narratives of faith are shaping today's world for a number of years. My interest stems in part from my conviction that it is crucial for more people to have an understanding of the promising and, sometimes, unhappy roles that religions have played in today's processes of globalisation. This topic also fascinates me because, as a scholar of religion, I am always curious about what we mean when we talk about things like 'narratives of faith' in the first place. Are there narratives that *aren't* 'narratives of faith'? No doubt there are, but what is it exactly that identifies a narrative as a narrative of faith? Is it a narrative's grounding within a widely-recognised religious tradition? Is it a community's enduring commitment to a particular narrative, whether or not that community is part of an institutional-ised religious tradition? Does a narrative's level of authority promote it from a regular narrative to a 'narrative of faith'? These are 'religious studies' questions I have been engaged with for a long time, and it is these questions that ultimately compelled me to write a book on the role of religion and secularity in the propa-gation of human rights.[1]

I think that most people would agree that the idea of human rights has been a preeminent vehicle for shaping the world – certainly in the twentieth century, but also very much so today. But is the idea of universal human rights a 'narrative of faith'? Is it something different from a narrative of faith? Certainly, today's human rights ideas and institutions are undergirded by a narrative of some sort – and a

---

1 J Reinbold, *Seeing the Myth in Human Rights* (Philadelphia: University of Pennsylvania Press, 2017).

powerful one, at that. The Preamble of the 1948 Universal Declaration of Human Rights is a striking example of this. It proclaims, among other things, that:

> [R]ecognition of the inherent dignity and of the equal and inalienable rights of all members of the human family is the foundation of freedom, justice and peace in the world.

And that:

> The advent of a world in which human beings shall enjoy freedom of speech and belief and freedom from fear and want has been proclaimed as the highest aspiration of the common people[s].

The Preamble then proceeds to assert that:

> [T]he peoples of the United Nations have in the Charter reaffirmed their faith in fundamental human rights, in the dignity and worth of the human person and in the equal rights of men and women and have determined to promote social progress and better standards of life in larger freedom.

And, in light of this, that the Declaration should be understood as:

> [A] common standard of achievement for all peoples and all nations, to the end that every individual and every organ of society, keeping this Declaration constantly in mind, shall strive by teaching and education to promote respect for these rights and freedoms and by progressive measures, national and international, to secure their universal and effective recognition and observance, both among the peoples of Member States themselves and among the peoples of territories under their jurisdiction.

Like all political preambles, the Declaration's opening lines are designed to convey authority and to inspire particular identities and behaviours. In other words, before the Declaration ever gets to its enumeration of particular rights, it narrates a foundation for these rights; it describes in the most forceful possible terms where these rights came from, how we know that we have them, and why it is that we have come to see the need for their reiteration at a given moment.

Political narratives like this are often permeated with elements that we might describe as faith claims, and the Preamble to the Declaration is no exception:

it postulates the existence of inherent human dignity and equal and inalienable rights, it enlists all people into membership in the human family, it claims to embody the highest aspirations of all humans, and it upholds itself as a vehicle capable of promoting not just particular rights but 'universal respect' for these rights. At its conclusion, the Preamble articulates its aspiration to create a world in which every individual and every organ of society will establish the Declaration as a point of political and ethical orientation – presumably out of a conviction that the Declaration presents the surest means of improving the lot of humans across the globe.

Given these various characteristics, is there anything that might challenge our understanding of the Declaration as a narrative of faith? One point of reservation might pertain to the fact that this document makes absolutely no reference to a deity, or even to a higher system of order like 'destiny' or 'providence' or 'Nature'. In this respect, the Declaration is radically immanent. Perhaps this is a reason to hesitate to think of this particular narrative as a 'narrative of faith'. Another reason that might give us pause in thinking of the Declaration as a narrative of faith is that the members of the First Commission on Human Rights, the people who spent two years drafting this document, emphatically denied that the Declaration presented a religious narrative of human rights. To the contrary, they worked diligently to create a preamble that would lay a thoroughly secular foundation for the Declaration's rights. As the Commission's chairwoman, Eleanor Roosevelt, describes the Commission's work:

> I happen to believe that we are born free and equal in dignity and rights
> because there is a divine Creator, and there is a divine spark in men. But, there
> were other [Commission members] who wanted it expressed in such a way
> that they could think in their particular way about this question, and, finally,
> these words were agreed upon because they stated in fact that all men are born
> free and equal, but they left each of us to put it in our own reason, as we say,
> for that end.[2]

Roosevelt's understanding of the Declaration's secular mandate was shared by almost all of her colleagues on the Commission.

I believe, however, that there are some very good reasons to analyse human

---

2 E Roosevelt, 'Making Human Rights Come Alive', in Allida M Black, ed., *What I Hope to Leave Behind: The Essential Essays of Eleanor Roosevelt* (New York: Carlson Publishing, 1995), p. 561.

rights as a narrative of faith. I am convinced that it is useful to evaluate human rights in this way because it provides some crucial insight into the history and logic of human rights, and insight also into some of the striking resistance that human rights ideas and institutions face today from a wide array of skeptics. In this chapter, I will explore the thesis of human rights as a narrative of faith and how this 'religious studies' approach to human rights might help us to understand certain forms of contemporary push-back against human rights – especially today's surprising opposition from many of the western liberal democracies that originally spearheaded the Universal Declaration of Human Rights itself. My own scholarly focus is the United States, so I will use contemporary American politics as a focal point for thinking about this brand of anti-human-rights discourse, but one could just as easily focus on recent developments in Britain in an inquiry such as this.

Seeing the myth in human rights

In my book, *Seeing the Myth in Human Rights*, I argued that there are some very good reasons for thinking of human rights as a powerful form of myth. Typically, of course, to associate human rights with 'myth' risks being perceived as advocating for a dismissal or even a rejection of human rights. Indeed, when the term myth is used in conjunction with human rights, it is almost always done so with the intention of discrediting either the idea or the substance of human rights. As a scholar of religion, however, I have argued not only that it is misleading to think of myth in this way but that this tendency to associate myth with error or duplicity actually prevents us from recognising some important insights that the category of myth sheds upon the history and the logic of human rights.

Thinking back to the Preamble of the Declaration, we might consider the fact that this document was advertised as emphatically secular even as its creators regularly used religious idioms of sacredness, veneration, and teleology to describe it. The Declaration proposes no mechanisms for the enforcement of its provisions, yet there is much evidence to indicate that it has come to command a significant 'moral' authority – and, indeed, that the First Commission on Human Rights actively aspired to imbue it with such a moral authority.[3] Ultimately, in fact, there is much in the historical record of the creation of the Declaration to indicate that many Commission members were deeply convinced of its capacity to transform the ethical and even the metaphysical landscape of international law.

---

3 Reinbold, *Seeing the Myth in Human Rights*, pp. 3–4.

The phenomenon of myth provides a valuable lens through which to make sense of these various conflicting elements in the Declaration. Far from understanding myth as a mode of erroneous or deceptive discourse, scholars in the field of religious studies understand myth as a form of human labour that serves the function of generating meaning, solidarity, and order within all manner of human communities. Far from being characterised by their inaccuracy or duplicity, myths are characterised within the study of religion by the particular authority they wield and the particular strategies their creators use to imbue them with this authority. In short, instead of offering arguments or strictures, myths are narratives that assert their descriptions of the world, and the moral imperatives stemming from these descriptions, in a way that makes them appear beyond dispute.

Mythmakers accomplish this authoritative assertion of information in a variety of ways – for example, by describing the prescriptions of supernatural beings, by narrating the feats of exemplary figures from earlier times, or by drawing connections between the present and a paradigmatic moment in the past. In all of their variety, however, mythopoeic narratives are distinguished by their efforts to set language to the task of, in the words of Roland Barthes, 'lending an historical intention a natural justification, and making the contingent appear eternal'.[4] The Universal Declaration of Human Rights obviously makes no appeal to supernatural realms or superhuman beings. It does, however, narrate its basic tenets in the unequivocal manner characteristic of myth. The framers of the Declaration aspired to generate a document capable of rectifying the horrors of World War II, and they aimed to do so not merely by enumerating certain rights but also by establishing, as Roosevelt put it, 'why we have rights to begin with'.[5] To accomplish this, the Commission worked to fortify the Declaration with a logic that would place its basic tenets beyond question. They worked, in other words, to create a secular narrative capable of wielding the authority of a religious one – a narrative that would appear to everyday people, in the words of one Commission delegate, 'as simple and as clear as the Decalogue'.[6]

Of course, an appreciation of the Declaration's mythopoeic qualities does not necessarily speak to the question of whether Commission members' efforts ultimately proved to be successful. The success of the Commission's mythmaking endeavours is a somewhat different question – and obviously a crucial question

---

4 R Barthes, *Mythologies*, transl. Annette Lavers (New York: Noonday Press, 1961), p. 142.
5 E Roosevelt, quoted in M Glendon, *A World Made New* (New York: Random House, 2002), p. 146.
6 Vladimir Koretsky, quoted in Reinbold, *Seeing the Myth in Human Rights*, p. 35.

where contemporary human rights are concerned.[7] Suffice it to say here that the scholarly category of myth allows us to appreciate the manner in which the First Human Rights Commission endeavoured, at a seminal moment in the history of international law, to create a narrative that would push deliberately against two longstanding human tendencies: first, the tendency to tie human rights to one's membership within a particular political community, and, second, the tendency to hearken to the realm of the divine when building a foundation for political ideals and practices. This twofold endeavour gave rise to a document the likes of which has never before been seen: a declaration that predicates its tenets upon a universal, secular human reality that it brings into existence through no other means than by professing to recognise this reality. This is a truly novel political manoeuvre, but, for all its novelty, it is also a manoeuvre that partakes of the logic of myth-making – a logic wherein language is set to the task of unequivocally presenting a vision of the world as well as a set of mandates appropriate to the maintenance of that vision. This unique narrative complicates conventional distinctions between 'religion' and 'secularism', and, in so doing, sheds new light not only on these often-take-for-granted categories, but on the nature of human rights themselves.

A clash of narratives

Today, we are living in a world in which the ideal of human rights remains embattled on a variety of fronts. One of the most surprising of these fronts is the resistance that human rights ideals and institutions are currently facing from within Western liberal democracies such as the United States. Now, there are obviously many possible ways to resist the ideals and institutions of human rights, and, frankly, some of these modes of resistance are more noteworthy than others. For example, there is little to be surprised about in the fact that the US government has in many ways resisted the logic of universal human rights from the Declaration's very inception – even in spite of the role that Roosevelt and other Americans played in drafting and advertising the Declaration. After all, one of the basic ideals of human rights is a notion, as Paul Kahn puts it, of 'equality among subjects', whether such subjects be people or the nations that those fundamentally equal people inhabit.[8] Like many modern legal formulations, human rights law

---

7 For a more detailed discussion, see Reinbold, *Seeing the Myth in Human* Rights, pp. 117–131.
8 P W Kahn, 'American Hegemony and International Law: Speaking Law to Power: Popular Sovereignty, Human Rights, and the New International Order', in *Chicago Journal of International Law* 1 (Spring 2000), p. 1.

is designed to resist hegemony; ideally, it postulates and enforces an equality among individuals within the domestic sphere and among states in the international sphere. Legal outcomes should, within such a system, be 'determined by identifying claims of right, not by measuring assertions of power'.[9] This principle of equality among subjects poses a significant discomfort to a nation such as the United States that has long enjoyed a certain political, economic, and military hegemony in relation to other nations. As Kahn puts it, 'appeals to international law have been one of the tools available to weaker states in their battles with more powerful states. Conversely, powerful states have been wary of adjudicatory mechanisms for settling disputes.'[10]

However, beneath the practical threat that human rights presents to the mechanisms and dynamics of national hegemony, such rights also present a more 'existential' threat to US interests that is perhaps less easy to discern. This threat is directly implicated in the mythopoeic logic of human rights that I have been exploring here; it has to do with the way in which the ideals and institutions of universal human rights butt up against deep-seated American conceptions of political legitimacy. Kahn maintains, '[Americans tend to] believe that unless an assertion of governmental authority can be traced to an act of popular sovereignty, it is illegitimate.'[11] Kahn refers to this as an American 'myth of popular sovereignty', and his use of the word 'myth' here is multifaceted.[12] Kahn's use of the word 'myth' refers in the first place to the basic deceptiveness of the notion of popular sovereignty given the variety of historical and structural elements in the American political system that stand in the way of pure popular sovereignty. In other words, Kahn uses the word myth in the first place in its more colloquial and common sense of a narrative that veils and perhaps even distorts the truth of things. Additionally, however, Kahn's use of the word myth meshes precisely with the 'religious studies' conception that I have described above. This second formulation of myth speaks to the manner in which the notion of popular sovereignty serves as a fulcrum for a whole matrix of visceral beliefs and commitments among Americans. Its deep-seated, visceral quality embodies precisely the type of allure that the First Human Rights Commission aspired to infuse into the Declaration – but, of course, the American narrative of popular sovereignty has had much more

---

9 Ibid., pp. 1–2.
10 Ibid., p. 1.
11 Ibid., p. 3.
12 Ibid.

time to take root and it wields the advantage of a kind of localism that universal human rights has always lacked.

In fact, as the First Human Rights Commission aspired to supply the Declaration with an innateness and authority that would shift this document from a mere enumeration of rights to a powerful narrative of faith, it conducted its work in direct tension with certain pre-existing American narratives: religious narratives, for example, and nationalist narratives. Some of these narratives, like that of popular sovereignty, operate in overt contradiction to the narrative of universal human rights. Such conflicting narratives are by no means unique to American interactions with human rights, though the American example is particularly interesting for the manner in which it pushes against the widespread tendency to associate 'cultural relativist' resistance to human rights primarily with so-called non-Western societies.[13] Notwithstanding this distinction, the tension between human rights universalism and American popular sovereignty is ultimately an embodiment of a broader tension lurking perennially at the heart of human rights: the question of, as Michael Freeman puts it, 'whether the priority that human rights discourse gives to human rights over other values is itself a universally valid value'.[14]

For a recent example of the deep-seated tension between the narrative of human rights and a particular narrative of American popular sovereignty, we need look no further than US Senator, and former Republican presidential contender, Ted Cruz. On 1 June 2017, the day that President Trump announced that the United States would withdraw from the Paris Climate Accord, Harvard professor Joyce Chaplin took to Twitter to note the irony that the United States, which had been 'created by' the international community in the 1783 Treaty of Paris, had now betrayed the international community by withdrawing from the Climate Accord.[15] Cruz responded, to the tune of over 21,000 likes, that a tenured chair at Harvard 'doesn't seem to know' how the US was created.[16] 'Not a treaty', asserted Cruz

13 For a helpful explanation of cultural relativism and its relation to human rights, see: J Donnelly, 'Cultural Relativism and Human Rights', in *Human Rights Quarterly* 6.4 (1984), pp. 400–419.

14 M Freeman, 'The Problem of Secularism in Human Rights', in *Human Rights Quarterly* 26.2 (2002), p. 376.

15 Joyce E Chaplin (JoyceChaplin1), 'The USA, created by int'l community in Treaty or Paris, betrays int'l community by withdrawing from #parisclimateagreement today', 1 June 2017, 1:55PM, Tweet.

16 Ted Cruz (tedcruz), 'Just sad. Tenured chair at Harvard, doesn't seem to know how USA was created. Not a treaty. Declaration+Revolutionary War+Constitution=USA', 1 June 2017, 8:02PM, Tweet.

in the same tweet: 'Declaration + Revolutionary War + Constitution = USA'.[17] Cruz's position, in other words, is that the US was created not through an international treaty process but through an almost totally autonomous combination of self-fashioning (in the form of both a declaration and a constitution) and victory in battle. Of course, the 'almost' of this process is crucial here; the American self-creation described by Cruz is not completely autonomous but rather hinges upon a particular external, international enabler: namely, the British – 'globalist' agent par excellence of the eighteenth century. It is difficult to overstate the importance of this element of the American narrative of popular sovereignty – this conviction that the US *earned* its national standing in the world, and through armed combat, no less. Lest his audience be left with any doubt about how this particular brand of combative meritocracy works, Cruz elaborates in a second tweet: the US is not a product of the international community but rather a product of 'force, the blood of patriots & We the People [*sic*]'.[18]

Such depictions of the genesis of the United States possess a localism and an assertive, self-affirming agency that is very hard for an international institution like the United Nations to replicate. As Cruz's tweets make clear, this proves true even for events from America's distant past. In a manoeuvre that bears the mark of highly effective mythmaking, Cruz deploys a narrative capable of viscerally calling forth a matrix of beliefs and commitments that have served to inspire a particular community over many generations. Moreover, as we can see from the final instalment in this series of tweets, Cruz is well aware of the power differential between these two competing narratives of the creation of the US: Chaplin's claim about the role of international treaty-making is, he asserts, 'like saying a plastic globe created the earth'.[19] In the face of Cruz's evocative narrative of national self-creation through combat, the idea of global governance is reduced, literally, to a hollow shell.

Cruz's response to Chaplin represents one example of the logic of populist resistance to human rights ideals and institutions – a cultural relativist critique, if you will – from within a liberal democracy. Though human rights do not specifically surface in this exchange, Cruz is articulating an aversion to the notion of

---

17 Ibid.
18 Ted Cruz (tedcruz), 'Lefty academics @ my alma mater think USA was "created by int'l community". No – USA created by force, the blood of patriots & We the People', 2 June 2017, 7:39AM, Tweet.
19 Ted Cruz (tedcruz), 'Treaty of Paris simply memorialized the fact, of our total victory at Yorktown. Her claim is like saying a plastic globe created the earth', 2 June 2017, 7:48AM, Tweet.

global governance that directly mirrors a brand of anti-human-rights discourse prevalent today among American political conservatives. Though this discursive resistance to human rights can take a variety of possible forms and lead to a variety of behaviours, one of the things we can see here is that Cruz is overtly framing a rejection of the idea of global governance as a vehicle for a return to America's true heritage. Within Cruz's formulation, a rejection of the ideal and the influence of global governance is one of the elements necessary to 'make America great again'.

This brand of resistance to the ideals and institutions of global governance is about more than just a desire to protect America's economic or political dominance – though it is unquestionably related to such concerns. The resistance that we see embodied in narratives such as the one put forth by Cruz in response to the invocation of the Treaty of Paris reveals a compulsion to push against perceived encroachments upon a particular American identity and a particular American system of values – an identity and a system of values that are upheld as indigenous to the American project itself, and therefore 'authentic' in a way that competing formulations are not. It is almost impossible to understand how certain Americans are primed to see human rights as such a threat if we fail to appreciate the manner in which universal human rights, even in their most secularised guise, aspire in the way of all narratives of faith to engender deep-seated loyalties that are designed to operate on a register wall beyond mere economic or political pragmatism. In aspiring to engender such loyalties, however, human rights always risk falling into intractable conflict with the more immediate and longstanding narratives that bind people to their parochial communities and identities. The current political landscape in the US should give us pause in presuming that human rights resisters come only from outside of the 'West' or outside of the 'Judeo-Christian' religious traditions. Today's political developments also afford us an understanding of the ongoing delicacy of the human rights project itself.

Bibliography

Barthes, R, *Mythologies*, transl. Annette Lavers (New York: Noonday Press, 1961).

Donnelly, J, 'Cultural Relativism and Human Rights', in *Human Rights Quarterly* 6.4 (1984), pp. 400–419.

Freeman, M, 'The Problem of Secularism in Human Rights', in *Human Rights Quarterly* 26.2 (2002), pp. 375–400.

Glendon, M, *A World Made New* (New York: Random House, 2002).

Kahn, P W, 'American Hegemony and International Law: Speaking Law to Power: Popular Sovereignty, Human Rights, and the New International Order', in *Chicago Journal of International Law* 1 (Spring 2000), pp. 1–16.

Reinbold, J, *Seeing the Myth in Human Rights* (Philadelphia: University of Pennsylvania Press, 2017).

Roosevelt, E, 'Making Human Rights Come Alive', in Allida M Black, ed., *What I Hope to Leave Behind: The Essential Essays of Eleanor Roosevelt* (New York: Carlson Publishing, 1995).

13

Interpretation of Islamic Principles: Muslim Movements and Ethical Social Imaginary in South India

Thahir Jamal Kiliyamannil

Introduction: invoking Islam in the contemporary

After the 1980s, a whole new set of Muslim movements emerged in South India, with regional and social articulations. Through these new movements, Islam has acquired renewed appearance in South India in the last three decades, as an Islamic ethos penetrated the contours of public avenues. These movements framed a social space with renewed interpretations of Islamic principles, through nuanced Islamic language and working modalities, which expands to the environs of secular space. If previous organisations mobilised the masses with a collective religious pursuit, in the new Muslim social movements the ideological chorus gave way to a multiplicity of voices. The change in language or mode of narrative is evident from the example of Muslim women's headscarves, which used to be debated as a 'religious necessity' and has now been defended as a 'constitutional choice/right'.[1] It is here that the complex phraseology of Muslim social movements attains excessive importance. They articulate their concerns

---

1 Campaigns by women's organisations like Girls Islamic Organisation (the female wing of Jamaat-e-Islami Hind) and Mujahid Girls and Women's Movement (MGM) during various controversies are textbook cases of the shift in language. They held public protests claiming wearing the scarf is Muslim women's 'conscious choice' and constitutional right, when it was banned from many competitive exams as a security measure to control plagiarism and malpractices.

in a secular constitutional language or in the universal language of human rights but without diminishing the Islamic characteristics of said concerns. The Social Democratic Party of India's (SDPI)[2] slogan 'freedom from hunger and freedom from fear'[3] is a perfect case of this blended phraseology. While the slogan is directly taken from the Qur'an 106:4,[4] it is used to articulate a secular concern affecting the public sphere[5] through a constitutional language whereby the alleviation of poverty and equal access to security are entrusted through constitutional safeguards.

The re-conceptualisation of Islam, as a pursuit of rights and means of defiance as pointed out by Irfan Ahmad,[6] is very much visible in the contemporary Muslim social movements which are entangled in the mix of religious and constitutional approaches. The Popular Front of India[7] uses the Qur'anic concept of *izzat* (might) as a synonym for self-respect. At the same time, they relate it to various movements from other marginalised communities that promote self-respect to produce a constitutional version and create horizontal solidarities with such communities. Likewise, Qarun (Korah), a historic figure in the Qur'an who is known for his vast wealth, is anachronistically depicted as a prototype of modern capitalist forces, while Nimrod, who tried to burn Prophet Abraham, is cited as an equivalent of modern fascist regimes which suppress freedom of religion. Since these movements do not merely consider the practice of Islam a matter of personal etiquette, but a social protocol, any principle which is irrelevant to the social upbringing of human beings is considered null and void. This corresponds to Ali Shariati's

---

2 Social Democratic Party of India (SDPI) is a political party formed in 2009 with the stated objective of empowering the marginalised communities.

3 The manifesto of SDPI released in the year 2009 highlights two fears which obstruct the organic development of citizens in the country; these are identified as fear of hunger and fear of violence, and a working method is suggested to remove them from the minds of common man.

4 Qur'an 106:4 talks about the mercy and benevolence shown by Allah to Quraysh and urges the worship of the Lord 'who has fed them, [saving them] from hunger and made them safe, [saving them] from fear'.

5 Without going into detail about debates on the (non)existence of the public sphere and counterpublics, this chapter takes into consideration the existence of a dominant public sphere as reflected in mainstream narratives.

6 I Ahmad, *Islamism and Democracy in India – The Transformation of Jamaat-e-Islami* (Princeton: Princeton University Press, 2010), p. 158.

7 Popular Front of India was formed by the merging of six organisations from different states in 2006. National Development Front in Kerala is the result of a coalition largely comprised of ex SIMI activists. They urge the mobilisation of marginalised communities into a political force, instead of remaining mere vote banks for different political parties in elections.

idea of social religion, where those rituals that do not serve a social purpose are considered of least importance.[8]

During my fieldwork in Kerala, I attended various Friday sermons and public speeches held by these organisations during their campaign against ISIS. In the initial stage, the campaign was titled 'ISIS is not Islam', followed by another stage which proclaimed: 'Islam is balanced.' Taking into consideration the criticism issued by Ashraf Kunnummal, who pointed out the necessity of understanding the political site of Muslims in the exercise of condemnation,[9] my interest is in the invoking of Islamic principles in the process. In their campaign, these movements stress the necessity of a vertical relation with God and a horizontal relation with human beings. Without a proper horizontal relationship with fellow human beings nurtured in love and mercy the vertical relationship with God is imperfect and impossible. They continuously quote the hadith 'God will not be merciful to those who are not merciful to mankind'[10] and argue that ISIS is not considering the horizontal relationships with human beings. The second stage of the campaign, 'Islam is balanced', is directly taken from the Qur'anic expression, 'Thus We have appointed you a middle/balanced nation.'[11] All extreme tendencies are criticised as an aberration from the perspective of this balanced/middle path, even if this extremity is expressed in asceticism.

In a private talk, a student leader from the Muslim Students Federation (MSF)[12] said, 'MSF doesn't have a moralistic position, as we have people from diverse backgrounds with diverse moral anxieties. Our focus is just obtaining possible constitutional safeguards and rights.' He further stressed that moralistic positions will characterise an organisation as reformist and theirs is just a political movement, seeking constitutional benevolence. At the same time, members of the MSF's parent organisation, the Muslim League, state that their religious commitment made them enter and participate in the political process. Though seemingly contradictory, both generations keep some sort of Islamic ethics in their discourse. The new turn from a reformist position towards a constitutionalist position effects a blurred distinction between political and religious stances. At the same time, it does not connote a secular divide, rather the development of a partnership in

---

8 A Shariati, *On the Sociology of Islam*, transl. H Algar (Berkeley: Mizan Press, 1979).
9 A Kunnummal, 'Muslims, Global Violence and Politics of Condemnation', in *Economic and Political Weekly* 51.11 (2016), pp. 17–19.
10 *Sahih al-Bukhari*, vol. 9, book 93, no. 473.
11 The Qur'an, 2:143.
12 MSF is the students' wing of electoral political party Indian Union Muslim League.

governmental and political acts and the deployment of a particular form of sub-jectivity informed by Islamic ethics.

Solidarity Youth Movement[13] occupied the public sphere of Kerala, a state in South India, through its continuous campaign on environmental issues. They talked extensively about problems related to development and displacement and took position in favour of displaced communities. They relentlessly struggled for the latter's rehabilitation and, in the due process, produced a narration of Islamic rights and humanity. In their campaign, they used the slogan '*janasevanam dhai-varadhanayanu*' (serving humanity is worshiping God), hence, redefining the customary interpretation of *ibadah* (worship) by connecting *ibadah* to social obligations and political articulations. The numerous drinking water projects they have carried forward are also interpreted in the same way. In their campaign, they evoke the hadiths which talk about the necessity of conserving the free flow of water[14] and remind their cadres about Allah's questioning on how one spends one's youth.[15] Through solidarity, the activities of their organisation provide an answer to this question. 'Vision 2016', a charity-oriented project run by Jamaat-e Islami, which adopted various villages in under-developed regions and promoted welfare activities in those areas also stems from this idea of Islam as a social obligation.

In another instance, Samastha Kerala Sunni Students Federation (SKSSF)[16] conducted an airport march against the fascist tendencies of the Modi govern-ment which is trying to erase the history of Islam and Muslim practices. They conducted the march on Ramadan 17, which commemorates the Battle of Badr led by Prophet Muhammed.[17] In their speeches, they pointed out that Badr is a reminder against the arrogance of the powerful and urged their cadres to follow the footsteps of soldiers of Badr. Invoking Badr, the strength of believers is used

---

13 Solidarity Youth Movement was formed in 2003 and described itself as a group of youth committed to promoting justice and welfare.

14 *Sahih al-Bukhari*, vol. 3, book 40, no. 543, says not to withhold water as it may prevent people from grazing their cattle, and hadith no. 547 says that such man who withholds water from travellers will not be looked at by Allah on the Day of Judgment.

15 Hadith reported by Hakim (4/306) says youth before old age is a benefit and has to be taken advantage of.

16 SKSSF, is the higher students' organisation of Samastha Kerala Jamiyyathul Ulama (the traditional Muslim group, who identify themselves as Sunni) formed on 19 February 1989 as part of its attempt to nurture moral life in all Muslim students under its fold.

17 The Battle of Badr was a key battle in the early days of Islam against the Quraysh (AH 2 Ramadan 17). It is one of the few battles specially mentioned in the Qur'an and the story of the battle has been passed down in generations as proof of divine intervention.

as a subtext to give hope to the oppressed and a warning to the oppressor. A simultaneous invoking of elements from Islamic tradition and an appeal to the language of human rights and equality is made, which is the very character of Islamist movements as defined by Salwa Ismail.[18] To articulate such a symbolic claim, the Indian National League (INL),[19] though it has a constitution like any other secular organisation, still uses the green flag and crescent as emblems.[20]

The *Companion* journal, run by the Students Islamic Organisation of India (SIO),[21] dedicated one volume to environmental ethics.[22] In the articles, they tried to develop an Islamic eco-theology, a religious call to protect the ecosystem. Various Qur'anic verses and hadiths were interpreted against materialist theories, arguing how the latter has given rise to the wrong practice of the survival of the fittest. The hadith, 'There is none amongst the Muslims who plants a tree or sows seeds, and then a bird, or a person or an animal eats from it, but is regarded as a charitable gift for him,'[23] and 'if the Resurrection were established upon one of you while he has in his hand a sapling, then let him plant it'[24] were used in enhancing the eco-theology, through which man-made ideologies were criticised. The hadith which maintains 'removal of what is injurious from the path [is branch of faith]'[25] was interpreted toward arguing that environmental ethics are a necessity for every Muslim. In other words, they argued that through replacing an anthropocentric worldview with a theocentric worldview, the innate Islamic values can render an eco-friendly vision, which will help to maintain proper balance in the ecosystem.

When it comes to gender issues, organisations for Muslim women have taken a renewed stance to enhance a centrifugal relation to liberal gender values without demeaning a centripetal relation to Islamic values and the Muslim community. Girls Islamic Organisation of India (GIO) has reinterpreted the hadith which talks about a model society where a woman will be free and secure to travel from *san'a* to *hadra mauth*.[26] They have taken the spirit of this hadith and described

18 S Ismail, *Rethinking Islamist politics: Culture, the State and Islamism* (New York: I B Tauris, 2006), p. 2.
19 INL was formed by Ibrahim Sulaiman Sait, when he resigned from Indian Union Muslim League after their pro-congress stand when Babri masjid was demolished.
20 Crescent is a symbol associated with Islam, from the Ottoman era onwards.
21 SIO is the student wing of Jamaat-e Islami, established in 1982.
22 *The Companion*, June 2017.
23 *Sahih al-Bhukhari*, vol. 3, book 39, no. 513.
24 *Sahih Musnad Ahmad*, no. 12491.
25 *Sahih al-Muslim*, book 1, no. 60.
26 *Sahih al-Bukhari*, vol. 4, book 5, no. 809.

themselves as a group which envisages a world where girls can travel more freely from the Himalayas to Kanyakumari[27] with their heads straight and thoughts high.[28] Instead of a non-contextual liturgical translation of the hadith, GIO adapted the principle of the hadith to contribute meaningfully to their socio-historic location, thus addressing contemporary gender concerns. It is imperative to note that a silent stance on the issue of *mahram*[29] is a mark of adopting modern contextual values, with a nuanced mix of tradition.

With new interpretations that are outside the traditional Islamic scholarship, as detailed above, new Muslim movements are beginning to debate the questions of environmental activism, gender justice, nation building and caste violence; which in turn changes their priorities and develops a broader democratic approach. The shift from the puritan idea of an 'Islamic state' to a contemporary idea of the 'welfare state'[30] gives some insight into a change in perceptions of imagining Islam and Islamic movements. These contemporary movements have led to different trends and internal transformations within the community. They confront the existing conceptual categories of community (*ummah*), constitutionalism, rights and duties, while attempting to expand their relationship with other marginal communities like Dalits and Adivasis. The possibilities of reading Islam in multiple contexts stems from re-interpretation practices available in Islamic scholarship.

Authority and legitimacy in question: ulama and organisations

Learning and teaching the Qur'an has always been a debatable topic. Even the translatability and existing translations of the Qur'an are controversial topics and it is still encouraged in Qur'anic debates not to talk about interpretations. The primary hesitance towards translations arises from the language of Qur'an being considered eternal and universal, unbound by historicity or context. Therefore, hermeneutical attempts at understanding the Qur'an may be devoid of the historical context of the revelation and language of text. Limited literal translation has been the minimum level of available interpretational possibility. 'According to this methodology, readers retrieve the text's meaning through analysis of the Arabic

---

27 Himalaya is the northern end and Kanyakumari is the southern end of the Indian territory.
28 GIO brochure, 2011.
29 As per classic texts on Islamic jurisprudence, *mahram* is an unmarriageable kin who has to escort the woman during longer journeys.
30 Halim Rane talked about similar trends in Muslim majority countries like Malaysia and Turkey. See: H Rane, 'The Relevance of a Maqasid Approach for Political Islam Post Arab Revolutions', in *Journal of Law and Religion* 28.2 (2013), pp. 504–505.

grammar, syntax, and morphology.'[31] However, one interesting fact is that, even those who reject the independent interpretation of Qur'an, tend to contextualise and historicise Islamic principles and moral stories to suite the present situation.[32]

Most of the studies about the re-interpretation of Islam have been focused on scholarly interventions and exegesis. For instance, Shahram Akbarzadeh and Abdullah Saeed have analysed the official ulama (who became bureaucrats or part of the ruling elite) and their religious legitimacy.[33] Scholars like Qasim Zaman have examined the role of ulama in the Muslim society and the authoritative nature of their viewpoints.[34] John J Donohue and John L Esposito have argued that the interpretation and application of sharia was the domain of a class of scholars whose main task was to interpret the law and advise the ruler.[35] The scrutiny of the ulama, hence, would be sought even in the matters related to social and political issues. For that reason, Talal Asad has considered the ulama as authoritative sources in the discursive formation of Islam. In short, ulama have been the legitimising actors of the lives of Muslims, including in the social and political arenas. Though there has been a decline in the popularity of ulama due to various reasons,[36] traditionally, their final decision on the Islamicity of an issue has functioned as a concluding remark.

With the advent of modern social organising and forms of mobilisation, along with a gradual retreat of ulama into the sphere of the religious, the Islamicity of an issue or act is no longer decided entirely by the ulama. Rather, social movements from the Muslim community emerge as actors who are responsible for

---

31 A Duderija, 'Traditional and Modern Qur'anic Hermeneutics in Comparative Perspective', in *International Qur'anic Studies Association* (2015), available at: https://iqsaweb.wordpress.com/2015/03/23/duderija_hermeneutics.

32 For instance, one such faction of Muslims in Kerala known as AP Sunni faction, used the metaphor of *buraq* (prophet's vehicle/carrier to the seventh sky) to suite the claim for use of luxury cars.

33 S Akbarzadeh and A Saeed, eds., *Islam and Political Legitimacy* (London: Routledge, 2003).

34 M Q Zaman, *The Ulama in Contemporary Islam: Custodians of Change* (Princeton: Princeton University Press, 2010).

35 J J Donohue and J L Esposito, eds., *Islam in Transition: Muslim Perspectives* (Oxford: Oxford University Press, 1982).

36 The evolution of modern print culture, and the ulama's collaboration with the ruling elite and seeking of patronage are some of the reasons listed for their decline in popularity. For details, see: S Akbarzade and A Saeed, eds., *Islam and Political Legitimacy*; and F Robinson, 'Technology and Religious Change: Islam and the Impact of Print', in *Modern Asian Studies* 27.1 (1993), pp. 229–251. Without devaluing the mentioned reasons, this chapter is trying to understand the impact of Muslim social movements on the authority of ulama.

legitimising Muslim life. An organisation's take on an issue or act decides the Islamicity of that act. In place of the scholar, in this case, the organisation itself becomes the interpreter, as and when required. This does not imply that scholarly interventions are completely absent in the process, but it stresses the importance of collective efforts.[37] In a way, traditional Muslim leadership which was primarily associated with the ulama has been challenged with new actors coming into the stage of political leadership, making a shift from centralised leadership to plural leaderships.

In the South Indian context, which this chapter focuses on, organisations obtained their modern structure after the 1920s. Initially, the ulama used to control the organisation, which is no longer the case with the presence of rebel voices and parallel marginal voices. This gives rise to further interesting facts on the shift of legitimacy. If it was the ulama's affiliation or fatwa which gave legitimacy to organisations, now it is an organisational affiliation which gives authenticity to the ulama. This can be best understood with the resigning or expulsion of scholars from organisations and subsequent disrespect for them among the community. Often, when eminent scholars are expelled, their views and stances are disregarded as authentic the moment they are no longer affiliated with the organisations. The expulsion of Kanthapuram A P Aboobacker Musliyar[38] from the scholarly wing of the traditional Sunni sect, Samastha Kerala Jamiyyathul Ulama, and Inayathulla Subhani and Khalid Moosa Nadvi from Jamaat-e-Islami Hind provide ample evidence. Even though they were senior leaders who enjoyed scholarly prestige in their respective organisations, they were hurled abuses soon after their respective expulsions. In other words, they ceased to be 'legitimate ulama' the moment they were ousted from the organisational structure, a fact which proves the authority of the organisations.

Ijtihad and new interpretative possibilities in the context of Muslim movements[39]

Ijtihad was always considered as a function of the ulama, and the traditional

---

37 Some groups like Kerala Samasthana Jamiyyathul Ulama still adhere to the ulama's authority.
38 He was the supreme council member of Samastha Kerala Jamiyyathul Ulama, and the leader of its youth wing. Later due to some difference of opinion with their stance, he was expelled from both organisations. He immediately formed Samatha Kerala Sunni Jamiyyathul Ulama (SKSJU), of which he is the supreme leader.
39 Ijtihad is the method of resolving new legal problems, which are not directly answered

scholarship has enlisted various characteristics necessary for a person to do ijtihad (or become a mujtahid). In all those scholarly discourses, the burden and duty of ijtihad falls upon the individual scholar. While social movements take charge of the legitimate space previously occupied by the ulama, ijtihad becomes a 'collective act'. Amidst ever-growing disciplinary boundaries, interdisciplinary approaches and the amount of knowledge being produced in each field, it has become increasingly difficult for a single individual to be a mujtahid.[40] Though the authority to issue fatwas is restricted to the ulama, the vast and extensive knowledge makes it difficult to be a 'learned one' in all disciplines, which in turn makes each person specialised in certain areas and he/she will be deemed fit to give fatwas in that special area only.[41] Here the possibility of collective ijtihad also arises, making organisations the absolute authority. Different people in the organisation can specialise in particular areas and they together can produce a coherent and comprehensive interpretation.[42]

Without having the burden of conforming to the liturgical aspect of a text, the new Muslim social movements are re-conceptualising sharia in a new frame, developing a new etiquette based on *maqasid-al-sharia* (principles of sharia).[43] The five basic principles defined accordingly are the preservation of religion, life, lineage, intellect and property.[44] This new interpretation has resulted in significant changes in reconfiguring the working modalities of these organisations. The Popular Front of India has made establishment of a social order based on freedom, justice and security for all one of their objectives. Their vision statement reads:

in the Qur'an and the hadith. For details see, F Opwis, 'Maslaha in Contemporary Islamic Legal Theory', in *Islamic Law and Society* 12.2 (2005), pp. 182–223.

40 Mujtahid is one who is qualified to exercise ijtihad in broadening or reshaping Islamic law. Female variant of the same is *mujtahida*.

41 Wael Hallaq has shown how the fatwas are closely related to the act of ijtihad. For details, see: W B Hallaq, 'Ifta' and Ijtihad: A Developmental Account', in B Messick and D S Powers, eds., *Islamic Legal Interpretation: Muftis and their Fatwas* (Massachusetts: Harvard University Press, 1996), pp. 32–43.

42 This further accelerates a difference in *taqlid* (the act of conforming to the scholar), where *taqlid* is not inclined towards the ulama, but the collective. Debates between Noushad Ahsani and AP Sunni faction also points to the question of authority and legitimacy.

43 For details, see: M H Kamali, *Shari'ah law: An Introduction* (Oxford: Oxford University Press, 2008).

44 According to Asghar Ali Engineer, the key values forming the basis of the Qur'an which characterise this Islamic paradigm are justice (*'adl*), benevolence (*iḥsān*), equality (*musawāh*), peace (*salām*), reason (*'aql*), and wisdom (*ḥikmah*). Quoted in Y Sikand, *Muslims in India Since 1947: Islamic Perspectives on Inter-faith Relations* (London: Routledge, 2004), p. 15

This organisation is a move towards co-ordination and management of such efforts for the achievement of socio-economic, cultural and political empowerment of the deprived and the downtrodden and the nation at large. It will try to establish an egalitarian society in which freedom, justice and security are enjoyed by all.[45]

The focus on freedom, justice and security clearly correlates with the values of *maqasid-al-sharia*. Similarly, affirming justice, basic rights and freedoms as objectives is featured in a speech by People's Democratic Party's (PDP)[46] chairman Abdul Nazer Mahdani, who addressing a protest gathering demanding land for the landless declared: 'I am a committed Muslim and every Muslim has the obligation to support the poor, Adivasis and Dalits… It is my duty to stand by you to fight for your rights… If needed, to be a martyr dying for this cause.'[47]

There have been attempts to reduce such new activism, emphasising constitutional safeguards as a mere survival mechanism in the majoritarian state structure. But considering the vibrant jurisprudential explorations in these spheres and the emerging immanent critiques from the Muslim community, such a reductive reading is inimical and promotes false stereotypes. Also, from the universality of these debates and their tandem with global geo-politics, it is quite clear that the process of participation in contemporary social and political realms is not only due to external factors, but also inspired by the internal debates on jurisprudence, including that of *maslaha*. 'Literally, *maslaha* means a cause or source of something good and beneficial. In English it is frequently rendered as "public interest", although it is much closer in meaning to well-being, welfare, and social.'[48] The Welfare Party of India's[49] proposed aim of a welfare state draws direct parallels with *maslaha*. Rather than reading it as Qur'anic values supplanting constitutional values, the movements are trying to re-align sociality within the available boundaries.

By analysing various works concerning the role of Islam in politics, Halim

---

45 From Popular Front of India's updated Constitution (Rules and Regulations) 2014, p. 4.
46 People's Democratic Party (PDP), was launched in 1992 by Islamic scholar Abdul Nazer Mahdani with the stated objective of Muslim-Dalit-Backward caste alliance. 'Power to Avarnas, Liberation for Oppressed' is the slogan of PDP.
47 'Madani in Chengara Bhoomi Samaram', YouTube, 17 March 2013, available at: https://www.youtube.com/watch?v=kmFHbEAil6A.
48 Opwis, 'Maslaha in Contemporary Islamic Legal Theory', pp. 182–183.
49 A political party launched by Jamaat-e-Islami Hind in 2011, with the aim of promoting value-based politics.

Rane argues that 'what is missing in this discussion is attention to the capacity of Islamic political parties to draw on Islamic tradition and evolve in response to modernity through a focus on Islam's higher objectives or a *maqasid* approach.'[50] The nascent Islamic scholarship among the new Muslim social movements focuses primarily on a *maqasid* approach. The special section dedicated to *maqasid-al-sharia* in the Islamic Academic Conference conducted by the Students Islamic Organisation of India[51] and the continuous articles published by *Prabodhanam*[52] on *usool-ul-fiqh* and *maqasid-al-sharia* tries to make the *maqasid* approach accessible to the masses, and thereby achieves a discursive shift in Muslim articulations.

The *maqasid* approach customarily connotes that the better interpreter can produce enhanced meanings and derivations. The interpreter assumes higher authority over the text. Ebrahim Moosa contends that, even in such a nuanced purposive interpretive approach, 'the text remains sovereign, ignoring the reader or marginalising the "community of the text" and their experiences as credible participants in the textual process.'[53] It invariably implies that meaning lies within the community. But when community is diversified in umpteen ways, it produces the possibility of multiple meanings. Moreover, in contemporary times, Muslim community is defined through the existing organisations and different sociological and theological sects. Thus, following Ebrahim Moosa, and taking his claim forward, I would argue that the meaning of Islam lies also with the organisations and hence they can be called interpretative movements, which in turn makes Islam dynamic, interactive and contemporaneous. Muslim movements redefine themselves in the process of becoming interpretative, which stems from the idea of *tajdeed* (renewal/revival) and *ijtihad* (interpretation/independent reasoning), allowing for the fluidity of community contours.

---

50 H Rane, 'The Relevance of a Maqasid Approach for Political Islam Post Arab Revolutions', in *Journal of Law and Religion* 28.2 (2013), p. 490.

51 The conference was organised by the Kerala Chapter of Student Islamic Organisation of India, focusing mainly on the themes of Islamic Epistemology, *fiqh* and *usool-ul-fiqh* and Islamic Political thought. The conference was held on the Campus of Al Jamia Al Islamia, Santhapuram on 14–15 January 2012.

52 A weekly magazine run by the Kerala chapter of Jamaat-e-Islami Hind.

53 E Moosa, 'The Debts and Burdens of Critical Islam', in O Safi, ed., *Progressive Muslims: On Justice, Gender and Pluralism* (Ipswich, MA: Ebsco Publishing, 2008), p. 123.

Conclusion: Islamic ethos in public avenues

Contemporary scholarship on the entry of Islam into the public sphere has diverse narratives centred on some basic questions like 'whether or not Islam fits into norms of secularity'[54] or 'can Islam meet the political, social, and economic demands of modernity'?[55] For some scholars, invoking religious principles seems anachronistic and hence illegitimate and must be refuted.[56] When it comes to Islam, antagonism increases to a new level owing to the perennial secular predicaments on the entry of Islam into the public, fuelled by its allegedly fanaticised image. Hence an immediate possible reading of the re-interpretation of Islamic principles by Muslim movements might debunk it as pretentious and peripheral. But as José Casanova has proposed, 'the publicisation of religion is not an infringement on secularity per se but rather a condition for its maturation.'[57] However, his approach has been critiqued from several quarters, including by Talal Asad and Armando Salvatore, citing the specific ways in which Islam has to adapt and adopt the Western secular notions and principles of the public sphere.

If it is the complex historical and normative relationship between Christianity and secularism that continues to inform the modern contours and shape of the public sphere in European society,[58] in India, the parallel is the relationship between Hinduism and secularism. Hence, the legal ordering of democracy, human rights and religious liberty are defined in terms of a Hindu moral ethos. The case of Hadiya[59] is a perfect example, where she was forced into house arrest for converting to Islam. The response of Muslim organisations is quite interesting, as most of them considered the house arrest a serious encroachment on the right to profess religion. They criticised the external fascist pressures on the judiciary as going out of the bounds of constitutional safeguards. In other words, Muslim

---

54 A Salvatore, 'Power and Authority within European Secularity: From the Enlightenment Critique of Religion to the Contemporary Presence of Islam', in *The Muslim World* 96.4 (2006), p. 543.

55 Donohue and Esposito, eds., *Islam in Transition: Muslim Perspectives*, p. 3.

56 For example, see L Swaine, *The Liberal Conscience: Politics and Principle in a World of Religious Pluralism* (New York: Columbia University Press, 2010).

57 Quoted in Salvatore, 'Power and Authority within European secularity', p. 544.

58 For details, see: T Asad, *Formations of the Secular: Christianity, Islam, Modernity* (Stanford: Stanford University Press, 2003); and P G Danchin, 'Islam in the Secular Nomos of the European Court of Human Rights', in *Michigan Journal of International Law* 32 (2011), pp. 663–747.

59 Hadiya is a 24-year-old woman who denounced Hinduism, embraced Islam, and married a Muslim a man. Her conversion has led to furious controversy, with High Court of Kerala annulling her marriage, leading to the house arrest of Hadiya alleging the case is a 'love jihad' (where Muslim men seduce and convert Hindu women in an organised attempt).

movements invoked the constitution, which is based on a Hindu ethos,[60] to counter the judicial encroachment on religious liberty.

Responding to the secular government's legal ordering, the Solidarity Youth Movement argues: 'Hadiya's side represents democracy which has ethical content and shade of divine thought, while the other side represents politics of fascist goons, who tries to annihilate Hadiya.'[61] What is interesting about the qualifiers of democracy which Solidarity propounds is the unsettling of hegemonic Eurocentric notions of secular democracy through bringing in new aspects of Islamic ethos. By enhancing the ethical content inscribed in the democracy, they are catalysing new forms of politics and reconfiguring the genealogical premises of the Hindu liberal order existing in India. Formulating the Islamic content of democracy becomes a simultaneous critique of Islamic jurisprudential antagonism to democracy and liberal antagonism to the public entry of Islam. Through such an amendment to the established formulation of religion and public, Muslim movements are accelerating the paradox of (im)possible/(im)permissible division between religion and the public sphere.

As Nilüfer Göle contends, on the one hand, 'public Islam' testifies to a shift in the orientation of the Islamic movement from macro-politics toward micro-politics, and on the other hand, it challenges the borders and the meanings of the secular public sphere.[62] Similarly, analysing Islamic articulations in Muslim majority countries, Asef Bayat contends that Muslims are reconciling their religious advocacy in tandem with the values and concerns of human rights and democratic discourses. He calls such attempts of conceptualising and rationalising the modalities of Islamism in social, political and intellectual domains as post-Islamism, which 'represents an endeavour to fuse religiosity and rights, faith and freedom, Islam and liberty'.[63] Are these movements at the verge of a post-Islamist

---

60 Somewhere else, I have argued that constitutional debates in the assembly show how Hindu ethics were deliberately inserted into the constitution. For details, see: K M T Jamal, 'Mathethara-Desheeya Udgrandanavum Nyoonapaksha Samudaya Chodyangalum: Niyama Nirmana Sabhayile Islam Pedi', in V Hikmathullah, ed., *Islamophobia: Prathivicharangal* (Calicut, 2017); Tejani, *Indian Secularism: A Social and Intellectual History, 1890–1950*; and, P Singh, 'Hindu Bias in India's "Secular Constitution": Probing Flaws in the Instruments of Governance', in *Third World Quarterly* 26.6 (2005), pp. 909–926.
61 From the pamphlet issued by Solidarity Youth Movement, 2017, (Translation mine).
62 N Göle, 'Islam in Public: New Visibilities and New Imaginaries', in *Public Culture* 14.1 (2002), p. 173.
63 A Bayat, 'Islam and Democracy: What is the Real Question?', in A Bayat, ed., *Islam and Democracy: What is the Real Question* (Amsterdam: Amsterdam University Press, 2007), p. 19.

turn, trying to overcome the public limit of religion through reified re-impetrations and thereby transcending the 'proper place of religion' in public? Or do these reinterpretations by Muslim social movements just contribute to, as Saba Mahmood has argued, 'producing a particular kind of religious subject who is compatible with rationality and exercise of liberal political rule',[64] which, as the project of the empire, becomes a ploy in marketing Islamic liberalism? Or are they succumbing to becoming Islamic constitutionalists?[65] The answer, which might not be singular, has to unravel in the course of action in the liminal space available for public religion. Rather than delegitimising any invoking of Islamic concepts and rejecting the existence and concerns of Muslim social movements, conceding and engaging through an immanent criticism might generate a positive imagination of a new social and political order in South India.

Bibliography

Ahmad, I, *Islamism and Democracy in India – The Transformation of Jamaat-e-Islami* (Princeton: Princeton University Press, 2010).

Akbarzadeh, S, and Saeed, A, eds., *Islam and Political Legitimacy* (London: Routledge, 2003).

Asad, T, *Formations of the Secular: Christianity, Islam, Modernity* (Stanford: Stanford University Press, 2003).

Bayat, A, 'Islam and Democracy: What is the Real Question?', in A Bayat, ed., *Islam and Democracy: What is the Real Question* (Amsterdam: Amsterdam University Press, 2007).

Danchin, P G, 'Islam in the Secular Nomos of the European Court of Human Rights', in *Michigan Journal of International Law* 32 (2011), pp. 663–747.

Donohue, J J, and Esposito, J L, eds., *Islam in Transition: Muslim Perspectives* (Oxford: Oxford University Press, 1982).

---

64 S Mahmood, 'Secularism, Hermeneutics, and Empire: The Politics of Islamic Reformation', in *Public Culture* 18.2 (2006), p. 344.

65 Bruce K Rutherford analysed the theoretical works of Egypt's prominent Islamic thinkers as well as the documents issued by Muslim Brotherhood to argue that 'a distinctively Islamic conception of constitutionalism has emerged that legitimates many of the key goals of liberal governance, including constraints on state power; governmental accountability, and protection of some civil and political rights'. For further information, see B K Rutherford, 'What do Egypt's Islamists Want? Moderate Islam and the Rise of Islamic Constitutionalism', in *The Middle East Journal* 60.4 (2006), p. 707.

Duderija, A, 'Traditional and Modern Qur'anic Hermeneutics in Comparative
    Perspective', in *International Qur'anic Studies Association* (2015), available
    at: https://iqsaweb.wordpress.com/2015/03/23/duderija_hermeneutics.

El Fadl, K A, 'Islamic Law and Muslim Minorities: The Juristic Discourse on
    Muslim Minorities from the Second/Eighth to the Eleventh/Seventeenth
    Centuries', in *Islamic Law and Society* 1.2 (1994), pp. 141–187.

Esposito, John L, ed., *The Oxford Dictionary of Islam* (Oxford: Oxford
    University Press, 2004).

Göle, N, 'Islam in Public: New Visibilities and New Imaginaries', in *Public
    Culture* 14.1 (2002), pp. 173–190.

Hallaq, W B, 'Ifta' and Ijtihad: A Developmental Account', in B Messick and
    D S Powers, eds., *Islamic Legal Interpretation: Muftis and their Fatwas*
    (Massachusetts: Harvard University Press, 1996), pp. 32–43.

Haq, M U, *Islam in Secular India* (Simla: Indian Institute of Advanced Studies,
    1972).

Ismail, S, *Rethinking Islamist politics: Culture, the State and Islamism* (New
    York: I B Tauris, 2006).

Jamal, K M T, 'Mathethara-Desheeya Udgrandanavum Nyoonapaksha
    Samudaya Chodyangalum: Niyama Nirmana Sabhayile Islam Pedi', in V
    Hikmathullah, ed., *Islamophobia: Prathivicharangal* (Calicut, 2017).

Kamali, M H, *Shari'ah law: An Introduction* (Oxford: Oxford University Press,
    2008).

Kunnummal, A, 'Muslims, Global Violence and Politics of Condemnation', in
    Economic and Political Weekly 51.11 (2016), pp. 17–19.

Mahmood, S, 'Secularism, Hermeneutics, and Empire: The Politics of Islamic
    Reformation', in *Public Culture* 18.2 (2006), p. 344.

Moosa, E, 'The Debts and Burdens of Critical Islam', in O Safi, ed., *Progressive
    Muslims: On Justice, Gender and Pluralism* (Ipswich MA: Ebsco Publishing,
    2008), pp. 111–127.

Opwis, F, 'Maslaha in Contemporary Islamic Legal Theory', in *Islamic Law and
    Society* 12.2 (2005), pp. 182–223.

Rane, H, 'The Relevance of a Maqasid Approach for Political Islam Post Arab
    Revolutions', in *Journal of Law and Religion* 28.2 (2013), pp. 489–520.

Robinson, F, 'Technology and Religious Change: Islam and the Impact of Print',
    in *Modern Asian Studies* 27.1 (1993), pp. 229–251.

Rutherford, B K, 'What do Egypt's Islamists Want? Moderate Islam and the
    Rise of Islamic Constitutionalism', in *The Middle East Journal* 60.4 (2006),
    pp. 707–731.

Safi, O, ed., *Progressive Muslims: On Gender, Justice, and Pluralism* (Ipswich MA: Ebsco Publishing, 2008).

Salvatore, A, 'Power and Authority within European Secularity: From the Enlightenment Critique of Religion to the Contemporary Presence of Islam', in *The Muslim World* 96.4 (2006), pp. 543–561.

Shariati, A, *On the Sociology of Islam*, transl. H Algar (Berkeley: Mizan Press, 1979).

Sikand, Y, *Muslims in India Since 1947: Islamic Perspectives on Inter-faith Relations* (London: Routledge, 2004).

Singh, P, 'Hindu Bias in India's "Secular Constitution": Probing Flaws in the Instruments of Governance', in *Third World Quarterly* 26.6 (2005), pp. 909–926.

Swaine, L, *The Liberal Conscience: Politics and Principle in a World of Religious Pluralism* (New York: Columbia University Press, 2010).

Tejani, S, *Indian Secularism: A Social and Intellectual History, 1890–1950* (Bloomington: Indiana University Press, 2008).

Zaman, M Q, *The Ulama in Contemporary Islam: Custodians of Change* (Princeton: Princeton University Press, 2010).

RELIGION
AND
SUSTAINABILITY

14

The Relationship of Ecological Science to the Christian Narrative

Caleb Gordon

The more we understand the effects of human activity on global ecological systems, the more the languages of science and religion require integration. Science and religion are ways of talking about the world which orient us to spatial and temporal roles, but our unprecedented ability to find global scientific consensus about the world's state and processes requires a deep re-examination of claims contained in the narratives of religious communities which are eligible for scientific scrutiny. This chapter focuses primarily on the relationship between Christianity and ecology. Many of the points apply to the relationships between other religions and ecology, but there are two reasons I focus on Christianity in particular: first, because it is a tradition I can speak about from within, and second, because Christianity is often cited as providing a narrative rationale for destruction and disruption of the earth's processes. I argue that the issue ecological science poses for Christianity is not that Christians believe things that science cannot prove, but that so many Christians still fail to acknowledge what science *can* prove, and thus resist responsibility for the consequences of many common behaviours. Christians are used to thinking about their ethics with reference to a narrative, but as technological power and scientific understanding have evolved, Christians must acknowledge that human influence within global systems factors crucially into the Christian telling of human history. 'Never before', Willis Jenkins writes, 'has a species understood that its story was renarrating life, and asked itself if it was telling the story well. The Anthropocene is an epoch of ethics because it is an epoch of domination by a moral species.'[1]

---

1 Willis Jenkins, *The Future of Ethics* (Washington , DC: Georgetown University Press, 2013), p. 2.

Perhaps the most difficult impediment posed by the realisation that humanity is creating its own ethical context – narrating its own story – is that within
some parts of Christianity this may necessitate a revised understanding of God's
ongoing relationship to the planet.[2] As I will argue over the course of this chapter,
the integration of ecological science with Christian ethics primarily serves to illustrate that ethics must move beyond analysing behaviour within the contexts we
find ourselves, and appreciate our role in *creating* ethical context as an additional
and crucial aspect of ethical deliberation.

Whether or not Christianity is uniquely culpable, it is certainly the case that
the dominant and exploitative hegemony of our present age most readily identifies
with the Christian tradition. As the technological historian Lynn White has argued,
it is not at all difficult to find appeals to texts and themes within the Christian tradition to justify deleterious treatment of the earth, suggesting that Christianity bears
'a huge burden of guilt'[3] for the ecological crisis. However, while understated in
his most famous article, White's emphasis is on the 'Western', European-cen-
tric interpretation of Christianity; he is speaking to the version of Christianity
best-known by his target audience. Acknowledging that this creates a degree of
ambiguity in what White simply refers to as 'Christianity', and that Christianity
is practised and interpreted in a variety of ways, inspires the inspection of what
it is to be truly 'Christian' as well as how the things we know about the world
shape that understanding. The heart of Christianity is found in the story of Jesus
Christ, who preached a simple, generous life ultimately defined by his choice to
willingly bear the guilt of others on a cross. Following in this example, though,
White's phrasing remains compelling – a burden of guilt *is* felt by the earth's
natural systems as well as the often tenuous existence of the world's majority
peoples, but *this* guilt is not their *own* guilt. The suffering they experience is due
to the activities of whoever takes part in the economic relationships which lead
to environmental degradation – making the dispersal of guilt both ambiguous
and ubiquitous, though it is certainly easy to identify many of the particularly
egregious examples.

But the ambiguity about causal responsibility – guilt – is less of an obstacle
than it may appear. In following Jesus, Christians need to be actively seeking the
relief of this burden for the sake of those who carry it, regardless of whether they

---

2 Thomas Berry, 'Christian Cosmology' (1984), in Mary Evelyn Tucker and John Grim, eds.,
The Christian Future and the Fate of Earth (New York: Orbis Books, 2009), pp. 26–27.
3 Lynn White, 'The Historical Roots of Our Ecologic Crisis', in *Science* 155.3767 (March
1967), p. 1206.

are its cause. It would be a huge mistake for Christians to simply shrug off White's assessment as a critique of flawed iterations of Christianity, for Christianity is not concerned merely with righteousness. It is an outward-facing orientation which brings life and nourishment to the afflicted: Christians should be compelled to care for the world's suffering even if there is no causal connection between the life of a given Christian and the suffering of someone else[4] (even though there certainly are connections between millions of Christians and millions of sufferers through the relationships of the civilisations and economic networks in which they respectively exist). This being the case, how much more acutely should the conscience of Christians be pricked when they admit causal relationships between their well-being and the misfortune of others! For Christians in the so-called 'developed world', accepting the historical and contemporary responsibility engendered through our lifestyles and inheritance clarifies the necessity of salvation for the rest of the world. Ecological science provides the framework for us to see how we tangibly affect the world, as well as the causes of effects we presently experience, and our emerging ability to assess causal relationships is the lens through which Christianity's mission and responsibilities must be observed.

Christianity, *properly understood*, does not justify a treatment of the earth which degrades its life-giving capacities and causes wanton suffering to its creatures. However, as mentioned, it is not difficult to trace the causes of the ecological crisis to professing Christians, and to behaviours which these Christians justify on the basis of their religious beliefs. For example, the Cornwall Alliance promotes a view that the world's poor will ultimately benefit from unregulated trade while also denying climate change.[5] Their rationale for these views is justified by their interpretations of scripture, but is inconsistent with the reality that unregulated global commerce has often resulted in the abuse of the weak, and that unregulated fossil fuel use is in fact warming the earth's atmosphere, resulting in rising seas and severe weather which are, again, most devastating to the poor. Such organisations exemplify the sort of thinking which leads to environmental degradation in the name of a Christianity which prioritises industrial and commercial ideals over truth. As Thomas Berry put it: 'The present disruption of all the basic life systems of Earth has come about within a culture that emerged from a biblical-Christian

---

4 Just consider the well-known parable of the Good Samaritan (Luke 10:25–37), in which a Samaritan helps a stranger (implied to be a Jew), but not because the Samaritan had anything to do with the stranger's misfortune; Jesus gives this example to illustrate the character of divine love as not following along lines of formal obligation, but an orientation toward care which manifests in the face of need.
5 See: www.cornwallalliance.org.

matrix.'[6] Christianity must ensure, then, that it does not contain claims which are properly the domain of ecological science, and commit to a willingness to re-conceive of causal relationships and Christian obligations in light of new information from ecological science.[7] Rather than undermining Christianity, however, ecological science gives heightened clarity and perspective to the meaning of Christianity in the 'Anthropocene' age. Rather than compromising or diluting the narrative on which Christianity is established, science compliments it and challenges believers to live a more genuine faith.

One of the first to write extensively on the integration of Christianity with ecology, Berry viewed the arrival of ecological science as 'the greatest change in human thought and consciousness since the rise of the Neolithic Period'.[8] It is not only that ecological science has deepened our understanding of the earth's processes by several orders of magnitude, but it is also an understanding that is different in kind to the narrative understandings that preceded it. 'Thus it is not only a difficulty for Christians,' Berry writes, 'it is a difficulty for human consciousness throughout the Earth community.'[9] He likens our need to understand Christianity within an ecological framework to the way Christianity has been understood within other frameworks throughout history, such as Hellenism, Neo-Platonism, Aristotelianism, humanism, and so on.[10] The Christian story and its values can and have been understood and shaped through other frameworks and now must be understood through the framework of ecology. But there is a crucial distinction here: while reference to these other frameworks is useful to show that Christianity has been enriched and expanded through other traditions of thought, there is not the same *necessity* for Christianity to be conceived through Neo-Platonism or humanism that there is for Christianity to be understood within an ecological framework.

Neo-Platonist, humanist, etc., are categorically different identifications to 'ecologist'; to describe oneself as the former refers to a system of concepts through which one *interprets* reality, while the latter has to do with *descriptions*

---

6 Thomas Berry, 'The Christian Future and the Fate of the Earth' (1989), in Mary Evelyn Tucker, Mary and John Grim, eds., *The Christian Future and the Fate of Earth* (New York: Orbis Books, 2009), p. 35.
7 Jenkins, *The Future of Ethics*, pp. 79–80. In this passage, Jenkins discusses the challenge White's essay presents to Christian thinkers to concede to the field of ecology what is properly its domain and re-construct values and narratives accordingly.
8 Berry, 'Christian Cosmology', p. 27.
9 Ibid.
10 Berry, 'Christian Cosmology', pp. 26–27.

of reality. The former entities are not falsifiable, but science is – in fact, this is what makes science what it is.[11] Science is an ongoing process of verification. Much of religion cannot be verified; the resurrection of Jesus, for example, is something no one in the present can either confirm or deny.[12] Importantly, Christianity knows this – this is why believing the claims of the Gospel narrative constitutes faith. Faith must be understood within a context of what we are able to verify, and we must be careful that faith does not make claims which are open to verification or disproof by scientific methods. With the increasing sophistication of ecological science, Christians no longer have the option of believing that their activities in one part of the world have no bearing on other parts of the world, even if this belief stems from conceptions of the world which arguably emerge from the 'biblical-Christian matrix'. Insofar as Christians deny the findings of ecological science, claims about the physical world that have been methodologically and mutually verified, we find parts of the tradition which must be modified or corrected.

So, Berry calls for a 'New Story',[13] a re-examination of Christianity within the framework of humanity's burgeoning ecological awakening. 'What is needed now', he writes, 'is not exactly a new religion but new religious sensitivities in relation to planet Earth that would arise in all our religious traditions.'[14] While faith is something personal and often ineffable, making it impossible to effectively adjudicate between the validity of different and potentially contradictory religious belief systems, the verifiability of ecological science means that the information it produces can both be shared between all religious faiths, and that, accordingly, it provides a framework within which all religious traditions can be imagined – even if those traditions posit past events, metaphysical realities, or eschatological outcomes which are not reproducible or verifiable. Berry refers

---

11 Karl Popper, 'Science as Falsification', in *Conjectures and Refutations* (London: Routledge and Keegan Paul, 1963), pp. 33–39. Popper argues that the defining characteristic of science is verification.

12 Though we would be remiss not to note, in this context, the significance of 1 Corinthians 15:26, which claims the resurrected Jesus appeared to '500 witnesses'. This is, effectively, the same method by which scientific postulates are confirmed; multiple persons observe the same thing and corroborate their results. Of course, we who live roughly 2000 years after these purported events are not able to confirm Jesus's resurrection for ourselves. Is relying on a community tradition established on the basis of hundreds of witnesses so different than relying on the reports of scientists regarding processes we cannot and likely will not ever understand ourselves? Both cases are similar in that they rely on the *reports of others* who claim verification.

13 Berry, 'Christian Cosmology', pp. 26–27.

14 Berry, 'The Christian Future and the Fate of the Earth', p. 45.

to the framework of ecological science as 'a new referent in terms of our moral activity'.[15]

When a Christian believes that their moral prerogative is to love their neighbour, for example, we must try to understand that prerogative in ecological terms. That is, when we wonder what it looks like to love a neighbour, we are asking a question about the physical world. Morality entails activity, and activity and process are precisely what ecological science describes. If ecological assessment of our activities reveal that we are not loving our neighbour, sincere Christians will modify their actions – ecological science can verify this in the terms first established by the religious tradition! If Christians think that to love is to care about the well-being of others, and they find that their actions are in fact causing harm, in order to act lovingly they must modify their actions according to the information they have received. At the very least, they are not permitted to callously deny harm.[16]

As Berry notes, the ecological movement exists in its own right;[17] it is certainly not necessary for someone to be Christian in order to care about the earth. Every living person has a vested interest in the well-being of the planet, and insofar as Western Christianity has historically included groups of people who see the claims of science as a threat to their faith, we understand why some Christians would be late to the conversation. But the dialogue between Christianity and ecology continues, and drawing boundaries around the kinds of claims each framework can make preserves the validity of faith and science on their own terms, even protecting them from each other. Once Christians understand that science cannot disprove the resurrection or an afterlife because those beliefs are not falsifiable, Christians are *forced* to take science seriously because it defines their moral relationships here on Earth – the very things which are of such interest *because* of the non-scientific, *faithful* beliefs Christians may hold regarding resurrection, afterlife, and the meaning of their existence as defined through the Christian narrative and the prerogatives it entails.

People claim to be 'Christian' from both ends of political, economic, and social spectrums; it has clothed and justified patriarchy and oppressive states as well as revolutionary egalitarian communities.[18] So rather than an anthropological

---

15 Berry, 'Christian Cosmology', p. 31.

16 This point alludes to discussion about predation and consumption of which the limited scope of this chapter does not permit a full treatment.

17 Berry, 'The Christian Future and the Fate of the Earth', p. 37.

18 Rosemary Radford Reuther, 'Ecofeminism: A Challenge to Theology', in Dieter T Hessel and Rosemary Radford Reuther, *Christianity and Ecology* (Cambridge, MA: Harvard

definition, we need a theological one. The priest and professor Oliver O'Donovan provides a helpfully simple and widely-agreed upon starting point: 'Christian ethics must arise from the gospel of Jesus Christ. Otherwise it could not be *Christian* ethics.'[19] Christianity must be defined in the terms of its origin as a religious tradition: in terms of its narrative. The Christian tradition has historically turned on the belief that what verifies Jesus's divinity is his resurrection, so Christian ethics proceed by the implication of the resurrection;[20] the nature of God was confirmed in the person of Jesus Christ. So how does the resurrection apply to ecology? Berry, curiously, hardly mentions it in his proposal for a 'New Story'. When he does allude to it, he seems more concerned that belief in an afterlife could cause Christians to neglect their responsibilities here and now on Earth. 'We long to pass over the river Jordan to that other world,' he writes, 'that we truly belong to this world is difficult for us.'[21] But ecological conscience needn't require leaving such beliefs behind. It actually makes them more meaningful: if belonging to the divine world is demonstrated through the expression of a Christ-like nature within the terrestrial one, it is necessary to be aware of the terrestrial conditions and relationships which provide the parameters for the expression of true divine character.

The reflections of Stanley Hauerwas echo O'Donovan in his suggestion that Christianity ought to be understood as the community which together believes that the nature of God is revealed in Jesus Christ.[22] This means that belief in the resurrection amounts to the belief that the divinity of the man Jesus was confirmed and his moral teachings validated; it means that the teachings of Jesus as contained

---

University Press, 2000), pp. 97–112. Reuther discusses the ways in which patriarchal societies adopted Christian language, concepts, and narratives while maintaining oppressive hierarchical social structures, and how this came to be seen as representative of 'Christianity', even though many of the first Christian communities were inspired to seek egalitarianism and radically different social structures according to their own interpretation of the Christian narrative. In other words, we cannot count on something being *called* 'Christian' to be representative of the changes Christianity might inspire; it may simply be more common to find that societies throughout history began calling themselves 'Christian' as though a conversion had taken place, without actually undergoing any substantial changes.

19 O O'Donovan, 'The Gospel and Christian Ethics', in *Resurrection and Moral Order* (Grand Rapids: William B. Eerdmans Publishing Company, 1994), p. 11.

20 O'Donovan, 'The Gospel and Christian Ethics', p. 13.

21 Berry, 'The Christian Future and the Fate of the Earth', p. 45.

22 Stanley Hauerwas, 'On Keeping Theological Ethics Theological', in John Berkeman and Michael Cartwright, eds., *The Hauerwas Reader* (Durham, NC: Duke University Press, 2001), p. 72.

in the gospels ought to give Christians their moral priorities. This is important because it sets the Christian Church apart from the rest of the world – not as though Christians must believe that they alone have access to morality,[23] but that in Jesus God's desires for humans are expressed. And the themes which rise most often and clearly from the gospel narrative are selflessness, humility, forgiveness, and identification and commiseration with the poor and the oppressed.

John Cobb, Jr writes that so long as Western Christians thought that their own affluence was part of the general advancement of humanity, it was possible to evade Jesus's teachings about limiting one's possessions and seeking to serve the poor. But now, with our increasing awareness that Western affluence is sustained at the expense of the global poor, the teachings of Jesus force a very difficult self-reflection for Western Christians: 'In a world divided between oppressor and oppressed, rich and poor, the Christian cannot remain identified with the oppressor and the rich.'[24] To do so is harshly inconsistent with the divine character Christians believe is revealed in Jesus Christ. In industrialised nations, per-person emission rates of carbon dioxide can be 60 to 100 times the per-person rates found across the poorest parts of Africa, Asia, and Latin America.[25] Furthermore, much of their prime agricultural land is exploited by European and North American corporations to grow food, even 'organic' food, which is exported by plane to Western supermarkets while local inhabitants experience extreme poverty.[26] Thus, Michael Northcott writes, 'The strongest moral case for mitigating global warming is that it is already life-threatening to those who are least able to defend themselves, and have no responsibility in its causation.'[27]

While this moral claim does not depend on Christianity for its justification, Christianity can see itself as having a unique and potentially *missional* role to play in the resolution of these problems.[28] If Christians believe that in Jesus the nature of God is revealed and understand the Church as the community testifying to this belief, the Church must be a locus of response and action to the systematic injustices that ecological science reveals and confirms. In its responsibility to the poor and in its love for the creation God also loves, the burden Christianity bears in righting those wrongs *is* one of guilt – and while it is certainly Christ-like to bear the guilt of others, Christians must also be willing to accept and repent of

---

23 Berry, 'The Christian Future and the Fate of the Earth', p. 38.
24 Cobb, 'Christian Existence in a World of Limits', p. 183.
25 Michael Northcott, *Moral Climate* (New York: Orbis Books, 2007), p. 49.
26 Ibid.
27 Northcott, *Moral Climate*, pp. 55–56.
28 Jenkins, *The Future of Ethics*, p. 72.

their own in keeping with the preaching of Jesus.[29] The poor bear the guilt of others all the time, whether they choose to or not. This recognition, especially as the result of the findings of ecological science, is a necessary condition to the development of a genuine Christianity in much of the West and other especially affluent parts of the world. It is not enough that it is Christ-like to bear the guilt of others – Christians cannot be said to live a genuine faith so long as they refuse to recognise and repent of the guilt others bear on their behalf.

Examples of ecological responsibility, bearing the guilt of others, and efforts to coordinate community responsibilities such as shared infrastructure are all available to affluent, Western Christians. At the most basic, this means picking up after oneself and trying to avoid single-use items, but to bear others' guilt means picking up after others and anticipating needs to avoid waste. On a slightly larger scale, this may mean transitioning away from the use of personal motor vehicles where possible, and buying as locally as possible to reduce packaging waste and unnecessary fuel expenditures – in addition to learning about where products originate and whether their exportation relies on exploitation. When flying or other fuel-dependent transport is unavoidable, there are carbon-offsetting schemes such as myclimate.org[30] where individuals may volunteer a payment which then goes to carbon-offset projects around the world. Organisations such as A Rocha[31] and the John Ray Initiative[32] promote science education amongst Christians and incentivise the development of strategies for Church communities to live with a greater sense of responsibility as well as practical sustainability and minimal waste. While such initiatives as the above remain somewhat marginal in the grand scheme, their existence are examples of tangible response to the need for Christian ecological responsibility and attempts to shape Christian life in response to that recognition. At the very least they represent possibilities of future action in line with Christian belief for those Christians who find themselves unable to disentangle their sense of Christian responsibility and vocation from what they have learned about the world.

Hauerwas notes that 'through most of Christian history Christians have not thought it possible to distinguish so easily between what they believe and what they do.'[33] Christians must be willing to believe what has been systematically verified, and their response cannot be separated from the beliefs which define

---

29 Matthew 4:17.
30 See: https://www.myclimate.org/.
31 See: http://www.arocha.org/en.
32 See: https://www.jri.org.uk/.
33 Haerwas, 'Christian Ethics', pp. 47–48.

Christianity as such; information provided by ecological science must not be partitioned away from ethical consideration because alternative ideas about how the world works have been erroneously attributed to scripture. When we look at the global poor from the perspective of Christianity, we find that, in the words of Jon Sobrino, 'the poor are bearers of truth... a crucified people is like an inverted mirror in which the First World, on seeing itself disfigured, comes to know itself in its truth.'[34] The global poor are in the image of Christ, and denying the role of global consumerism in suffering throughout the world is to turn away from the global poor in the same manner as those who in their self-interest crucified God rather than confront their sin.

For the poor and oppressed, Christianity is a religion of hope, a promise of justice and restoration in a world which appears, 'objectively, hopeless'.[35] For those in the developed world who are not suffering from injustice but are more often its comfortable beneficiaries, we do not need to re-imagine Christianity; we urgently need to see how we fit into the existing narrative. We need to look to ecology and its illumination of the extended and often unintentional consequences of our habits and choices so as not to be the oppressor from whom salvation is required. 'We need a prophetic vision of a world,' Cobb writes, 'into which God might transform ours through transforming us.'[36] I would not say that we need an entirely 'new story'. Ecology is a new way of talking about the earth and its history, but while it is new it also harmonises and connects with the stories we already inhabit. And so within the context of these old stories, ecological science can tell us who we are; it reveals to us the roles we are playing, the character we express. Will we respond to the face of Christ in the suffering of the world, or will we turn our backs? But even if not a 'new story', the introduction of an ecological framework to ethical thought should certainly mark the beginning of a new chapter in the Christian narrative. And indeed, as Willis Jenkins so provocatively suggests, we must recognise that it is a chapter which we are writing ourselves.

34 Jon Sobrino, *No Salvation Outside the Poor: Prophetic-Utopian Essays* (New York: Orbis Books, 2008), p. 60.
35 Cobb, 'Christian Existence in a World of Limits', p. 176.
36 Cobb, 'Christian Existence in a World of Limits', p. 185.

Bibliography

Berry, Thomas, 'Christian Cosmology' (1984), in Mary Evelyn Tucker and John Grim, eds., *The Christian Future and the Fate of Earth* (New York: Orbis Books, 2009).

Berry, Thomas, 'The Christian Future and the Fate of the Earth' (1989), in Mary Evelyn Tucker and John Grim, eds., *The Christian Future and the Fate of Earth* (New York: Orbis Books, 2009).

Cobb, Jr, John B, 'Christian Existence in a World of Limits', in *Religion and Environmental Crisis* (Athens, GA: University of Georgia Press, 1986).

Grim, John, and Evelyn Tucker, Mary, *Ecology and Religion* (Washington: Island Press, 2014).

Hauerwas, Stanley, 'Christian Ethics', in John Berkeman and Michael Cartwright, eds., *The Hauerwas Reader* (Durham, NC: Duke University Press, 2001).

Hauerwas, Stanley, 'On Keeping Theological Ethics Theological', in John Berkeman and Michael Cartwright, eds., *The Hauerwas Reader* (Durham, NC: Duke University Press, 2001).

Jenkins, Willis, *The Future of Ethics* (Washington , DC: Georgetown University Press, 2013).

Northcott, Michael, *Moral Climate* (New York: Orbis Books, 2007).

O'Donovan, O, 'The Gospel and Christian Ethics', in *Resurrection and Moral Order* (Grand Rapids: William B. Eerdmans Publishing Company, 1994).

Popper, Karl, 'Science as Falsification', in *Conjectures and Refutations* (London: Routledge and Keegan Paul, 1963).

Radford Reuther, Rosemary, 'Ecofeminism: A Challenge to Theology', in Dieter T Hessel and Rosemary Radford Reuther, *Christianity and Ecology* (Cambridge, MA: Harvard University Press, 2000).

Sobrino, Jon, *No Salvation Outside the Poor: Prophetic-Utopian Essays* (New York: Orbis Books, 2008).

White, Lynn, 'The Historical Roots of Our Ecologic Crisis', in *Science* 155.3767 (March 1967), pp. 1203–1207.

15

Gurmat – The Art of Spiritual Wisdom: How Peace *from* Mind through Knowledge of the Soul can Help Overcoming the Challenges of Humankind

Khushwant Singh

'I'm gonna make a change, for once in my life
It's gonna feel real good, gonna make a difference
Gonna make it right…
I'm starting with the man in the mirror
I'm asking him to change his ways
And no message could have been any clearer
If you wanna make the world a better place…'

– 'Man in the Mirror', 1987[1]

Eighty percent of people say they belong to a religion – and as religion inspires all followers to do good – why isn't our world a better place? The natural beauty of Mother Earth already makes it a wonderful place by itself. Yet, once humans are added to the equation, we see that all of the virtues that religions claim to encourage – humility, justice, solidarity, farsightedness, and a loving relationship with

---

1 Lyrics to a song by Michael Jackson, written by Glen Ballard and Siedah Garrett.

our fellow beings and nature – are not prevailing on Earth. How can we then speak of ourselves as developed beings, let alone good?

What peaceful visitors from another galaxy would observe

Evolution has always been an integral part of life. And since the onset of industrialisation, the Earth has especially been undergoing decisive changes. There is little doubt that an observer from another galaxy would acknowledge the cultural, medical, infrastructural and technological achievements of our world. But, by comparing the present condition of the planet with its magnificence before human beings began 'cultivating' it, the witness would point out that we have paid a high price. We are the only species on Earth that is capable of destroying the whole planet – either quickly with atomic warfare or slowly through the destruction of the environment. We are the only species that restricts its fellow's rights. We are the only species that limits access to basic needs like food, water (and health services) by a system of remuneration. And, we are the only species that causes suffering through undignified treatment, prejudices, deceit, discrimination on the grounds of origin or so-called religion, the denial of free speech, psychological torture and even violence and abuse.

There are many other critical examples an outside observer could point to. We consume resources faster than our planet can renew them. The wonder of biodiversity is fading away on both land and under water. More and more toxic substances enter into the biological cycle every second. And, to satisfy our desire for cheap food products, deforestation, livestock farming and the use of genetically modified foods and hormones have become normal.

Approximately two billion people live in conditions of fragility and conflict. Violence causes more than one million deaths every year. Human rights violations are prevalent in all parts of the world. More than 50 percent of the world's population live on less than a few Euros per day. The richest 20 percent of the world's population consume 80 percent of all resources. The wealthiest one percent owns more than the rest of all other people put together. Nonetheless, most nations continue with interest-led policies in the same way as rich business people, shareholders and multinational corporations carry on to maximise their profits without having much ethical concerns for society and the environment. Using loopholes for 'legal' tax breaks is a widely acknowledged practice even after major financial crises. At the same time, more and more people see no other option than to leave their homes and immigrate due to poverty and violence. Conspicuous is that refugees and displaced people mainly find shelter in poor neighbouring regions, and not in countries whose riches are clearly tied to colonial pasts and the on-going practice of exploiting natural resources in so-called developing countries.

Side effects: a spoiled seed never produces a beautiful flower

Why has a spoiled seed never produced a beautiful flower? Because it is against the laws of nature.[2] Similarly, the supposedly developed lifestyle of material affluence and recklessness has created neither more justice nor peace *from* mind. The number of people suffering from loneliness, depression, insecurities, performance pressure, obesity, chronic maladies, and diseases like cancer is increasing. Excessive consumption of meat, unhealthy industrial processed foods, alcohol and cigarettes, as well as using hormones is widely socially accepted. More and more people are permanently stressed. It has even become a signifier for being 'successful'. Closely linked is the rise of a 'throw-away' and 'the grass is always greener' mentality as the growing number of affairs and divorces illustrates.[3]

Aftereffects of the Internet

A new factor that is decisively changing our lives is the Internet. Its achievements are outstanding. At the same time, it reinforces disorientation and hyper-individualisation. It has created space for superficial exchange and self-expression. The dissemination of shallow information and fake news, inhumane and denunciatory content – often well protected behind the walls of anonymity – contribute to the decline of a quality-oriented and respectful discussion culture, and in the worst case lead to hatred and violence. The free access to pornography creates additional problems. Another challenge is that women feel a growing pressure to conform to the beauty ideals of models who edit not only their pictures, but also their bodies surgically and put themselves on display on the web.

It has also become more difficult to consciously be present in the now, and to have a meaningful and uninterrupted conversation because we let ourselves be

---

2 All insights in this essay are derived from *Gurbani*, the key scriptures of the Sikh Religion. AGGS refers to the (*Adi*) *Guru Granth Sahib*. The number indicates the page in the standard edition, then the name of the writer follows, e.g. Kabir. M. 1/2 etc. refers to the specific author among the ten enlightened ones. DG refers to the writings of Gur Gobind Singh in the *Dasam Granth*, which is of special importance for baptised Sikhs. The number indicates the page in the standard edition. Original key terms from *Gurbani* are added in italics in parenthesis.
3 ਬੂਝਿ ਵਿਸਰਜੀ ਗਈ ਸਿਆਣਪ ਕਰਿ ਅਵਗਣ ਪਛੁਤਾਇ ॥ AGGS: 76, M. 1; ਜੈਸਾ ਬੀਜੇ ਸੋ ਲੁਣੈ ਜੇਹਾ ਪੁਰਬਿ ਕਿਨੈ ਬੋਇਆ ॥ AGGS: 309, M. 4.

permanently distracted by mobile devices. We are continuously craving for the next visual, sensory and emotional highlight.

We cannot solve a problem on the same level where it arose

Despite the well-known fact that prevention is better than cure, human history shows that we are prone to repeat our mistakes.[4] Yet, the ostensible side-effects of the current 'Western' lifestyle have not discouraged 'developing' countries from striving for a similar consumption-oriented lifestyle. As the ecological footprint of developing counties expand, we are faced with a dire reality: if the world's seven billion people all live according to current 'Western standards', we will need five earths for sufficient resources.

Political, social and religious debates about why a large proportion of people still face existential challenges, although sufficient wealth is available, remain side issues. Although there are well-functioning technologies in the field of renewable energies, nuclear and fossil forms of energy production are still dominant energy suppliers.

It is a source of hope that slowly more people are becoming aware of the challenges illustrated. It is encouraging that efficiency and economic growth are being questioned as the only solutions to the world's problems. Politicians are being asked more and more to move from a predominantly interest-oriented governance culture to a value-oriented model. Incoherence in politics is also being steadily exposed, for example, when governments criticise human rights valuations while exporting weapons to countries that oppress minorities. It is also laudable that climate summits are held, and that nearly all countries have agreed to achieve the UN Sustainable Development Goals (SDGs) of the 2030 Agenda. But as long as there are no legally binding sanctions for those who fail to achieve these goals, it remains a well-intentioned exercise. Furthermore, it is problematic that the current values and systemic assumptions – foremost the growth paradigm along with measuring development purely based on the gross national product (GNP) – are not scrutinised. From the viewpoint of *Gurmat*, timeless spiritual wisdom that is at the heart of the Sikh Religion, it is not possible to solve problems on the same level they arose from.[5] Einstein also reminded us of this. It is a psychological fact that

---

4 ਕਬੀਰ ਮਨੁ ਜਾਨੈ ਸਭ ਬਾਤ ਜਾਨਤ ਹੀ ਅਉਗਨੁ ਕਰੈ ॥ AGGS: 1376, Kabir; ਪਾਪੁ ਬੁਰਾ ਪਾਪੀ ਕਉ ਪਿਆਰਾ ॥ AGGS: 935, M. 1.
5 ਝੂਠਾ ਉਰਝਿ ਸੁਰਝਿ ਨਹੀ ਜਾਨਾ ॥ AGGS: 341, Kabir.

we need to change the context if we want to change our behaviour. A drug addict is unlikely to overcome addiction while living with other addicts.

The power of spirituality touches our heart

Gurmat helps us understand that neither technological, economic nor political solutions alone can provide the answers we need today; all shortcomings in the world are expressions of an inner blemish. Consequently, we have to understand the root causes of our difficulties. To be able to do this, the wisdom of spirituality is needed. It not only explains the origins of our problems but also has the power to inspire behavioural change. Knowledge and statistics rarely make us change our attitude. However, spiritual wisdom, brought to life by truthful devotees, does. These devotees touch our heart, acting without professional, monetary or interest-led motivation. They act without missionary, communal or nationalistic zeal. They are not stung by narcissism and do not crave fame. They inspire us through their humble wisdom. They do what they say. Their impressive insights follow extraordinary selfless deeds. They have the courage to stand against commonly held beliefs, even if they are marginalised and have to give up their physical life. Even today, the heroic sacrifices of figureheads of *Gurmat*, like Gur Arjan, Gur Tegh Bahadar, Gur Gobind Singh and his four sons, are remembered not just by Sikhs. These devotees took a firm stand against injustice, fanatic rulers, religious intolerance, the oppression of minorities, and the caste system.[6]

To understand how *Gurmat* can help us overcome the challenges we are facing, let us explore its basics.

Basics of *Gurmat*

Sikhi – also known as Sikhism – is based on timeless spiritual wisdom revealed to three-dozen enlightened ones who originated from different cultural and social backgrounds. It developed into a unique religion between the 14th and 16th century in Panjab on the Indian subcontinent. Today, around 25 million people regard themselves as Sikhs, students of truth. Sikh men are traditionally recognisable by their uncut hair and beard along with a turban that express a humble and natural way of life. Sikhs who take on the responsibility to become role models

---

6 ਨਾਨਕ ਦੁਨੀਆ ਕੀਆਂ ਵਡਿਆਈਆਂ ਅਗੀ ਸੇਤੀ ਜਾਲਿ ॥ AGGS: 1290, Kabir; ਜਉ ਤਉ ਪ੍ਰੇਮ ਖੇਲਣ ਕਾ ਚਾਉ ॥ ਸਿਰੁ ਧਰਿ ਤਲੀ ਗਲੀ ਮੇਰੀ ਆਉ ॥ AGGS: 1412, M.1; ਤੇਰੋ ਜਨੁ ਹੋਇ ਸੋਇ ਕਤ ਡੋਲੈ ਤੀਨਿ ਭਵਨ ਪਰ ਛਾਜਾ ॥ AGGS: 856, Kabir; ਜਾਣਹੁ ਜੋਤਿ ਨ ਪੂਛਹੁ ਜਾਤੀ ਆਗੈ ਜਾਤਿ ਨ ਹੇ ॥ AGGS: 349, M. 1.

join the order of *khalsa* (pure ones who know the art of love) through baptism *(khande di pahul)* and wear five religious articles, known as *kakar*.[7] The common spiritual descent is symbolised by collective family names. Women use the name Kaur (prince) and men Singh (lion). The majority of Sikhs live in the Indian state of Panjab, in Delhi, the United Kingdom, North America and Australia.

The original insights of the enlightened ones, who regarded themselves as humble devotees (*das, jan, garib*) and messengers of the One (*bolae bole*) are called *Gurmat* or *Sikh Mat*.[8] These insights were preserved based on the specially developed script-language, *Gurmukhi*, in written form (*pothi*), to enable seekers of truth access to the revealed wisdom. Gur Nanak, born in 1469, the first in the line of ten enlightened ones, initiated the compilation process. The writings, called *Gurbani*, are comprised of exceptionally beautiful poetry and melodies, and unite a multitude of languages and metaphors, and cannot be understood or translated literally.[9] The discoveries of enlightened ones like Bhagat Kabir, Ravidas and Shekh Farid were consciously included. This was to highlight that the revelation of truth is bound neither to a specific time, religious background, social class or a person, nor is a spiritual role-model elected, but selected.[10] Gur Gobind Singh, the last in the line of the ten enlightened ones, completed the key anthology for Sikhs, which is today known as *Guru Granth Sahib*.

Gurmat, the insights of *Gurbani*, inspires us to acknowledge our common spiritual origin and trust in the wisdom of the name- and formless One. It focuses on the unifying impact of spirituality in everyday life, and encourages an ethical attitude that strengthens our individual as well as communal well-being, whilst respecting cultural diversity. *Gurmat* values lifelong spiritual development, and a life marked by truthfulness, modesty and far-sightedness. Ultimately, *Gurmat* offers wisdom to those who want to move beyond beliefs and intellectuality and understand the deeper purpose of life. It explains holistically the nature of the soul and Oneness (*ik oankar*) of all existence, and how we can live in tune with the Divine Will (*hukam*), which is a prerequisite to achieving full enlightenment.[11]

7 ਕਹੁ ਕਬੀਰ ਜਨ ਭਏ ਖਾਲਸੇ ਪ੍ਰੇਮ ਭਗਤਿ ਜਿਹ ਜਾਨੀ ॥ AGGS: 655, Kabir.
8 ਬੋਲਾਇਆ ਬੋਲੀ ਖਸਮ ਦਾ ॥ AGGS: 74, M. 5; ਗੁਰਮਤਿ ਜਿਨੀ ਪਛਾਣਿਆ ਸੇ ਦੇਖਹਿ ਸਦਾ ਹਦੂਰਿ ॥ AGGS: 27, M. 3; ਸਿਖ ਮਤਿ ਸਭ ਬੁਧਿ ਤੁਮ੍ਹਾਰੀ ਮੰਦਿਰ ਛਾਵਾ ਤੇਰੇ ॥ AGGS: 795, M. 1.
9 ਗੁਰੁ ਕੁੰਜੀ ਪਾਹੂ ਨਿਵਲੁ ਮਨੁ ਕੋਠਾ ਤਨੁ ਛਤਿ ॥ AGGS: 1237, M. 5; ਪੋਥੀ ਪਰਮੇਸਰ ਕਾ ਥਾਨੁ ॥ AGGS: 1226, M. 5; ਗੁਰਬਾਣੀ ਹਰਿ ਅਲਖੁ ਲਖਾਇਆ ॥ AGGS: 336, M. 4.
10 ਹਰਿ ਜੁਗੁ ਜੁਗੁ ਭਗਤ ਉਪਾਇਆ ਪੈਜ ਰਖਦਾ ਆਇਆ ਰਾਮ ਰਾਜੇ ॥ AGGS: 451, M. 4.
11 ਮੰਦਾ ਮੂਲਿ ਨ ਕੀਚਈ ਦੇ ਲੰਮੀ ਨਦਰਿ ਨਿਹਾਲੀਐ ॥ AGGS: 474, M. 2.

Nad – the voice of the Divine Will

According to *Gurmat*, the One is an all-inherent, omnipotent yet forgiving director, who communicates through the voice (*nad, shabad, bani*) of the inner pure part of the soul (*antaratma*). The One acts as the creator, sustainer and innovator through its creation and creatures and embodies the purest form of wisdom, virtues, and responsibility.[12] Unconditionally, the One provides everything essential to sustain life and ensures cosmic order through universal laws and interdependent cycles. The One governs everything from the viewpoint of a higher Divine Will, which always has the long-term good of all in mind. In this sense, all things that happen are spiritually meaningful. In the course of evolution, all beings have the possibility of spiritual self-exploration and enlightenment. Accordingly, the enlightened ones never prayed for anything worldly, only for the gift of enlightenment.[13]

There is only one religion

The enlightened ones carefully analysed existing religious texts and traditions, and disclosed contradictions and hypocritical behaviour. They scrutinised ancient Vedic wisdom, and concluded that it had carried the essence of truth (*nam*) but had lost it through an increased focus on outward practices such as rituals, idol worship, and the capitalisation of religion through payments for prayers and other 'religious services'. They put forward critique not for missionary purposes, but to help seekers deconstruct old conditionings and un-reflected attitudes.[14] The pious ones highlighted that devotion to the truth is impossible as long as we are hungry for worldliness. They spoke in favour of recalling the heart of spirituality – which is love for humanity combined with transcendence.[15]

---

12 ਗੁਰਮੁਖਿ ਨਾਦੰ ਗੁਰਮੁਖਿ ਵੇਦੰ ਗੁਰਮੁਖਿ ਰਹਿਆ ਸਮਾਈ ॥ AGGS: 2, M. 1; ਬਾਣੀ ਪ੍ਰਭ ਕੀ ਸਭੁ ਕੋ ਬੋਲੈ ॥ AGGS: 294, M. 5; ਅੰਤਰ ਆਤਮੈ ਜੋ ਮਿਲੈ ਮਿਲਿਆ ਕਹੀਐ ਸੋਇ ॥ AGGS: 791, M. 5; ਇਕੁ ਸੰਸਾਰੀ ਇਕੁ ਭੰਡਾਰੀ ਇਕੁ ਲਾਏ ਦੀਬਾਣੁ ॥ AGGS: 7, M. 1.
13 ਸਾਹਿਬੁ ਮੇਰਾ ਏਕੋ ਹੈ ॥ AGGS: 350, M. 1; ਤੂ ਅਣਮੰਗਿਆ ਦਾਨੁ ਦੇਵਣਾ ਸਭਨਾਹ ਜੀਆ ॥ AGGS: 585, M. 3; ਨਾਨਕ ਚਿੰਤਾ ਮਤਿ ਕਰਹੁ ਚਿੰਤਾ ਤਿਸ ਹੀ ਹੋਇ ॥ AGGS: 955, M. 5; ਜਾਨ ਕੋ ਦੇਤ ਅਜਾਨ ਕੋ ਦੇਤ ਜਮੀਨ ਕੋ ਦੇਤ ਜਮਾਨ ਕੋ ਦੇ ਹੈ ॥ DG: 75; ਹੁਕਮੈ ਅੰਦਰਿ ਸਭੁ ਕੋ ਬਾਹਰਿ ਹੁਕਮ ਨ ਕੋਇ ॥ AGGS: 1, M. 1; ਸਤਿਗੁਰੁ ਸਭਨਾ ਦਾ ਭਲਾ ਮਨਾਇਦਾ ਤਿਸ ਦਾ ਬੁਰਾ ਕਿਉ ਹੋਇ ॥ AGGS: 302, M. 4; ਵਿਣੁ ਤੁਧੁ ਹੋਰੁ ਜਿ ਮੰਗਣਾ ਸਿਰਿ ਦੁਖਾ ਕੈ ਦੁਖ ॥ ਦੇਹਿ ਨਾਮੁ ਸੰਤੋਖੀਆ ਉਤਰੈ ਮਨ ਕੀ ਭੁਖ ॥ AGGS: 958, M. 5; ਅੰਮ੍ਰਿਤੁ ਹਰਿ ਕਾ ਨਾਮੁ ਹੈ ਵਰਸੈ ਕਿਰਪਾ ਧਾਰਿ ॥ AGGS: 1281, M. 3.
14 ਜਿਨ ਮਨਿ ਹੋਰੁ ਮੁਖਿ ਹੋਰੁ ਸਿ ਕਾਂਢੇ ਕਚਿਆ ॥ AGGS: 488, Shekh Farid; ਅਵਰ ਉਪਦੇਸੈ ਆਪਿ ਨ ਕਰੈ ॥ AGGS: 269, M. 5; ਵੇਦਾ ਮਹਿ ਨਾਮੁ ਉਤਮੁ ਸੋ ਸੁਣਹਿ ਨਾਹੀ ਫਿਰਹਿ ਜਿਉ ਬੇਤਾਲਿਆ ॥ AGGS: 919, M. 3; ਸਾਸਤ ਬੇਦ ਸਿਮ੍ਰਿਤਿ ਸਭਿ ਸੋਧੇ ਸਭ ਏਕਾ ਬਾਤ ਪੁਕਾਰੀ ॥ AGGS, M. 3, 919; ਪਤਿਆ ਅਣਪਤਿਆ ਪਰਮ ਗਤਿ ਪਾਵੈ ॥ AGGS: 197, M. 5.
15 ਭੁਖੇ ਭਗਤਿ ਨ ਕੀਜੈ ॥ ਯਹ ਮਾਲਾ ਅਪਨੀ ਲੀਜੈ ॥ AGGS: Kabir, 656; ਸਾਚੁ ਕਹੋਂ ਸੁਨ ਲੇਹੁ ਸਭੈ ਜਿਨ ਪ੍ਰੇਮ ਕੀਓ ਤਿਨ ਹੀ ਪ੍ਰਭ ਪਾਇਓ ॥ DG: 14.

The enlightened ones did not value self-perception and self-attributions, the outward 'religious' appearance or the (religious) title of a person per se, but instead the degree of applied spiritual wisdom in daily life. To illustrate this point, they state that it is difficult to be a true Muslim. For a Muslim respects the Divine Will, is gracious, pure-hearted, and is not afraid of physical death. Similar attributes are subscribed to a true Hadji and Yogi. In the metaphorical language of *Gurbani*, labels like Hadji and Yogi are used to describe a spiritual person. Truly spiritual people are not lobbyists but act beyond group-led interests. They never make a business out of religion and do not seek worldly power, especially not in the name of religion. Instead, they offer spiritual guidance to all those (in responsible positions) who strive to rule. *Gurbani* calls people who are masters of spirituality saints (*sant*), or even heroes (*sura*).[16] It is in this sense that *Gurmat* says that there is only the one religion of truthfulness (*sach dharam*).[17] Accordingly, the pious ones unanimously stated that they did not belong to any prevalent religion. They reached the realm of everlasting spiritual bliss neither through a confession to a faith, the observance of food regulations, dogmas, codes of conduct, nor through practices such as recitations, chanting of mantras, yoga and meditation, fasting or pilgrimages – but through spiritual self-exploration (*khoj*). The enlightened ones explained that they were able to dissociate from their body, mind, and emotions with the help of spiritual wisdom. They attribute their enlightened state, which they describe as beyond liberation (*mukti*), to the grace of the only one true and infallible wondrous 'Guru', the name- and formless Enlightener.[18]

Do not worship the messenger

The pious ones emphasised that only that is to be regarded as truth and divine

---

16 ਚਿਟੇ ਜਿਨ ਕੇ ਕਪੜੇ ਮੈਲੇ ਚਿਤ ਕਠੋਰ ਜੀਉ ॥ AGGS: 571, M. 1; ਭਾਵੈ ਲਾਂਬੇ ਕੇਸ ਕਰੁ ਭਾਵੈ ਘਰਰਿ ਮੁਡਾਇ ॥ AGGS: 1365, Kabir; ਮੁਸਲਮਾਨੁ ਕਹਾਵਣੁ ਮੁਸਕਲ ਜਾ ਹੋਇ ਤਾ ਮੁਸਲਮਾਨੁ ਕਹਾਵੈ ॥ AGGS: 141, M. 1; ਜੋ ਦਿਲੁ ਸੋਧੈ ਸੋਈ ਹਾਜੀ ॥ AGGS: 1081, M. 5; ਐਸਾ ਜੋਗੀ ਵਡਭਾਗੀ ਭੇਟੈ ਮਾਇਆ ਕੇ ਬੰਧਨ ਕਾਟੈ ॥ AGGS: 208, M. 5; ਪ੍ਰਿਗੁ ਤਿਨਾ ਕਾ ਜੀਵਿਆ ਜਿ ਲਿਖਿ ਲਿਖਿ ਵੇਚਹਿ ਨਾਉ ॥ AGGS: 1245, M. 1; ਜਿਸ ਕੈ ਅੰਤਰਿ ਰਾਜ ਅਭਿਮਾਨੁ ॥ ਸੋ ਨਰਕਪਾਤੀ ਹੋਵਤ ਸੁਆਨੁ ॥ AGGS: 279, M. 5; ਜਨ ਨਾਨਕ ਤਿਸੁ ਬਲਿਹਾਰਣੈ ਜੋ ਆਪਿ ਜਪੈ ਅਵਰਾ ਨਾਮੁ ਜਪਾਏ ॥ AGGS: 140, M. 4; ਜਿਨਾ ਸਾਸਿ ਗਿਰਾਸਿ ਨ ਵਿਸਰੈ ਹਰਿ ਨਾਮਾਂ ਮਨਿ ਮੰਤੁ ॥ ਧੰਨੁ ਸਿ ਸੇਈ ਨਾਨਕਾ ਪੂਰਨੁ ਸੋਈ ਸੰਤੁ ॥ AGGS: 319, M. 5; ਗੁਰ ਕਾ ਸਬਦੁ ਮਨੇ ਸੋ ਸੂਰਾ ॥ AGGS: 1023. M. 1.

17 ਬੋਲੀਐ ਸਚੁ ਧਰਮੁ ਝੂਠੁ ਨ ਬੋਲੀਐ ॥ AGGS: 488, Shekh Farid; ਸਰਬ ਧਰਮ ਮਹਿ ਸ੍ਰੇਸਟ ਧਰਮੁ ॥ ਹਰਿ ਕੋ ਨਾਮੁ ਜਪਿ ਨਿਰਮਲ ਕਰਮੁ ॥ AGGS: 266, M. 5.

18 ਨਾ ਹਮ ਹਿੰਦੂ ਨ ਮੁਸਲਮਾਨ ॥ AGGS: 1136, M. 5; ਜਪੁ ਤਪੁ ਸੰਜਮੁ ਧਰਮੁ ਨ ਕਮਾਇਆ ॥ AGGS: 12, M. 1; ਰਾਮ ਰਾਮ ਸਭੁ ਕੋ ਕਹੈ ਕਹਿਐ ਰਾਮੁ ਨ ਹੋਇ ॥ AGGS: 491, M. 3; ਵਰਤ ਨ ਰਹਉ ਨ ਮਹ ਰਮਦਾਨਾ ॥ AGGS: 1136, M. 5; ਮਾਸੁ ਮਾਸੁ ਕਰਿ ਮੂਰਖੁ ਝਗੜੇ ਗਿਆਨੁ ਧਿਆਨੁ ਨਹੀ ਜਾਣੈ ॥ AGGS: 156, M. 1; ਗੁਰ ਗਿਆਨੁ ਪਦਾਰਥੁ ਨਾਮੁ ਹੈ ਹਰਿ ਨਾਮੋ ਦੇਇ ਦਿੜਾਇ ॥ AGGS: 759, M. 4; ਰਾਜੁ ਨ ਚਾਹਉ ਮੁਕਤਿ ਨ ਚਾਹਉ ਮਨਿ ਪ੍ਰੀਤਿ ਚਰਨ ਕਮਲਾਰੇ ॥ AGGS: 534, M. 5; ਭੁਲਣ ਅੰਦਰਿ ਸਭੁ ਕੋ ਅਭੁਲੁ ਗੁਰੂ ਕਰਤਾਰੁ ॥ AGGS: 60, M.1.

which is effective and irrefutable in this life (*iha, lok*) and in the hereafter (*uha, parlok*). They pointed out that neither they nor their scriptures ought to be worshipped, since the messenger is just the finger that directs the thirsty to the source. They reminded devotees of their obligation to never confuse the creator with its creation, and the original source of wisdom with the messenger. Consequently, they inspired seekers not to regard *Gurbani* as merely an object of reading and singing, but to contemplate the deeper meaning of the insights (*bhuje bujanhar*), to internalise the wisdom and bring this wisdom to life by being a truthful and virtuous person.[19]

Dharam Juddh – let us start with the one in the mirror

Gurmat takes us on a voyage of understanding not only our personal destiny and the challenges we are facing, but the root cause for life itself. This journey begins with a conscious look in the mirror.[20] All forms of pollution, whether environmental, social or emotional, are the result of inner pollution. Pollution, equivalent to vices, is described as darkness. It is a lack of spiritual insight.[21] The first step to betterment is to pause, reflect, and accept the deficiencies. The second is to acknowledge that the good must always be dared. There is no day without night, no insight without ignorance. Good (*pun*) and evil (*pap*) are close to each other.[22] The key difference is that the good needs patience and devotion. It is the art of reaching the inner summit where the fire of egoism (*trishna*) is quenched by the coldness of wisdom (*hemkunt, hevai ghar*). Evil comes easily and takes only seconds to destroy. Hence, falling down is not an art.[23]

---

19 ਨਾਨਕ ਦਾਸੁ ਮੁਖ ਤੇ ਜੋ ਬੋਲੈ ਈਹਾ ਊਹਾ ਸਚੁ ਹੋਵੈ ॥ AGGS: 681, M. 5; ਸਚੁ ਪੁਰਾਣਾ ਹੋਵੈ ਨਾਹੀ ਸੀਤਾ ਕਦੇ ਨ ਪਾਟੈ ॥ AGGS: 956, M. 1; ਗੁਰਿ ਕਹਿਆ ਸਾ ਕਾਰ ਕਮਾਵਹੁ ॥ ਗੁਰ ਕੀ ਕਰਣੀ ਕਾਹੇ ਧਾਵਹੁ ॥ AGGS: 933, M. 1; ਏ ਅਖਰ ਖਿਰਿ ਜਾਹਿਗੇ ਓਇ ਅਖਰ ਇਨ ਮਹਿ ਨਾਹਿ ॥ Kabir: 340; ਲੋਗੁ ਜਾਨੈ ਇਹੁ ਗੀਤੁ ਹੈ ਇਹੁ ਤਉ ਬ੍ਰਹਮ ਬੀਚਾਰ ॥ AGGS: 335, Kabir; ਊਤਮ ਕਰਣੀ ਸਬਦ ਬੀਚਾਰ ॥ AGGS: 158, M.3; ਦਾਤਿ ਪਿਆਰੀ ਵਿਸਰਿਆ ਦਾਤਾਰਾ ॥ AGGS: 676, M. 5; ਬੂਝੈ ਬੂਝਨਹਾਰੁ ਬਿਬੇਕ ॥ AGGS: 285, M. 5; ਹਰਿ ਜਨ ਐਸਾ ਚਾਹੀਐ ਜੈਸਾ ਹਰਿ ਹੀ ਹੋਇ ॥ AGGS: 1372, Kabir.
20 ਆਪਨੜੇ ਗਿਰੀਵਾਨ ਮਹਿ ਸਿਰੁ ਨੀਵਾਂ ਕਰਿ ਦੇਖੁ ॥ AGGS: 1378, Shekh Farid; ਬੰਦੇ ਖੋਜੁ ਦਿਲ ਹਰ ਰੋਜ ਨਾ ਫਿਰੁ ਪਰੇਸਾਨੀ ਮਾਹਿ ॥ AGGS: 727, Kabir.
21 ਮਨਿ ਮੈਲੈ ਸਭੁ ਕਿਛੁ ਮੈਲਾ ਤਨਿ ਧੋਤੈ ਮਨੁ ਹਛਾ ਨ ਹੋਇ ॥ AGGS: 558, M. 3; ਫਰੀਦਾ ਜੇ ਤੂ ਅਕਲਿ ਲਤੀਫੁ ਕਾਲੇ ਲਿਖੁ ਨ ਲੇਖ ॥ AGGS: 1378, Shekh Farid.
22 The relationship between good and evil is discussed in many traditions, such as *Yang* and *Yin* in Daoism, or *Jetzer ha-Tov* and *Jetzer ha-Ra* in Judaism. See also *Voices from Religions on Sustainable Development*, published by the German Federal Ministry for Economic Cooperation and Development (BMZ), 2016.
23 ਕਾਇਆ ਅੰਦਰਿ ਪਾਪੁ ਪੁੰਨ ਦੁਇ ਭਾਈ ॥ ਦੁਹੀ ਮਿਲਿ ਕੈ ਸ੍ਰਿਸਟਿ ਉਪਾਈ ॥ AGGS: 26, M. 3; ਤ੍ਰਿਸਨਾ ਬੂਝੈ ਹਰਿ ਕੈ ਨਾਮਿ ॥ AGGS: 682, M. 5; ਗੁਰੁ ਦਾਤਾ ਗੁਰੁ ਹਿਵੈ ਘਰੁ ਗੁਰੁ ਦੀਪਕੁ ਤਿਹ ਲੋਇ ॥ AGGS: 137, M. 1.

The enlightened ones are living examples of masters of the spiritual martial arts, called *dharam juddh*. *Dharam* encompasses all aspects of a spiritual and responsible life: being honest and doing good by knowing the difference between right (*khara*) and wrong (*khota*), and being watchful of temptations. The weapon is the sword of wisdom (*gian khaddag*). Like a scalpel, it removes the evil and preserves the necessary. But *dharam* also stands selflessly for the truth in society. Since this requires courage and sacrifices for the wellbeing of all people without expecting any reward, it is called spiritual war, *dharam juddh*.[24]

The primeval sin of conceit

The starting point of life as we know it lies in a spiritual deception (*bharam*) and not – as often asserted – in former sinful actions (*karam*). No sins could have been committed by the very first beings. We have to go back even further.[25]

The realm of truthfulness (*sach khand, par brahm*), harbours all enlightened souls. Together they form the ocean of eternal bliss (*sukh sagar*). This metaphor indicates what is explicitly described in *Gurbani* in different places: The One is a unity (*ek*), yet formed by many (*anek*). This unanimous choir of all enlightened souls governs the universe through its Divine Will.[26] As long as creation did not exist, the One was dormant (*sun samadhi*), and no Will had to be exercised. Then, at a time that can never exactly be determined, existence came into being and the Divine Will was necessary to direct the fate of time (*ekankar*). This phenomenon of falling asleep along with a contraction of all existence, and awaking along with expansion, repeats itself time and time again.[27]

Some souls, or drops of the ocean of bliss – to continue with the metaphor – succumb to the conceit that they have more than enough wisdom to independently guide the destinies of the cosmos. As a consequence, they are released from the

---

24 ਹਕੁ ਹਲਾਲੁ ਬਖੋਰਹੁ ਖਾਣਾ ॥ AGGS: 1084, M. 5; ਗੁਰਮੁਖਿ ਖੋਟੇ ਖਰੇ ਪਛਾਣੁ ॥ AGGS: 942, M. 1; ਇਹੁ ਸਰੀਰੁ ਸਭੁ ਧਰਮੁ ਹੈ ਜਿਸੁ ਅੰਦਰਿ ਸਚੇ ਕੀ ਵਿਚਿ ਜੋਤਿ ॥ AGGS: 309, M. 4; ਗਿਆਨ ਖੜਗ ਪੰਚ ਦੂਤ ਸੰਘਾਰੇ ਗੁਰਮਤਿ ਜਾਗੈ ਸੋਇ ॥ AGGS: 1414, M. 3; ਕਬੀਰ ਸੇਵਾ ਕਉ ਦੁਇ ਭਲੇ ਏਕੁ ਸੰਤੁ ਇਕੁ ਰਾਮੁ ॥ AGGS: 1373, Kabir; ਸੂਰਾ ਸੋ ਪਹਿਚਾਨੀਐ ਜੁ ਲਰੈ ਦੀਨ ਕੇ ਹੇਤ ॥ AGGS: 1105, Kabir; ਅਵਰ ਬਾਸਨਾ ਨਾਹਿ ਪ੍ਰਭ ਧਰਮ ਜੁੱਧ ਕੇ ਚਾਇ ॥ DG: 1133.

25 ਜਬ ਕਛੁ ਨ ਸੀਓ ਤਬ ਕਿਆ ਕਰਤਾ ਕਵਨ ਕਰਮ ਕਰਿ ਆਇਆ ॥ AGGS: 748, M. 5.

26 ਸਚ ਖੰਡਿ ਵਸੈ ਨਿਰੰਕਾਰੁ ॥ AGGS: 8, M. 1; ਤੈਸੇ ਬਿਸ੍ਵ ਰੂਪ ਤੇ ਅਭੂਤ ਭੂਤ ਪ੍ਰਗਾਟ ਹੋਇ ਤਾਹੀ ਤੇ ਉਪਜਿ ਸਬੈ ਤਾਹੀ ਮੈ ਸਮਾਹਾਂਗੇ ॥ ਅਨੇਕ ਹੈ ਫਿਰਿ ਇਕੁ ਹੈ ॥ DG: 8; ਸਾਗਰ ਮਹਿ ਬੂੰਦ ਬੂੰਦ ਮਹਿ ਸਾਗਰੁ ਕਵਣੁ ਬੁਝੈ ਬਿਧਿ ਜਾਣੈ ॥ AGGS: 878, M. 1.

27 ਸੁੰਨ ਸਮਾਧਿ ਅਨਹਤ ਤਹ ਨਾਦ ॥ AGGS: 292 M. 5; ਕਈ ਬਾਰ ਪਸਰਿਓ ਪਾਸਾਰ ॥ ਸਦਾ ਸਦਾ ਇਕੁ ਏਕੰਕਾਰ ॥ AGGS: 276, M. 5; ਸਾਚੇ ਤੇ ਪਵਨਾ ਭਇਆ ਪਵਨੈ ਤੇ ਜਲੁ ਹੋਇ ॥ AGGS: 19, M. 1.

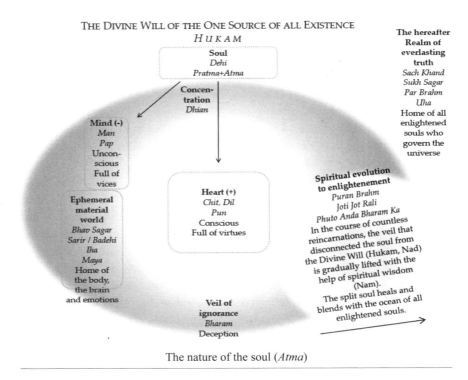

THE DIVINE WILL OF THE ONE SOURCE OF ALL EXISTENCE

HUKAM

Soul
Dehi
Pratma+Atma

Concen-
tration
Dhian

The hereafter
Realm of
everlasting
truth
Sach Khand
Sukh Sagar
Par Brahm
Uha
Home of all
enlightened
souls who
govern the
universe

Mind (-)
Man
Pap
Uncon-
scious
Full of
vices

Ephemeral
material
world
Bhav Sagar
Sarir / Badehi
Iha
Maya
Home of
the body,
the brain
and emotions

Heart (+)
Chit, Dil
Pun
Conscious
Full of virtues

Spiritual evolution
to enlightenement
Puran Brahm
Joti Jot Rali
Phuto Anda Bharam Ka
In the course of countless
reincarnations, the veil that
disconnected the soul from
the Divine Will (Hukam, Nad)
is gradually lifted with the
help of spiritual wisdom
(Nam).
The split soul heals and
blends with the ocean of all
enlightened souls.

Veil of
ignorance
Bharam
Deception

The nature of the soul (*Atma*)

spiritual ocean into the ephemeral material world (*bhav sagar*).[28] From the perspective of the universe, new life is born the moment a soul incarnates a body
(*jivatma*). It is with this understanding that our world is described as a therapeutic
learning place for all fallen souls who are out of tune. Hence, we all carry the
blemish of conceit and egoism in us and produce a cacophony of opinions that
again is a key reason for our problems. The degree of deception and ignorance
influences our inclination towards immorality.

Ultimately, the act of being born is an act of grace because the body is needed
to experience the supposed oppositions of joy and suffering, understanding and
ignorance, so that the incarnated soul can gradually realise its disease, heal, unite
and return home.[29]

28 ਭਰਮੇ ਭੂਲੇ ਆਵਉ ਜਾਉ ॥ AGGS: 229, M. 3; ਭਰਮੇ ਭੂਲਾ ਦਹ ਦਿਸਿ ਧਾਵੈ ॥ AGGS: 277, M. 5; ਜੰਮਣੁ
ਮਰਣਾ ਹੁਕਮੁ ਹੈ ਭਾਣੈ ਆਵੈ ਜਾਇ ॥ AGGS: 472, M. 1; ਹਉ ਆਇਆ ਦੂਰਹੁ ਚਲਿ ਕੈ ਮੈ ਤਕੀ ਤਉ ਸਰਣਾਇ ਜੀਉ
॥ AGGS: 763 M. 5.
29 ਜੋ ਜੋ ਦੀਸੈ ਸੋ ਸੋ ਰੋਗੀ ॥ ਰੋਗ ਰਹਿਤ ਮੇਰਾ ਸਤਿਗੁਰੁ ਜੋਗੀ ॥ AGGS: 1140 M. 5; ਸੰਸਾਰੁ ਰੋਗੀ ਨਾਮੁ ਦਾਰੂ ਮੈਲੁ
ਲਗੈ ਸਚ ਬਿਨਾ ॥ AGGS: 678, M. 1; ਹਮ ਅਵਗਣਿ ਭਰੇ ਏਕੁ ਗੁਣੁ ਨਾਹੀ ਅੰਮ੍ਰਿਤੁ ਛਾਡਿ ਬਿਖੈ ਬਿਖੁ ਖਾਈ ॥

Good and evil – the nature of our soul

The illustration above aims to help us understand the nature of the soul, and why the healing process is comparable to the balancing act on a sword.[30]

Like the sun, the soul (*pratma, atma*) forms the background of life. Its rays give birth to a body with a consciousness. The soul (*dehi*) controls the heart and breathing, therefore, they are beyond our control. The body (*sarir*) and the brain (*tirkuti*) are instruments that are freshly provided after each reincarnation. Metaphorically speaking, the soul is split (*dal*). It is like a medal, with two sides that work antagonistically. The worldly unconscious outer part of the soul, the mind (*man*), is prone to identify with all ephemeral phenomena (*maya*), including the biological body (*badehi*), thoughts, desires, emotions, as well as material objects. It is the power of the mind that creates worldly 'progress', but also all evil attitudes. Whenever our attention (*dhian*) is outside, our brain is working; therefore, thinking eludes energy. On the collective level, capitalism emerges from our mind as it provides the best framework to entertain its insatiable desires.[31]

The inner and pure part of the soul – also called heart (*dil, chit*), home (*nij ghar*) and temple (*gurduara*) – is in tune with the truth (*gur ka bhana*), and therefore is conscious of our spiritual origins. The heart is the source of all virtues and realisation, and provides energy through its ability to create understanding. The intellect (*aqal, bhudi*) is the force that processes all experiences and sensory impressions. The more insight about its spiritual origin a soul gains, the stronger its light. The more light, the more subtleties of existence are understood. A fully illuminated intellect (*bibek bhudi*) makes the mind vanish. It only uses the brain where it is necessary to function in the material world; otherwise, it remains focused on the inner centre. It is important to understand in this context that the realm of truth and ephemerality both exist in the here and now. Time is an illusion.[32]

AGGS: 1406, Bal; ਆਪੁ ਆਪੁਨੀ ਬੁਧਿ ਹੈ ਜੇਤੀ ॥ ਬਰਨਤ ਭਿੰਨ ਭਿੰਨ ਤੁਹਿ ਤੇਤੀ ॥ DG: 1387; ਝਗੜਾ ਕਰਦਿਆ ਅਨਦਿਨੁ ਗੁਦਰੈ ਸਬਦਿ ਨ ਕਰੈ ਵੀਚਾਰੁ ॥ AGGS: 549, M. 3; ਯਾ ਜੁਗ ਮਹਿ ਏਕਹਿ ਕਉ ਆਇਆ ॥ AGGS: 251, M. 5.

30 ਖੰਨਿਅਹੁ ਤਿਖੀ ਵਾਲਹੁ ਨਿਕੀ ਏਤੁ ਮਾਰਗਿ ਜਾਣਾ ॥ AGGS: 918, M. 3; ਬਾਣੀ ਬਿਰਲਉ ਬੀਚਾਰਸੀ ਜੇ ਕੋ ਗੁਰਮੁਖਿ ਹੋਇ ॥ AGGS: 929, M. 1.

31 ਦੇਹੀ ਗੁਪਤ ਬਿਦੇਹੀ ਦੀਸੈ ॥ AGGS: 900, M. 5; ਬੀਉ ਬੀਜਿ ਪਤਿ ਲੈ ਗਏ ਅਬ ਕਿਉ ਉਗਵੈ ਦਾਲਿ ॥ AGGS: 468, M. 1; ਮਨ ਤੂੰ ਜੋਤਿ ਸਰੂਪੁ ਹੈ ਆਪਣਾ ਮੂਲੁ ਪਛਾਣੁ ॥ AGGS: 441; M. 3.

32 ਇਹ ਬਾਣੀ ਮਹਾ ਪੁਰਖ ਕੀ ਨਿਜ ਘਰਿ ਵਾਸਾ ਹੋਇ ॥ AGGS: 935, M. 1; ਗੁਰਦੁਆਰੈ ਲਾਇ ਭਾਵਨੀ ਇਕਨਾ ਦਸਵਾ ਦੁਆਰੁ ਦਿਖਾਇਆ ॥ AGGS: 922, M. 3; ਬੁਝੈ ਦੇਖੈ ਕਰੈ ਬਿਬੇਕ ॥ AGGS: 279, M. 5; ਸਤਿਗੁਰ ਕਾ ਭਾਣਾ ਕਮਾਵਦੇ ਬਿਖੁ ਹਉਮੈ ਤਜਿ ਵਿਕਾਰ ॥ AGGS: 65, M. 3; ਨਾਨਕ ਦਇਆਲੁ ਹੋਆ ਤਿਨ ਉਪਰਿ ਜਿਨ ਗੁਰ ਕਾ ਭਾਣਾ ਮੰਨਿਆ ਭਲਾ ॥ AGGS: 1115, M. 4; ਹਾਥ ਪਾਉ ਕਰਿ ਕਾਮੁ ਸਭੁ ਚੀਤੁ ਨਿਰੰਜਨ ਨਾਲਿ ॥ AGGS: 1376, Kabir; ਭਵ ਸਾਗਰ ਸੁਖ ਸਾਗਰ ਮਾਹੀ ॥ AGGS: 323, Kabir.

When the wave dies in the ocean

Returning home is difficult. Because the mind – a product of the original conceit – is as easy to seduce by transience as a little wave is carried away by the wind. Once the wave rises, there is turmoil. As soon as the wind vanishes, the wave dies and becomes a part of the serene ocean again. However, a drop that has been blown away from the ocean, cannot reach home easily. At some stage, it cannot even hear the sound of the ocean. Similarly, we come to the conviction that we are soulless, biological machines, when the mind is working at full force. Out of this, a material-oriented lifestyle emerges, where we are hardly able to deconstruct our identification with the body, objects, mind-made ideologies, identities, beliefs or fictional categories and boundaries with real impacts such as nation states. Since each of us influences and is being influenced by the existing structures, an overwhelming mind-oriented conditioning increases over time. When we become mind-oriented (*manmukh, mayadhari*) and eventually succumb to the mind (*apna bhana*), we are not only ready in our thoughts to harm others, but use our intellect to plan and commit terrible deeds without regret – even in the name of religion. This stage of ignorance leads to an ongoing entanglement in the cycle of birth and death.[33]

The five thieves – transforming negative energies to positive

In order to reach peace *from* the mind, and heal, a prerequisite is addressing the offspring of the original deceit, called the five thieves (*panch chor, dhut*). They consume positive energies, and are inherent to the mind. Therefore, they need to be subdued and transformed through the food of spiritual wisdom (*brahm gian, langar*): desire (*kam*) into an awareness of natural necessities; anger (*krodh*) into righteousness; greed *(lobh)* into a sense of well-being for everyone; emotional attachment *(moh)* into unconditional and subject-independent love; and selfishness *(ahankar)* into selflessness. Based on our past, the force of the five thieves vary. Accordingly, our healing process is individualistic.[34]

---

33 ਆਪਣੈ ਭਾਣੈ ਜੋ ਚਲੈ ਭਾਈ ਵਿਛੁੜਿ ਚੋਟਾ ਖਾਵੈ ॥ AGGS: 601, M. 3; ਮਾਇਆਧਾਰੀ ਅਤਿ ਅੰਨਾ ਬੋਲਾ ॥ ਸਬਦੁ ਨ ਸੁਣਈ ਬਹੁ ਰੋਲ ਘਚੋਲਾ ॥ AGGS: 313, M. 3; ਲਖ ਚਉਰਾਸੀਹ ਭਰਮਦੇ ਭੂਮਿ ਭੂਮਿ ਹੋਇ ਖੁਆਰੁ ॥ AGGS: 27, M. 3; ਮਨਮੁਖਾ ਨੋ ਫਿਰਿ ਜਨਮੁ ਹੈ ਨਾਨਕ ਹਰਿ ਭਾਏ ॥ AGGS: 450, M. 4.
34 ਇਸੁ ਦੇਹੀ ਅੰਦਰਿ ਪੰਚ ਚੋਰ ਵਸਹਿ ਕਾਮੁ ਕ੍ਰੋਧੁ ਲੋਭੁ ਮੋਹੁ ਅਹੰਕਾਰਾ ॥ AGGS: 600, M. 3; ਬ੍ਰਹਮ ਗਿਆਨੀ ਕਾ ਭੋਜਨੁ ਗਿਆਨ ॥ AGGS: 273, M. 5; ਲੰਗਰੁ ਚਲੈ ਗੁਰ ਸਬਦਿ ਹਰਿ ਤੋਟਿ ਨ ਆਵੀ ਖਟੀਐ ॥ AGGS: 967, Balvand Te Sata.

The poison of hubris itself contains the antidote

Through each of countless reincarnations, we are given the possibility to overcome our blemishes. The Enlightener therefore helps us to climb the ladder of spiritual evolution (*vigas*) step after step, and finally we reach the last stage as a human being. Here, we get the opportunity for complete healing (*sabat surat, ik man ik chit*) through enlightenment (*param gati*).[35] It is reached after all worldly desires, including to be born again, have vanished and we are attuned to the Divine Will (*gurmukh*). Then we wake up from our current dream state (*phalke uth*). The veil of ignorance is lifted and the egg of illusion dissolves (*phuto anda bharam ka*). The wave (*joti*) and ocean (*jot*) become one. A completely healed soul (*puran brahm*) is ready to return home from the diaspora it has intermittently regarded as its home. Through self-fertilisation by spiritual wisdom, it is born back into the ocean of bliss (*janam padarath*). But as a human being, we have to be especially cautious since there is a high danger of being trapped by the very powerful mind and having to begin all over again.[36]

The mystery behind all this is that the separating poison of hubris itself contains the antidote. In this sense, the cosmic theatre is primarily not about redemption from suffering or a state of emptiness. Rather, the highest art lies in humbly realising the limits of our power, reminding ourselves of the constant need for wisdom through an intimate and harmonious bonding with the One.[37]

The only lasting gift we can give ourselves is enlightenment

We are like a lantern whose light is pure. Yet, without regular cleansing, our lamp will collect soot on the inside. All efforts to clean it from the outside are in vein. Similarly, efforts with the body, on a technical or structural level, can never clean

---

35 ਲਖ ਚਉਰਾਸੀਹ ਜੋਨਿ ਸਬਾਈ ॥ ਮਾਨਸ ਕਉ ਪ੍ਰਭਿ ਦੀਈ ਵਡਿਆਈ ॥ AGGS: 1075, M. 5; ਨਾਨਕ ਭਗਤਾ ਸਦਾ ਵਿਗਾਸੁ ॥ AGGS: 2, M. 1; ਹਉ ਆਇਆ ਦੂਰਹੁ ਚਲਿ ਕੈ ਮੈ ਤਕੀ ਤਉ ਸਰਣਾਇ ਜੀਉ ॥ AGGS: 763, M. 5; ਨਾਪਾਕ ਪਾਕੁ ਕਰਿ ਹਦੂਰਿ ਹਦੀਸਾ ਸਾਬਤ ਸੂਰਤਿ ਦਸਤਾਰ ਸਿਰਾ ॥ AGGS: 1084, M.5; ਜਿਨਾ ਇਕ ਮਨਿ ਇਕ ਚਿਤਿ ਧਿਆਇਆ ਸਤਿਗੁਰ ਸਉ ਚਿਤੁ ਲਾਇ ॥ AGGS: 1423, M. 3; ਅੰਮ੍ਰਿਤ ਬਾਣੀ ਹਰਿ ਹਰਿ ਤੇਰੀ ॥ ਸੁਣਿ ਸੁਣਿ ਹੋਵੈ ਪਰਮ ਗਤਿ ਮੇਰੀ ॥ AGGS: 103, M. 5.

36 ਗੁਰਮੁਖਿ ਮਨੁ ਸਮਝਾਈਐ ਆਤਮ ਰਾਮੁ ਬੀਚਾਰਿ ॥ AGGS: 18, M. 1; ਜੈਸਾ ਸੁਪਨਾ ਰੈਨਿ ਕਾ ਤੈਸਾ ਸੰਸਾਰ ॥ AGGS: 808, M. 5; ਤੈ ਜੀਵਨ ਜਗਿ ਸਚੁ ਕਰਿ ਜਾਨਾ ॥ AGGS: 794, Ravidas; ਗੁਰ ਸਤਿਗੁਰ ਕਾ ਜੋ ਸਿਖੁ ਅਖਾਏ ਸੁ ਭਲਕੇ ਉਠਿ ਹਰਿ ਨਾਮੁ ਧਿਆਵੈ ॥ AGGS: 305, M. 4; ਫੂਟੋ ਆਂਡਾ ਭਰਮ ਕਾ ਮਨਹਿ ਭਇਓ ਪਰਗਾਸੁ ॥ AGGS: 1002, M. 5; ਜੋਤੀ ਜੋਤਿ ਰਲੀ ਸੰਪੂਰਨੁ ਥੀਆ ਰਾਮ ॥ AGGS: 846, M. 5; ਛੋਡਿ ਪਰਦੇਸਹਿ ਧਾਇਆ॥ AGGS: 1348, M. 5; ਪੂਰਨ ਬ੍ਰਹਮੁ ਰਵਿਆ ਮਨ ਤਨ ਮਹਿ ਆਨ ਨ ਦ੍ਰਿਸਟੀ ਆਵੈ ॥ AGGS: 531, M. 5; ਜੇ ਇਕੁ ਹੋਇ ਤ ਉਗਵੈ ਰੁਤੀ ਹੂ ਰੁਤਿ ਹੋਇ ॥ AGGS: 468, M. 1; ਇਸੁ ਪਊੜੀ ਤੇ ਜੋ ਨਰੁ ਚੂਕੈ ਸੋ ਆਇ ਜਾਇ ਦੁਖੁ ਪਾਇਦਾ ॥ AGGS: 1075, M. 5; ਜਨਮ ਪਦਾਰਥੁ ਜੀਤੀਐ ਜਪਿ ਹਰਿ ਬੈਰਾਗਰ ॥ AGGS: 1318, M. 4.

37 ਹਉਮੈ ਦੀਰਘ ਰੋਗੁ ਹੈ ਦਾਰੂ ਭੀ ਇਸੁ ਮਾਹਿ ॥ AGGS: 466, M. 2; ਦੁਖੁ ਦਾਰੂ ਸੁਖੁ ਰੋਗੁ ਭਇਆ ਜਾ ਸੁਖੁ ਤਾਮਿ ਨ ਹੋਈ ॥ AGGS: 469, M. 1; ਮੁਕਤਿ ਬਪੁੜੀ ਭੀ ਗਿਆਨੀ ਤਿਆਗੇ ॥ AGGS: 1078, M. 5.

the root cause of inner pollution. The enlightened ones have demonstrated that the miracle of inner self-cleaning and realisation of the Divine Will is possible. They knew the greatest mystery in life: The only lasting gift we can give ourselves is enlightenment.[38]

Being a guest on this planet

Once we start considering the beauty and profoundness of spiritual wisdom, we and our planet will flourish. For this, the most important step is a shift in education. The more we teach about the necessity of considering cyclic thinking, which includes giving back to Mother Earth what we have taken, the more our future generations will consider alternative economic models – like Gross National Happiness, which measures development based on the satisfaction of citizens and the environment. Our current crisis shows that it is not enough to teach how to become successful professionals within a capitalist society. We need to nourish virtues and explain the implications of being guests on this planet as well as the nature of the soul from an early age. We need to create space for open and reflected dialogues with spiritually wise people, and disseminate well-founded and independent publications (instead of interest-led articles or top listed websites and Wikipedia entries on Google). For this, we neither need institutions nor major financial investments.[39]

When spiritual insights become more popular, it will also be easier to assess which are of especial importance to solve specific problems of humankind. Ultimately, the wisdom of spirituality is an offer. It can be integrated in every (secular) sphere of life, whether politics, economy, medicine or psychotherapy. When we apply it on a larger scale, we will be able to strengthen inner and outer peace, and promote sustainable development without side effects – and leave a memorable legacy for our heirs, on this beautiful blue planet.

Valuing the aesthetics of simplicity and naturalness, and transcending the human-made, leads to peace *from* mind. To be pure in the midst of impurity (*jivan mukat*), and to love in the midst of hatred – this is the art of *Gurmat*.

---

38 ਬਾਹਰਿ ਢੂਢਤ ਬਹੁਤੁ ਦੁਖੁ ਪਾਵਹਿ ਘਰਿ ਅੰਮ੍ਰਿਤੁ ਘਟ ਮਾਹੀ ਜੀਉ ॥ AGGS: 598; M.1; ਸਚੁ ਤਾਂ ਪਰੁ ਜਾਣੀਐ ਜਾ ਆਤਮ ਤੀਰਥਿ ਕਰੇ ਨਿਵਾਸੁ ॥ AGGS: 468, M. 1; ਹੈਨਿ ਵਿਰਲੇ ਨਾਹੀ ਘਣੇ ਫੈਲ ਫਕੜੁ ਸੰਸਾਰੁ ॥ AGGS: 1411, M. 1; ਏਹ ਕਿਨੇਹੀ ਦਾਤਿ ਆਪਸ ਤੇ ਜੋ ਪਾਈਐ ॥ AGGS: 474, M. 5; ਆਪਣ ਹਥੀ ਆਪਣਾ ਆਪੇ ਹੀ ਕਾਜੁ ਸਵਾਰੀਐ ॥ AGGS: 474, M. 1.

39 ਹੋਇ ਪੈ ਖਾਕ ਫਕੀਰ ਮੁਸਾਫਰੁ ਇਹੁ ਦਰਵੇਸੁ ਕਬੂਲੁ ਦਰਾ ॥ AGGS: 1083, M. 5; ਹੋਇ ਇਕਤੁ ਮਿਲਹੁ ਮੇਰੇ ਭਾਈ ਦੁਬਿਧਾ ਦੂਰਿ ਕਰਹੁ ਲਿਵ ਲਾਇ ॥ AGGS: 1185, M. 5.

The beauty of truth

Egoism and superficiality are like weeds.
They spread with the speed of the wind.
The truth stands.
Quiet.
Lonely.
Shines in the midst of the mud.
Like a lotus.[40]

---

40 ਜੋ ਹਰਿ ਲੋੜੇ ਸੋ ਕਰੇ ਸੋਈ ਜੀਅ ਕਰੰਨਿ ॥ AGGS: 134, M. 5; ਰੁਖੀ ਸੁਖੀ ਖਾਇ ਕੈ ਠੰਢਾ ਪਾਣੀ ਪੀਓ ॥ ਫਰੀਦਾ ਦੇਖਿ ਪਰਾਈ ਚੋਪੜੀ ਨਾ ਤਰਸਾਏ ਜੀਉ ॥ AGGS: 1379, Shekh Farid; ਜੀਵਨ ਮੁਕਤਿ ਸੋ ਆਖੀਐ ਮਰਿ ਜੀਵੈ ਮਰੀਆ ॥ AGGS: 449, M. 4; ਆਈ ਪੰਥੀ ਸਗਲ ਜਮਾਤੀ ਮਨਿ ਜੀਤੈ ਜਗੁ ਜੀਤੁ ॥ AGGS: 6, M. 1; ਅਲਿਪਤੁ ਰਹਉ ਜੈਸੇ ਜਲ ਮਹਿ ਕਉਲਾ ॥ AGGS: 384, M. 5; ਕਬੀਰ ਜਿਹ ਮਾਰਗਿ ਪੰਡਿਤ ਗਏ ਪਾਛੈ ਪਰੀ ਬਹੀਰ ॥ ਇਕ ਅਵਘਟ ਘਾਟੀ ਰਾਮ ਕੀ ਤਿਹ ਚੜਿ ਰਹਿਓ ਕਬੀਰ ॥ AGGS: 1373, Kabir.

16

Understanding the Islamic Perspective on Environment: Doctrine and Ethics

Emmanuel Karagiannis

Introduction

In the last 10–15 years, Muslims around the world have shown strong interest in organising themselves for the protection of the environment. As a result, a number of eco-Muslim initiatives have been launched in the Middle East and beyond. In September 2010, for example, the Royal Aal al-Bayt Institute for Islamic Thought organised a conference on Islam and Environment in Amman, Jordan, where more than one-hundred Muslim leaders from forty countries discussed environmental issues from an Islamic perspective. In addition, there are efforts outside the Middle East to bring together concerned Muslims of different backgrounds for the purpose of improving environmental cooperation. The African Muslim Environmental Network, one of the most active environmentalist networks, consists of groups and organisations from Kenya, Zambia, Tanzania, Zimbabwe and South Africa. This trend of environmentalism goes beyond organised efforts to protect the environment; there is a lively debate about faith-based solutions to the ecological crisis. This chapter aims at providing an overview of the relationship between Islam and the environment.

Understanding Islamic ecotheology

Ecotheology is a subcategory of theology that examines the connection between religion and nature.[1] The term 'Islamic ecotheology' refers to the study of Muslim

---

1 There is an extensive bibliography on ecotheology. See, for instance: Robert J Jacobus,

creed (*aqidah*) in relation to environmental issues. Also, it focuses on the essence of religious ideas about humankind's relationship with nature. But Islam was not established in isolation from other religions. In fact, Islam came to integrate pre-Islamic norms, values and beliefs. The Muslim faith was certainly influenced by religions that existed in the Middle East before the seventh century.[2] For many centuries, the inhabitants of the Arabian Peninsula were polytheists or followed Judaism and Christianity. Nevertheless, Islam has a rather unique understanding of man's relationship with nature that is centred on theosophy (the nature of divinity), cosmogony (the origin of the universe), and ontology (the nature of humankind).

The Qur'an maintains that humankind is one of the many creations of Allah, although it has been at the centre of His plan for the world. In effect, humans have the status of first among equals (*primus inter pares*) because Islam essentially adheres to the idea of the equality of all living beings. The ultimate goal is submission to God in order to achieve salvation. Consequently, humanity's relationship with the environment is dictated by rules emanating from the Qur'an and the *ahadith*. The former offers general guidelines about the role of humans on earth, the use of water, and the place of animals in the world. The latter reports the Prophet's concerns and suggestions about the protection of the environment and nonhumans. Therefore, sharia (Islamic law) aspires to regulate every aspect of human life, including the relationship with the environment.[3]

Islamic environmental ethics

The moral relationship between human beings and the environment has been the subject of intense study. Tongjin Yang has argued that 'environmental ethics deals with the ethical problems surrounding environmental protection, and it aims to provide ethical justification and moral motivation for the issue of global

---

'Understanding Environmental Theology: A Summary for Environmental Educator', in *The Journal of Environmental Education* 35.3 (2004), pp. 35–42; Allan M Savage, 'Phenomenological Philosophy and Orthodox Christian Scientific Ecological Theology', in *Indo-Pacific Journal of Phenomenology* 8.2 (2008), pp. 1–9; Celia Deane-Drummond, *Eco-Theology* (London: Darton, Longman & Todd Ltd, 2008).

2 Daniel Brown, *A New Introduction to Islam*, second edition (Oxford: Wiley-Blackwell, 2009), p. 187.

3 Safei El-Deen Hamed, 'Seeing the Environment Through Islamic Eyes: Application of Shariah to Natural Resources Planning and Management', in *Journal of Agricultural and Environmental Ethics* 6.2 (1993), pp. 145–164.

environmental protection'.[4] The task of Muslim ethics is to understand how believers can live in accordance with the Islamic principles.[5] In this way, several scholars have argued that Islamic sources have set up the basis of Islam's environmental ethics which are based on three concepts: *tawhid* (unity), *khilafa* (trusteeship), and *akhirah* (accountability).[6]

The unity of God is the most fundamental concept of the Muslim faith. Therefore, it has been widely discussed within the Muslim world. The 18th-century preacher and scholar Muhammad ibn Abd al-Wahhab, who advocated purification of the faith and return to the Islam practised by the first generations of Muslims in the Arabian Peninsula, argued that there are three types of tawhid: *tawhid arruboobiyyah*, whereby power rests in one God alone; *tawhid al-uloohiyyah*, which dictates that all worship is directed solely to God; and *tawhid al-asmaa wa'al-sifat*, which obliges the believer to accept literally the names and attributes of God found in the Qur'an and the *ahadith* without inquiring about their exact nature.[7] The unity of God means that He alone is responsible for the creation of nature and humankind. Therefore, Islam has considered Allah as the sole Creator of the universe. In fact, two of Allah's names, the Maker of Order and the Shaper of Beauty, reflect His primordial role in organisation of the environment.

The concept of *khilafa* entails certain obligations because God entrusted the earth to human beings. A hadith reported by Sahih Muslim states that, 'The world is sweet and green (alluring) and verily Allah is going to install you as vicegerent in it in order to see how you act.'[8] The Qur'an states that when God decided to create human beings, he told the angels, 'I am going to place a ruler in the earth. They said: Wilt Thou place in it such as make mischief in it and shed blood? And we celebrate Thy praise and extol Thy holiness. He said: Surely I know what you

---

4 Tongjin Yang, 'Towards an Egalitarian Global Environmental Ethics', in H A M J ten Have, ed., *Environmental Ethics and International Policy* (Paris: UNESCO, 2006), p. 23.
5 See, for example: Muhammad Khalid Masud, 'Muslim Perspectives on Global Ethics', in William M Sullivan and Will Kymlicka, eds., *The Globalization of Ethics: Religious and Secular Perspectives* (Cambridge: Cambridge University Press, 2007).
6 Iqtidar H Zaidi, 'On the Ethics of Man's Interaction with the Environment: An Islamic Approach', in *Environmental Ethics* 3.1 (Spring 1981), pp. 35–47; Mawil Izzi Dien, 'Islamic Environmental Ethics, Law and Society', in J Ronald Engel and Joan G Engel, eds., *Ethics of Environment and Development* (London: Belhaven, 1990); Marjorie Hope and James Young, 'Islam and Ecology', in *Cross Currents* 44.2 (Summer 1994); Lisa Wersal, 'Islam and Environmental Ethics: Tradition Responds to Contemporary Challenges', in *Zygon* 30.3 (1995), pp. 451–459.
7 See: Natasha J DeLong-Bas, *Wahhabi Islam: From Revival and Reform to Global Jihad* (Oxford: Oxford University Press, 2004), pp. 56–58.
8 Sahih Muslim, Book 49, Hadith 12, available at: https://sunnah.com/muslim/49/12.

know not' (2:30). Additionally, the Qur'an states that 'Surely We offered the trust to the heavens and the earth and the mountains, but they refused to be unfaithful to it and feared from it, and man has turned unfaithful to it. Surely he is ever unjust, ignorant' (33:72). That means that humankind's stewardship over nature is not without limitations, because humans are imperfect.

Thus, humankind has been given by God a very important responsibility that has to be fulfilled. It follows that every man and woman has inherited power and accountability regarding the protection of earth.[9] The Qur'an states that, 'And surely We have honoured the children of Adam, and We carry them in the land and the sea, and We provide them with good things, and We have made them to excel highly most of those whom We have created' (17:70). Consequently, the Book commands humans to live in a harmonious world: 'And when it is said to them, Make not mischief in the land, they say: We are but peacemakers' (2:11). In effect, Islam favours sustainable development of natural resources. A verse from the Qur'an commands the believer to 'Eat of the good things We have provided for you, and be not inordinate in respect thereof, lest My wrath come upon you; and he on whom My wrath comes, he perishes indeed' (20:81). Human beings do not have the right to utilise natural resources unconditionally. They must avoid exploitation of the environment.

The concept of *akhirah* refers to the afterlife when every human being would be held accountable by God for his or her deeds. It follows that those who have performed more good deeds would end up in *Jannah* (Paradise) and those whose bad deeds outweigh the good ones would be sent to *Jahannam* (Hell). Besides, Islam establishes the principle of 'generational responsibility'. A hadith reported by Anas maintains that 'if any one deprives an heir of his inheritance, Allah will deprive him of his inheritance in Paradise on the Day of Resurrection'.[10] The allegorical meaning of this hadith is that every generation must maintain a high quality of living conditions. It is an obligation shared by all individuals, not only Muslims. The aforementioned verses are addressed to all humans because Islam is a universal religion that claims to possess the final book of divine revelation. Thus, the Islamic view is that, irrespective of religious affiliation, all people have a responsibility to protect God's earthly creation.

Furthermore, the Islamic tradition provides a set of Islamic ethical principles

9 Ali Mohammad al-Damkhi, 'Environmental Ethics in Islam: Principles, Violations, and Future Perspectives', in *International Journal of Environmental Studies* 65.1 (February 2008), p. 16.
10 Oliver Leaman, *The Qur'an: An Encyclopedia* (London: Routledge, 2006), p. 412.

that can help humankind in its mission, including *adl* (justice), *shura* (consultation), *al-mizan* (balance), *maslaha* (public interest), *ihsan* (excellence), and *wasat*
(middleness).[11] While the list of Islamic ethical principles is far from complete,
these are the main ones found in the existing literature. They provide a normative
framework for the development of modern Islamic thought on environment that
will be discussed in the next subsection.

The concept of justice ('*adl*) has been at the heart of Islamic tradition and
thought. The main aim of Islamic revelation is to create an ethical and just social
order on earth.[12] Two of the 99 names of God are related to justice: 'Upholder of
Justice' (*Al-Muqsit*) (3:18); and the 'Just' (*Al-Adl*) (16:90). The concept itself can
be found throughout the Qur'an; for example, a verse states, 'Certainly We sent
Our messengers with clear arguments, and sent down with them the Book and the
measure, that men may conduct themselves with equity. And We sent down iron,
wherein is great violence and advantages to men' (57:25). According to Sa'id ibn
Jubayr, an early Islamic scholar, '*adl* has four significations:

> [Firstly,] *al-'adl* in the administration of justice in accordance with God's
> command 'and when you judge between the people, judge with justice' (4:61).
> [Secondly,] *al-'adl* in speech, as construed in this command 'and when you
> speak, be just' (6:153). [Thirdly,] *al-'adl* [in the meaning of] ransom [because]
> God said 'and beware a day when no soul will in aught avail another; and no
> counterpoise ('*adl*) shall be accepted from it [the soul], nor any intercession
> shall be profitable to it' (2:113). [Fourthly,] *al-'adl* in the sense of attributing
> to God [because] 'the unbelievers ascribe equals to their Lord' (6:1).[13]

Although all Muslims believe that justice is a God-given virtue, there are dif-
ferent perceptions of its essence. Most Sunnis view justice as compliance with
God's actions and commands which can be understood only through revelation.[14]
Therefore, it is not possible to provide a rationale for God's wishes and decisions.
It follows that human reason cannot fully comprehend or explain the nature of

---

11 Muhammad Muinul Islam, 'Towards a Green Earth: An Islamic Perspective', in *Asian
Affairs* 26.4 (October-December 2004), p. 51.
12 Abdulaziz Abdulhussein Sachedina, *The Just Ruler (al-suktan al-adil) in Shi'ite Islam:
The Comprehensive Authority of the Jurist in Imamite Jurisprudence* (Oxford: Oxford
University Press, 1988), p. 120.
13 Ibid, p. 122.
14 See: Majid Khadduri and R K Ramazani, *The Islamic Conception of Justice* (Baltimore:
Johns Hopkins University Press, 2001), pp. 1–4.

divine justice. The Shia perspective on justice is different from the Sunni perspective. Most Shias argue that human reason can explain and understand God's actions and His divine commands. Thus, Godly justice must align with human notions of justice.[15] Moreover, *al-'adl* has been connected to the return of Mahdi (the hidden imam).[16] According to one Shia hadith, '[Mahdi] would fill up the earth with equity and justice as it would have been fraught with injustice and tyranny.'[17] He will rule for some years before the Judgment Day (*Yawm ad-Din*); although each individual has a responsibility for his actions, Allah will judge them according to His will.

The concept of *shura* (collective consultation) can also contribute to the formation of environmental ethics. There are two verses in the Qur'an referring to consultation: 'And those who respond to their Lord and keep up prayer, and whose affairs are (decided) by counsel among themselves, and who spend out of what We have given them' (42:38), and 'So pardon them and ask protection for them, and consult them in (important) matters' (3:159). Sheikh Yusuf al-Qaradawi has argued that '*Shura* has always been good for the Muslim society, and autocracy has always been evil since the beginning of mankind on this planet'.[18] Likewise, Fethullah Gülen has claimed that *shura* 'is a method, a process of government, and way of life for Muslims'.[19] The opinion of these two Islamic scholars is very important because they have a large following in the Middle East and beyond. In essence, the concept inherently includes the belief that all humans are equal in rights and responsibilities.

The notion of *al-mizan* (balance) can provide the ethical basis for the development of a new model of sustainable development. Nature has been created by God as a whole of absolute perfection and beauty. Its very existence is based on

15 Najam Haider, *Shi'I Islam: An Introduction* (Cambridge: Cambridge University Press, 2014), p. 18.

16 The adherents of Shia Islam believe that Mahdi was the twelfth imam, or the so-called 'hidden imam', who was born and disappeared but will return to bring justice. The occultation of Mahdi can be divided into two periods: the minor occultation (874–941) when he used his deputies to maintain contact with followers and the major occultation (941 to the present) when the hidden imam is not in contact with the faithful. See: Richard Martin, *Encyclopedia of Islam and the Muslim World* (New York: Macmillan, 2004), p. 421.

17 Bihar al-Anwar, *The Promised Mahdi*, vol. 13 (Mumbai: Ja'fari Propagation Centre, no date), p. 274.

18 Yusuf al-Qaradawi, 'Shura and Democracy', available at: https://archive.islamonline. net/?p=5662.

19 Leonid Sykiainen, 'Democracy and the Dialogue between Western and Islamic Legal Cultures: The Gülen Case', in Robert A Hunt and Yüksel A Aslandoğan, eds., *Muslim Citizens of the Globalized World* (Somerset, NJ: The Light, 2007), p. 126.

balance, harmony (*itidal*), and peace. God created the world with balance and humanity has the obligation not to distort it. The Qur'an states that, 'Surely We have created everything according to a measure' (54:49). Qaradawi has analysed the significance of a hadith that states 'whoever cuts down a lute-tree, Allah would direct his head to the Hell-fire'; from his point of view, it commands the protection of basic elements of nature which provide a balance between creatures.[20] Hence all elements submit to His will and exist according to His commandments. Humans are obliged to serve God's plan by not disturbing the cosmic balance. Furthermore, Fazlun Khalid has argued that 'nature is a vehicle to perform good deeds; nature is a blessed gift (*ni'ma*) of God's beauty. It is not humankind's to possess or destroy; the Muslim is expected to treat nature with respect and deep gratitude to its Creator and any transformation of it must have a purpose and benefit to all.'[21]

The concept of *maslaha* (public interest) has deep roots in the Islamic tradition. Historically speaking, Muslim jurists have advocated the establishment of conservation zones (*hima*) and wildlife sanctuaries (*harim*) where commercial use of the land is not permitted.[22] In the early Islamic era, the *hima* system was restricted to Mecca and Medina where the Prophet and the Rightly Guided Caliphs grazed the horses used by their armies.[23] This tradition survived until recently. During the 1960s, there were over 3,000 *hima*s in Saudi Arabia, varying in size from 10 to 1,000 hectares, but less than a dozen remain today.[24] The rationale for the maintenance of these protected zones was based on the concept of *maslaha*.[25]

In addition, the notion of *ihsan* (excellence) relates to inner beauty and intimacy to God. Accordingly, *ihsan* can manifest in activities such as geometry, calligraphy and gardening. Those who embrace *ihsan* will seek to live in peace

---

20 Yusuf al-Qaradawi, *Education and Economy in the Sunnah* (Cairo: Al-Falah Foundation, 2005), p. 23.
21 Fazlun M Khalid, 'Islam, Ecology and Modernity: An Islamic Critique of the Root Causes of Envrionmental Degradation', in Richard C Foltz, Frederick M Denny and Azizan Baharuddin, eds., *Islam and Ecology – A Bestowed Trust* (Cambridge, MA: Harvard University Press, 2003).
22 Arthur Saniotis, 'Muslim and Ecology: Fostering Islamic Environmental Ethics', in *Contemporary Islam* 6 (2012), p. 158.
23 Mawil Izzi Dien, *The Environmental Dimensions of Islam* (Cambridge: Lutherworth, 2000), p. 43.
24 David L Johnston, 'Intra-Muslim Debates on Ecology: Is Shari'a Still Relevant?', in *Worldviews* 16 (2012), p. 233.
25 Johnston, 'Intra-Muslim Debates on Ecology: Is Shari'a Still Relevant?', p. 227.

with the environment and its different components.[26] In fact, it has been claimed that it 'constitutes the highest form of worship'.[27]

Moreover, the concept of *wasat* can be applied to environmental issues. According to the Qur'an, 'And therefore, we made you the Community of the Middle so that you be to the people witnesses and the Messenger be a witness to you' (2:143). Many Islamic scholars have interpreted the verse as a God-given request for moderation. For instance, Yusuf al-Qaradawi has argued that 'Wasatiyya is the balance between mind and Revelation, matter and spirit, rights and duties, individualism and collectivism, inspiration and commitment, the Text (i.e. the Qur'an) and personal interpretation (*ijtihad*).'[28] Practically speaking, believers must avoid anything that is extreme and excessive in their conduct vis-à-vis the environment.

Conclusion

It can be argued that the Muslim faith perceives the relationship between humanity and the environment as mutually complementary; humanity cannot exist without the natural world. Therefore, God and his Messenger have requested Muslims to protect the environment and its resources. But this is not all. Humans are God's guardians on earth and have a special mission, which is to enforce His will on the rest of the earth. The Qur'an and *ahadith* have called Muslims to be careful and gentle toward the environment. In this way, the believer would draw closer to the divine. It is both a spiritual and a practical obligation to obey the divine rules and respect the Godly order. To sum up, Islam as a religion has explored the relationship between humanity and nature, favouring a balanced approach that permits their harmonious co-existence.

Bibliography

al-Anwar, Bihar, *The Promised Mahdi*, vol. 13 (Mumbai: Ja'fari Propagation Centre, no date).

---

26 AbdulGafar O Fahm, 'Factor Contending with Environmental Sustainability in Nigeria: An Islamic Approach', in Proceedings of the Social Sciences Research, 9–10 June 2014, Kota Kinabalu, Malaysia.

27 Mahmoud M Ayoub, *Islam: Faith and History* (London: Oneworld Publications, 2005), p. 4.

28 Ana Belén Soage, 'Yusuf al-Qaradaqi: The Muslim Brothers' Favorite Ideological Guide', in Barry Rubin, *The Muslim Brotherhood: The Organization and Policies of a Global Islamist Movement* (London: Palgrave Macmillan, 2010), p. 30.

Ayoub, Mahmoud M, *Islam: Faith and History* (London: Oneworld Publications, 2005).

Belén Soage, Ana, 'Yusuf al-Qaradaqi: The Muslim Brothers' Favorite Ideological Guide', in Rubin Rubin, *The Muslim Brotherhood: The Organization and Policies of a Global Islamist Movement* (London: Palgrave Macmillan, 2010), p. 30.

Brown, Daniel, *A New Introduction to Islam*, second edition (Oxford: Wiley-Blackwell, 2009).

al-Damkhi, Ali Mohammad, 'Environmental Ethics in Islam: Principles, Violations, and Future Perspectives', in *International Journal of Environmental Studies* 65.1 (February 2008).

Deane-Drummond, Celia, *Eco-Theology* (London: Darton, Longman & Todd Ltd, 2008).

DeLong-Bas, Natasha J, *Wahhabi Islam: From Revival and Reform to Global Jihad* (Oxford: Oxford University Press, 2004).

Fahm, AbdulGafar O, 'Factor Contending with Environmental Sustainability in Nigeria: An Islamic Approach', in Proceedings of the Social Sciences Research, 9–10 June 2014, Kota Kinabalu, Malaysia.

Haider, Najam, *Shi'I Islam: An Introduction* (Cambridge: Cambridge University Press, 2014).

Hamed, Safei El-Deen, 'Seeing the Environment Through Islamic Eyes: Application of Shariah to Natural Resources Planning and Management', in *Journal of Agricultural and Environmental Ethics* 6.2 (1993), pp. 145–164.

Hope, Marjorie, and Young, James, 'Islam and Ecology', in *Cross Currents* 44.2 (Summer 1994).

Izzi Dien, Mawil, *The Environmental Dimensions of Islam* (Cambridge: Lutherworth, 2000).

Izzi Dien, Mawil, 'Islamic Environmental Ethics, Law and Society', in J Ronals Engel and Joan G Engel, eds., *Ethics of Environment and Development* (London: Belhaven, 1990).

Jacobus, Robert J, 'Understanding Environmental Theology: A Summary for Environmental Educator', in *The Journal of Environmental Education* 35.3 (2004), pp. 35–42.

Johnston, David L, 'Intra-Muslim Debates on Ecology: Is Shari'a Still Relevant?', in *Worldviews* 16 (2012).

Khadduri, Majid and Ramazani, R K, *The Islamic Conception of Justice* (Baltimore: Johns Hopkins University Press, 2001).

Khalid, Fazlun M, 'Islam, Ecology and Modernity: An Islamic Critique of the Root Causes of Envrionmental Degradation', in Richard C Foltz, Frederick M Denny and Azizan Baharuddin, eds., *Islam and Ecology – A Bestowed Trust* (Cambridge, MA: Harvard University Press, 2003).

Leaman, Oliver, *The Qur'an: An Encyclopedia* (London: Routledge, 2006).

Martin, Richard, *Encyclopedia of Islam and the Muslim World* (New York: Macmillan, 2004).

Masud, Muhammad Khalid, 'Muslim Perspectives on Global Ethics', in William M Sullivan and Will Kymlicka, eds., *The Globalization of Ethics: Religious and Secular Perspectives* (Cambridge: Cambridge University Press, 2007).

Muinul Islam, Muhammad, 'Towards a Green Earth: An Islamic Perspective', in *Asian Affairs* 26.4 (October-December 2004).

al-Qaradawi, Yusuf, *Education and Economy in the Sunnah* (Cairo: Al-Falah Foundation, 2005), p. 23.

al-Qaradawi, Yusuf, 'Shura in Islam', Fatwa no. 84768, 4 September 2002, available at: http://www.islamweb.net/emainpage/index.php?page=showfatw a&Option=FatwaId&Id=84768.

Sachedina, Abdulaziz Abdulhussein, *The Just Ruler (al-suktan al-adil) in Shi'ite Islam: The Comprehensive Authority of the Jurist in Imamite Jurisprudence* (Oxford: Oxford University Press, 1988).

Sahih Muslim, Book 49, Hadith 12, available at: https://sunnah.com/ muslim/49/12.

Saniotis, Arthur, 'Muslim and Ecology: Fostering Islamic Environmental Ethics', in *Contemporary Islam* 6 (2012).

Savage, Allan M, 'Phenomenological Philosophy and Orthodox Christian Scientific Ecological Theology', in *Indo-Pacific Journal of Phenomenology* 8.2 (2008), pp. 1–9.

Sykiainen, Leonid, 'Democracy and the Dialogue between Western and Islamic Legal Cultures: The Gülen Case', in Robert A Hunt and Yüksel A Aslandoğan, eds., *Muslim Citizens of the Globalized World* (Somerset, NJ: The Light, 2007).

Wersal, Lisa, 'Islam and Environmental Ethics: Tradition Responds to Contemporary Challenges', in *Zygon* 30.3 (1995), pp. 451–459.

Yang, Tongjin, 'Towards an Egalitarian Global Environmental Ethics', in H.A.M.J ten Have, ed., *Environmental Ethics and International Policy* (Paris: UNESCO, 2006).

Zaidi, Iqtidar H, 'On the Ethics of Man's Interaction with the Environment: An Islamic Approach', in *Environmental Ethics* 3.1 (Spring 1981), pp. 35–47.

FROM IMAGINATION TO RELIGIOUS PRACTICE

17

Religious Leadership in Conflict Transformation: The Case of Christian Leadership in South Africa's Truth and Reconciliation Commission[1]

Megan Shore

Religious leadership has played an ambivalent role in conflict resolution in Africa (and throughout the world), at times stoking the conflict. In Kenya, there have been instances where church leaders and elders have incited violence. For example, the quasi-religious sect known as Mungiki, which started as a religious group, transformed into a politically inclined militia who have carried out killings, extortion, and organised crime encouraged by religious leaders.[2] And in Nigeria, religious riots between Christians and Muslims have killed hundreds in sporadic acts of violence since 1994, with religious leadership either encouraging the violence or doing nothing to prevent it.[3] On the other hand, there are instances where religious

1 This chapter draws heavily on work that was previously published in: M Shore, *Religion and Conflict Resolution: Christianity and the South African Truth and Reconciliation Commission* (Surrey: Ashgate Press, 2009).

2 M Gecaga, 'Religious Groups and Democratization in Kenya: Between the Sacred and the Profane', in *Kenya: The Struggle for Democracy* (London: Zed Books, 2007), pp. 58–89. S Sprenk, 'Leaving Mungiki: Some Express Skepticism As Violent Sect Receives Baptism', in *Christianity Today*, 11 February 2010, available at:
https://www.christianitytoday.com/ct/2010/february/18.15.html.

3 M Basedau, J Vüllers and P Körner, 'What Drives Inter-Religious Violence? Lessons from Nigeria, Côte d'Ivoire, and Tanzania', in *Studies in Conflict and Terrorism* 36.10 (2013), pp. 857–879. K Sulaiman, 'Religious Violence in Contemporary Nigeria:

leaders have organised rallies for peace, overseen fair elections, fostered civil peace education, and denounced politicians who were corrupt or incited tension for their own end. For example, the Acholi Religious Leaders Peace Initiative (ARLPI) is an interfaith forum of Muslim, Catholic, Protestant, and Orthodox Christian leaders who provide community-based mediation, advocacy, and peace-building activities during conflicts in northern Uganda.[4] Religious leadership, like religion itself, has the powerful potential to foster justice and peace; yet it can also mobilise hatred and violence. In many respects, the dominant approaches to international conflict resolution have had difficulties accounting for the often non-political and 'non-rational' forces that drive religious activities. Using the language of risk, these approaches have historically sought to mitigate the risk of religious actors inciting violence by isolating religion as an element that must be duly contained. As a result, international conflict resolution has generally adopted the position that organised religion is primarily, if not essentially, an instigator of violence and has tended to exclude religion as a source for peacebuilding. However, an alternative approach to conflict resolution, referred to as 'religious conflict resolution', suggests that religion can contribute constructively to conflict resolution and peacebuilding.[5] The general thesis is that, if religion plays a significant part in people's lives, and if religion plays a part in fuelling conflict, then religion must be at least taken into account for conflict resolution, for without this consideration, peacekeepers, diplomats, and mediators not only fail to deal with the fundamentals of the conflict, but they also miss potential peacebuilding resources offered by religious traditions.

This chapter will focus on the role that religious leadership can play in constructively contributing to conflict transformation. Religious conflict resolution will be the underlining premise: that is, my argument is based on the assumption that religion can contribute constructively to conflict resolution. First, I will focus on why religious leadership could be considered an asset in conflict transformation. I will then draw on the example of the role religious leadership, specifically Christian leadership, played in South Africa's transition from apartheid to democracy.[6] And

---

Implications and Options for Peace and Stability Order', in *Journal for the Study of Religion* 29.1 (2016), pp. 85–103, available at: http://www.reviewofreligions.org/2284/editorial-%E2%80%93-religious-violence-in-nigeria/.

4 The Acholi Religious Leaders Peace Initiative, see: http://www.arlpi.org/about-us.

5 M Shore, 'Christianity and Justice in the South African Truth and Reconciliation Commission: A Case Study in Religious Conflict Resolution', in *Journal of Political Theology* 9.2 (2008), pp. 164–165.

6 In South Africa, it was not just the Christian tradition, or just Christian leadership, that

I will conclude with some final reflections on the role religious leadership can play in international conflict resolution in general.

Assets of religious leadership

For the purpose of this chapter, religious leadership refers to a person who is recognised as having authority within a particular religious tradition. It includes recognisable figureheads such as clergy, imams, rabbis, and monks, as well as leaders of faith-based organisations and religious communities. Although religious leadership often refers to national and international leaders, it can also refer to local leaders, both religious and lay leaders, who have significant influence within their religious community. And although I am speaking specifically about leadership, in most instances religious leadership is connected with religious organisations and faith-based organisations.[7]

I suggest that there are at least four interconnected reasons that religious leadership can be considered an asset for conflict transformation.[8] The first reason is that religious leaders have the privileged position of authority and influence over many people, which crosses many boundaries of social, racial and political structures in society. Despite increasing secularism in certain parts of the world, and in Africa, religion still plays a prominent role in the lives of many, *particularly*

---

was involved in the anti-apartheid struggle and the transition to democracy. Religious leaders from Muslim, Jewish, Hindu, Buddhist, and Baha'i traditions played various roles. In fact, the South African Truth and Reconciliation Commission held a special institutional hearing on faith communities and their role in the apartheid. All of these traditions submitted reports, and all accepted the complicated relationship of agent, opponent and victim of apartheid. For further information on this, refer to: J Cochrane, J de Gruchy and S Martin, eds., *Facing the Truth: South African Faith Communities and the Truth and Reconciliation Commission* (Cape Town: David Philip Publishers, 1999). However, Christian leadership arguably played the most prominent and visible role in the transition. So much so that the TRC was often criticised for being overly or exclusively Christian. The purpose of this chapter is not to engage in this debate; I do so elsewhere, particularly in: Shore, 'Christianity and Justice in the South African Truth and Reconciliation Commission'. My purpose in this chapter is to use the South African TRC as a case study to examine the role of religious actors in conflict transformation, and in order to do this, I focus on Christian leadership because they were the most visible and as a result, there is a larger body of research to analyse.

7 United Nations Development Programme, 'UNDP Guidelines on Engaging with Faith -Based Organizations and Religious Leaders', New York, October 2014, available at: http://www.undp.org/content/dam/undp/documents/partners/2014_UNDP_Guidelines-on-Engaging-with-FBOs-and-Religious-Leaders_EN.pdf.

8 The four assets of religious leadership introduced here are developed in detail in: Shore, *Religion and Conflict Resolution*, pp. 24–26.

in Africa, and religious leadership continues to exact influence in people's lives. In these cases, to exclude or even marginalise religious leadership as a matter of principle would effectively mean removing a key social authority and institution, which for many could mean an attack on one's worldview and self-understanding.

Second, religious leadership has the ability to access ethical norms and moral frameworks that can provide direction and a moral language for religious people seeking answers to complex social and political situations. In other words, religious leaders can provide a moral discourse for people wanting to make sense of injustice and the consequences of conflict. And they have the ability to promote peace, just as they can promote militancy and intolerance. The key is for religious leaders to tap into the peacebuilding aspects of their traditions. In doing so, they have the capability to mobilise community, national, and international support toward peaceful resolutions.

Third, religious organisations and religious leadership often have access to broader networks of people and similarly aligned organisations. This can in turn provide logistical support in conflict resolution processes, and it allows them the potential to reach many people. Indeed, these are oftentimes the best equipped networks to serve as relays or go-betweens, whether in the form of communication or aid, in regions where government infrastructures or communication infrastructures have collapsed.

And finally, religious leadership can create a safe, and relatively neutral space in times of conflict. They are on the ground and have credibility as trusted leaders in a community. Indeed, religious leadership, and institutions, can help war-torn countries as they transition to just systems of governance and a stable peace in a variety of forms: for example, providing a physical venue for political or (quasi-) judicial processes, or working with victims of violence.

South Africa's Truth and Reconciliation Commission

South Africa is a country in which religious leadership, primarily Christian leadership, has played a prominent role in the countries' conflict transformation. The role of Christian leadership was significant in the anti-apartheid movement, as well as in the Truth and Reconciliation Commission (TRC), which was part of a negotiated settlement to help South Africa deal with over 40 years of official apartheid. To be clear at the outset, the churches and religious leaders were not always on the side of justice and peace in South Africa. Indeed, the response of the Christian churches to apartheid was always an ambivalent one.

Apartheid is the Afrikaans word for 'separation', it denotes 'aparthood' or 'apartness'. In South Africa, the term was used to justify racial separation to varying degrees. From the arrival of the Dutch in southern Africa until the early nineteenth century, an informal system of racial separation existed, first imposed by the Dutch and then by the British. It became an official policy in South Africa in 1948, when Daniel Malan, the chief architect of apartheid, and his National Party won the general election.[9] Apartheid was a system of systematic racism that affected almost every aspect of life, including interpersonal relations, residential patterns, and social, economic and political organisation. Resistance to this system, and subsequent violence and human rights abuses to stop the resistance, led to decades of bloody civil war.

The Christian churches in South Africa have historically had an ambivalent stance in terms of apartheid. On the one hand, Christianity, more specifically the Dutch Reformed Church (DRC), the dominant Christian tradition among Afrikaners in South Africa, was a significant contributor to the theory of apartheid. The first president of democratic, post-apartheid South Africa, Nelson Mandela, explains in his autobiography that apartheid 'policy was supported by the Dutch Reformed Church, which furnished apartheid with its religious underpinnings by suggesting that Afrikaners were God's chosen people and that blacks were subservient species. In the Afrikaner's worldview, apartheid and the church went hand in hand'.[10] The DRC provided theological, political and social justification for apartheid.[11] Through sermons, biblical commentaries, and theological justifications, the Dutch Reformed Church and other pro-apartheid denominations supported apartheid by claiming: a) that they were God's chosen people; and b) that God had given them South Africa as their promised land; and c) that Blacks were destined to be subservient.

On the other hand, there were Christian churches and leaders who refused to remain silent. But it was not until the 1960s and 1970s that religious leaders began an organised resistance against apartheid. When the government declared a state of emergency, it banned political opposition parties and sent anti-apartheid activists to prison or into exile in neighbouring countries. The result was that within the course of a few years, political resistance leaders were no longer on the scene to mobilise the resistance movements within South Africa. To fill this void,

---

9 Shore, *Religion and Conflict Resolution*, p. 36.

10 N Mandela, *Long Walk to Freedom: The Autobiography of Nelson Mandela* (New York: Brown and Company, 1995), p. 111.

11 L Graybill, *Religion and Resistance Politics in South Africa* (Connecticut: Praeger, 1995); J de Gruchy, *The Church Struggle in South Africa* (Michigan: Eerdmans, 2004).

a number of Christian churches emerged to challenge the system and Christian leaders became the vocal opponents of apartheid.[12]

Because a number of churches had international connections with organisations such as the World Council of Churches, the churches were often in a position to provide cover and infrastructure for the black resistance movement and anti-apartheid activists. Black Christians such as Allan Boesak, Mana Buthelezi and Frank Chikane, and to a lesser degree some prominent white Christians, such as Albert Nolan, John de Gruchy, and Denis Hurley, thought it was part of the gospel call to bring politics into the churches because there was no other public forum in which they were able to challenge the apartheid regime.[13] With public assemblies banned and anti-apartheid political parties declared unlawful, religious leadership created an alternative social location that was safe and relatively free from government interference. By the 1970s, a number of the religious leaders had an international reputation for leading the fight against apartheid.

After years of civil unrest, the negotiation for a peaceful transition in South Africa began in 1992, when a whites-only referendum was held to determine whether negotiations for new reforms and a new constitution would take place to address the racial injustice of apartheid. Sixty-eight percent voted in favour of continued reform, and this set the groundwork for negotiations between the ruling National Party, and the unofficial opposition group, the African National Congress, which eventually led to an Interim Constitution and the first democratic election in South Africa in 1994. In metaphorical terms, the options that South Africa had for dealing with its history of apartheid ranged from burying the past to exhuming it. Not wanting to bury its past, which would have allowed gross human rights abusers to walk away with impunity, South Africa chose to confront its history by establishing a truth commission.

The Interim Constitution laid the framework for the truth commission, and the Promotion of National Unity Act of 1995 established the South African Truth and Reconciliation Commission (TRC). The TRC was commissioned to write an official history of South Africa's apartheid era, with the aim of establishing as complete a picture as possible of human rights abuses. It was inaugurated in December 1995 and had a mandate of operating for three years. Due to the mammoth dimension of the task, this period was eventually extended until 2002.

---

12 C Villa-Vicencio, *Trapped in Apartheid: A Socio-theological History of the English-Speaking Churches* (New York: Orbis Books, 1988); D Johnston, 'The Churches and Apartheid in South Africa', in Douglas Johnston and Cynthia Sampson, eds., *Religion the Missing Dimension of Statecraft* (Oxford, Oxford University Press, 1994), pp. 177–207.
13 Shore, *Religion and Conflict Resolution*, pp. 48–54.

In terms of structure, the TRC consisted of three committees: 1) The Human Rights Violations Committee, which dealt primarily with victims and investigated alleged atrocities that occurred during the apartheid era; 2) The Amnesty Committee, which dealt primarily with perpetrators and where appropriate granted amnesty to those who applied and qualified; and 3) the Reparations and Rehabilitation Committee, which recommended compensation and awards to the victims.

Because the TRC was officially a political process, it was not obvious that Christianity should have been involved in the TRC, however, religion (specifically Christianity) and religious leaders shaped the mandate of the TRC, and in turn influenced how the process functioned.[14] As a newly declared democratic state, South Africa had now allied itself with other liberal democracies, all of which were formally secular and generally suspicious of the involvement of religion in politics. Although South Africa had adopted a secular constitution, it was never a secular society. On the contrary, most South Africans understood South Africa to be a Christian country, in which religion played an important role in both the public and private realms. As a result, if there was going to be open and honest dialogue in the TRC, then religion was inevitably going to play a vital, yet controversial, role in not only the stories told but also in the administration of the process.

The most profound impact of religion on the TRC was through the religious leadership that had a prominent role to play. Respected religious leaders who took on roles as Commissioners and staff of the TRC implemented the mandate which resulted in the functioning of the process itself. One of the most visible roles of religious leadership was through the actual leadership of the TRC. Of the seventeen commissioners that President Mandela appointed to the TRC, one-third were ordained ministers or religious leaders. The two most prominent leaders in the TRC were also Christian leaders. Archbishop Desmond Tutu, the first black Anglican Archbishop of Cape Town and a Nobel Peace Prize winner in 1984, was appointed chair, and Dr Alex Boraine, President of the South African Methodist Church and a member of South Africa's parliament from 1980 to 1986, was named deputy chair.[15]

Three other high-profile religious leaders were appointed as commissioners. Reverend Bongani Finca was a Presbyterian minister from the Eastern Cape. Dr

---

14 Along with Scott Kline, I explore the Christian language, ritual and concepts that permeated the TRC in: 'The Ambiguous Role of Religion in the South African Truth and Reconciliation Commission', in *Peace and Change: A Journal of Peace Research* 31 (2006), pp. 309–332. But for the purpose of this chapter I will focus on Christian leadership and actors.

15 Shore, *Religion and Conflict Resolution*, pp. 59–74.

Khoza Mgojo was the former president of the Methodist Church and president of the South African Council Churches.[16] Of course, the role religious leadership played in the TRC was not without controversy. Yet it was inevitable that religion would ultimately play a role in the process for it was one of the few institutions that had the organisational capacity, and the leadership, that could bridge various communities in South Africa, which it eventually did.

The pool of potential candidates for Commission posts were limited by the political realities of the 1970s and 1980s. In the face of government crackdowns and bannings, church leaders, such as Tutu, often emerged as anti-apartheid activists and quasi-political leaders. With little alternative, the religious leaders came forward as political leaders and spokespersons to fill the vacuum left by those forced into exile. Leaders such as Tutu were recognised as a leader in the struggle against apartheid, and they had hugely popular following that crossed racial and political boundaries.

There were at least three other roles in which religious leadership was involved in the TRC. First, religious leadership was involved in high-level administrative positions of the TRC. For example, Dr Charles Villa-Vicencio, theology professor and former head of the religious studies department at the University of Cape Town, was appointed director of research. This meant that he led the group that were in charge of the verification of human rights violations, as well as the editing and production of the final TRC report.

Second, religious leadership was involved in the on-the-ground functioning of the TRC. Through their role in leading national organisations, like the South African Council of Churches, or religious organisations and churches, mosques, and temples, religious leadership were able to provide networks through their national structure and grassroots connections. Indeed, these religious leaders were crucial to the success of the TRC since they had access to the people that the Commission planned to target, and they were able to create an awareness of its mandate and publicise its work through existing communication networks.

And finally, religious leadership provided logistics support in terms of offering office space for administrative work and arranging venues for public hearings. They were statement takers for collecting human rights violations, they accompanied witnesses to hearings, they offered counselling support, and they held workshops and provided resources in trauma counselling.

---

16 There was one high-profile Muslim leader, Ms Yasmin Sooka. She was a human rights lawyer and had been president of the South Africa chapter of the multi-faith body World Conference on Religion and Peace.

To be sure, South Africa has come a long way since the TRC. But with massive poverty and continued socio-economic injustice along racial lines there is still much to be done. The major challenge for religious leaders (and the churches and faith-based organisations) is to discover their role in the continued rebuilding of justice, which is essential to sustainable peace. Religious leadership had a clear and decisive role in challenging apartheid, and facilitating the first stage of justice in South Africa through the TRC.[17] As Hugo van der Merwe, Programme Manager at the Centre for the Study of Violence in Cape Town, explains, 'the TRC has provided the churches with many insights and channels to pursue, but the blurring of the line between politics and religion involved in the process has left the churches with little clarity about their responsibilities in the new society.'[18] The task they now face is how to overcome social divisions and build long-term justice in democratic South Africa, and to figure out their role in an increasingly secular society.

Lessons

In looking at the role religious leadership played in South Africa's transition from apartheid to democracy, I do not want to suggest that we should treat the South African process as a template that is applicable to every case. I think this example needs to be understood within the framework of religious conflict resolution; that is, it made sense in South Africa because religion had a role to play in fuelling the conflict and it had a role to play in people's lives. And perhaps more importantly, the political reality of apartheid meant that religious leaders were largely the ones who stepped in to fill the void in the anti-apartheid struggle when anti-apartheid activists were forced into exile or imprisoned. This examination of the role of religious leadership needs to be seen as a first step in a much broader project of understanding the complex and ambiguous role that religious leaders, and religion in general, can play in conflict processes and mechanisms. Based on this study, I see at least three general lessons that are particularly worthy of attention as we struggle to make sense of the role religious leadership can play in conflict resolution.

The first lesson concerns the extent to which religious leaders influence the structure and administration of a conflict resolution process. For example, in the case of South Africa, there were times when the TRC ran the risk of becoming

---

17 H van der Merwe, 'The Role of the Church in Promoting Reconciliation in Post–TRC South Africa', in Audrey Chapman and Bernard Spong, eds., *Religion and Reconciliation in South Africa: Voices of Religious Leaders* (Philadelphia: Templeton Foundation Press, 2003), p. 269.
18 Ibid., p. 280.

a religious event, at expense of the exclusion of those who have suspicion of religion or are anti-religious. It can become very hard to translate the religious aspects of conflict transformation process into the concrete social change that may be needed in resolving conflict. To avert some of the confusion, I would suggest that at the outset of any conflict resolution mechanism in which religious leaders play a significant role, it is imperative to establish basic guidelines for religious actors. It is true that conflict resolution mechanisms and processes vary widely, but at a minimum level these types of discussions may prepare political leaders, mediators, and local personnel to assess challenges that they may confront when bringing religious leadership into the process.

The second lesson has to do with reductionism. I see three forms of reductionism with respect to the involvement of religion and religious leadership. First, there is a *reductionism of the cause* of the conflict. Historically, if religion is an element in the conflict, then the conflict is reduced to a religious conflict and thus religion is excluded from the conflict resolution process. Second, there is the potential for *political reductionism*. This means that the conflict is reduced to political matters, such as power or statecraft. Thus only political means are considered in resolving it. And third there is *religious reductionism*. This is when religion is reduced to values such as justice or peace, which means that the only role religion can play in conflict resolution is to offer these values to the process. If religious leadership continues to speak out about injustice or about the inequities in conflict resolution processes, and they surely will, there can be a tendency to discredit these voices as inauthentic. To overcome these pitfalls of reductionism, there needs to be a more nuanced understanding of the role religion plays in conflict, and in turn the potential religion can play in conflict transformation. This can be developed through examining the role religion and religious actors already play on the ground in conflict situations. For example, in South Africa, religious leadership had been involved in a variety of roles and in the anti-apartheid movements (and continues to be today). Not only were they the organising forces in the struggle, they led grassroots initiatives, such as establishing and supporting sports clubs, theatres, and community organisations, that contributed to building peace.

And the final lesson has to do with integration. Often religious leadership works independently, and on the fringes, from the political government initiatives in conflict transformation. Often there is hostility toward religious leadership in conventional conflict resolution mechanisms and practices. What ends up happening is that the two can be seen as competing or duplicating forces. I would suggest that this is a result of the realist/secularist roots of conflict resolution, which in turn results in a misunderstanding of what religion is and what religious leadership can do in terms of conflict resolution. I would suggest that the best way to work toward integration of religious leadership in conflict transformation would be religious literacy on behalf of the diplomats and politicians who have historically led conflict transformation. Religious literacy includes education about the basic tenets of the worlds faiths, about the diversity of expressions and beliefs within traditions in relation to differing social and historical contexts, as well as education about the profound role that religions play in human social, cultural, and political life.

To be clear, I am not advocating for a manipulation of religion, rather a broader understanding of religion on the part of politicians, diplomats, etc., so that they can discover shared understanding as they work together to build peace. I am also not proposing a search for some universal religion, nor am I suggesting naively that all religious actors want peace. I am suggesting a broader understanding of religion because not only are opportunities for grassroots peacebuilding being missed by conventional conflict resolution approaches, in some cases these conventional approaches are exacerbating the violence.

In conclusion, I think that van der Merwe's observation about the blurring of lines between religion and politics is the crux of the challenge for religious leaders in conflict transformation. Bringing religious leadership into conflict resolution directly challenges conventional conflict resolution methods that have historically excluded religion, and religious leaders, as an asset in peacebuilding. These conventional approaches to conflict resolution have failed to recognise diverse forms of conflict, and have been unable to address the changing nature of conflict today. In short, religious conflict resolution proposes an alternative model to conventional conflict resolution that suggests that religious leadership can play a crucial role in resolving international conflict. It is crucial for politicians, diplomats and other peacebuilders to take religious leadership seriously in resolving conflict, and to collaborate with them – to share the table – because not doing so not only leads to failure in dealing with the fundamentals of the conflict, but results in missed potential peacebuilding resources in the religious traditions themselves.

Bibliography

The Acholi Religious Leaders Peace Initiative, available at: http://www.arlpi.
    org/about-us.
Basedau, M, Vüllers, J, and Körner, P, 'What Drives Inter-Religious Violence?
    Lessons from Nigeria, Côte d'Ivoire, and Tanzania', in *Studies in Conflict
    and Terrorism* 36.10 (2013), pp. 857–879.

Cochrane, J, de Gruchy, J, and Martin, S, eds., *Facing the Truth: South African Faith Communities and the Truth and Reconciliation Commission* (Cape Town: David Philip Publishers, 1999).

Gecaga, M, 'Religious Groups and Democratization in Kenya: Between the Sacred and the Profane', in *Kenya: The Struggle for Democracy* (London: Zed Books, 2007), pp. 58–89.

Graybill, L, *Religion and Resistance Politics in South Africa* (Connecticut: Praeger, 1995).

De Gruchy, J, *The Church Struggle in South Africa* (Michigan: Eerdmans, 2004).

Johnston, D, 'The Churches and Apartheid in South Africa', in Douglas Johnston and Cynthia Sampson, eds., *Religion the Missing Dimension of Statecraft* (Oxford: Oxford University Press, 1994), pp. 177–207.

Mandela, N, *Long Walk to Freedom: The Autobiography of Nelson Mandela* (New York: Brown and Company, 1995).

Van der Merwe, H, 'The Role of the Church in Promoting Reconciliation in Post–TRC South Africa', in Audrey Chapman and Bernard Spong, eds., *Religion and Reconciliation in South Africa: Voices of Religious Leaders* (Philadelphia: Templeton Foundation Press, 2003), pp. 269–281.

Shore, M, 'Christianity and Justice in the South African Truth and Reconciliation Commission: A Case Study in Religious Conflict Resolution', in *Journal of Political Theology* 9.2 (2008), pp. 161–178.

Shore, M, *Religion and Conflict Resolution: Christianity and the South African Truth and Reconciliation Commission* (Surrey: Ashgate Press, 2009).

Shore, M, and Kline, S, 'The Ambiguous Role of Religion in the South African Truth and Reconciliation Commission', in *Peace and Change: A Journal of Peace Research* 31 (2006), pp. 309–332.

Sprenk, S, 'Leaving Mungiki: Some Express Skepticism As Violent Sect Receives Baptism', in *Christianity Today* 11 (February 2010), available at: https://www.christianitytoday.com/ct/2010/february/18.15.html.

Sulaiman, K, 'Religious Violence in Contemporary Nigeria: Implications and Options for Peace and Stability Order', in *Journal for the Study of Religion* 29.1 (2016), pp. 85–103.

United Nations Development Programme, 'UNDP Guidelines on Engaging with Faith -Based Organizations and Religious Leaders', New York, October 2014, available at: http://www.undp.org/content/dam/undp/documents/partners/2014_UNDP_Guidelines-on-Engaging-with-FBOs-and-Religious-Leaders_EN.pdf.

Villa-Vicencio, C, *Trapped in Apartheid: A Socio-theological History of the English-Speaking Churches* (New York: Orbis Books, 1988).

18

Who Do You Trust? Enabling Cross-Religious Involvement in Public Life for a Peaceful and Equitable Future

Catriona Robertson

Who do you trust? Which voices are considered legitimate in public debate and policy making? How do we unlock the imagination of religious networks to enable them to play their part in civic society?

When New Labour's *Neighbourhood Renewal Programme*[1] began in 2001 and local places of worship were included in decision making on public services, there was often a combination of suspicion and blank unknowingness from the statutory side of things. Will they seek to promote their own religious beliefs? What about the unsavoury ones? Or are they after concessions – relaxed parking regulations at funerals, planning permission? And who are all these people anyway? One local authority Chief Executive once told me: 'All these churches and mosques and temples, it's all so chaotic out there!' When most government-citizen transactions are based on the individual, and increasingly online, how do we relate to religious communities, groups of people, social networks? Is it not easier to deal with citizens, tax-payers, patients and voters one by one? Parental choice in schools and the offer of several hospitals for treatment when you visit the GP has highlighted this trend. Surely these value-based groups only seek to benefit themselves?

---

1 Cabinet Office, A New Commitment to Neighbourhood Renewal: A National Strategy Action Plan, 2001, available at: http://webarchive.nationalarchives.gov.uk/20080102112409/ http://www.neighbourhood.gov.uk/publications.asp?did=85.

Mental wellbeing for minority communities

It turned out that, for the religious organisations, proselytising and garnering favours were the least of their concerns. It was the public sector strategies which failed and had been failing for decades, such as those addressing health inequalities,[2] that affected the lives of people in churches, mosques and temples and this is where they were able to make a difference. They cared when their people were sick, especially when this was preventable. They not only had suggestions about how things could be better, but were equipped to make it happen. All they needed was to be linked up to the professional services, invited to participate in policy-making and included in the delivery of services.

When mental illness statistics refused to change for the better in one London borough,[3] a local group volunteered to take the Chair of the mental health trust for a tour of the borough. They visited the Buddhist shrine, the local mosque, black-led churches, synagogues, gurdwaras and Hindu temples. Instead of a community engagement employee (often an entry-level post) giving out some leaflets on post-natal depression or recommending a Beat the Blues mobile app,[4] the chair of the Trust met, on equal terms, senior religious leaders with large congregations, sometimes of over a thousand. For these congregations and their families, many of them from minority ethnic backgrounds, their religious network was often the first port of call when they hit trouble and places of worship were where they came to when life got tough. I have seen a similar case in an Ethiopian church at the end of an incense-filled service – i.e. people bringing their application forms for school places or housing benefit to the priest or leaders for help. These religious leaders understand how the system works and can support members of the congregation who do not. I have also seen such cases in small mosques.

Instead of problems to be solved, the Chair of the Mental Health Trust began to see these religious leaders as part of the solution, capable people with sophisticated webs of relationships and a great deal of influence. Slowly, key people from these religious organisations began working with the Mental Health Trust. They underwent professional training and became qualified systemic family therapists.[5] They are now able to spot issues that can be helped at an early stage. They are not

---

2 The Marmot Review, 2010, available at: http://www.instituteofhealthequity.org/.
3 Chair of St George's and South West London Mental Health Trust visited places of worship in Wandsworth in 2008. See: http://wcen.co.uk/timeline/.
4 See: https://www.beatingthebluesus.com/.
5 Black pastors and Muslim leaders trained as family therapists in 2016; see: http://wcen.co.uk/training/.

only able to refer individuals to the relevant service with confidence, but able to use their therapeutic understanding and skills in a pastoral setting. Two other good things happened. When the congregations became more aware of mental wellbeing, the stigma of talking about it dropped. And the mental health services gained huge insights into the lives of the population they served and began to locate their counselling and therapy in community sites where people felt comfortable and safe, rather than the usual clinical settings. Hence, a whole new way of sustaining good mental health has been imagined and crafted into existence.

Public servants sitting around the Neighbourhood Renewal table, and its successors, did get a bit nervous when, for example, a Black pastor mentioned the story of the Good Samaritan, or an imam quoted from the Qur'an – was this allowed? There is a strong body of opinion which wants religion to be kept private. The pastor and the imam had a story, whereas the public servant was often beholden to a spreadsheet. It took a long time to build two-way, solid trust. The reality, of course, is that we need both. We need public accountability for money spent, but we also need the imagination to see how things could be, and the confidence, energy and commitment to get there. Allowing religious groups to play to their strengths and be themselves – stories, scriptures and all – allowed something entirely new to happen in the face of failure on the part of the authorities.

The Mental Health Trust and its commissioning body, the Clinical Commissioning Group, had run out of ideas on mental health inequalities – they knew that minority groups lacked trust in the services but the leaflets and pop-up stalls and IAPT[6] schemes could not harness the enthusiasm of these relational social networks, religious institutions that really cared about the distress in their communities and knew it did not have to be that way. Bringing together people from several religious traditions helped mitigate concerns that the services were not 'neutral'.

At the start of the Welfare State, post WWII, many people knew who ran the local hospital – their name and probably where they lived. Now, very few of us know who is responsible. The gap between public services – whether it's the NHS, the police, local authorities or education – and ordinary people has widened. Following the banking crisis, there has been both less money for public services and a political return, perhaps as a result of the end of the Cold War and the failure of Communism, to the idea of small government. There are fewer people employed to make links between ordinary communities and local statutory services and

---

6 Improving Access to Psychological Therapies: https://www.england.nhs.uk/mental-health/
adults/iapt/.

fewer people working at local level on public policy. Some have said that the New Labour years were unnecessarily managerial,[7] obsessed with targets and outputs. However, it is hard for those charged with managing a system to think simultaneously of creative ways of improving it.

It also turned out that churches and mosques and temples had a long heritage and centuries-old traditions; and far from being irrelevant to public policy, they were likely to outlive not only the current round of initiatives but successive governments in the centuries to come. Day by day, week by week, scriptures and tradition encourage the imagination of a better life, a better world.

You can see this in the faith-based aid organisations. Christian Aid's strapline used to be: 'We believe in life before death.' 'Recognise the whole human race as one', is Khalsa Aid's slogan. Muslim Hands says, 'United for the Needy', and Penny Appeal, 'Small Change, Big Difference'. Tzedek says, 'Jewish action for a just world'. They all want to make a difference because they can imagine a world without famine, without injustice, without ill health, without violence and suffering.

The Hebrew scriptures say, 'My people will abide in a peaceful habitation, in secure dwellings, and in quiet resting places,'[8] articulating what makes for the best kind of living arrangements – I will return to city living later. The Qur'an's often-quoted sura[9] also has an imagined future: 'I (God) made you into different tribes and nations so that you may know one another.' This implies networks of people who are interested in each other. The heavenly city described in the Book of Revelation[10] has not only an abundance but a diversity of life.

Living well together while remaining different

The Christian Muslim Forum[11] has recently put a toe in the water on public policy, and it relates to that passage from the Qur'an about living well together when we are different. The Government-commissioned Casey Review[12] on integration and opportunity gave us a chance to explore these issues more deeply and to ask the

7 C Dillow, *The End of Politics: New Labour and the Folly of Managerialism* (Petersfield: Harriman House, 2007).
8 Isaiah 32:18.
9 Qur'an 49:13.
10 Revelation 21–22.
11 See: www.christianmuslimforum.org.
12 Casey Review, 2016, available at: https://www.gov.uk/government/publications/the-casey-review-a-review-into-opportunity-and-integration.

questions that most concern us. We have a group of Christians and Muslims from different backgrounds and with very different views, but all deeply rooted in the realities of Muslim and Christian life in this country. We meet regularly and try to understand the underlying complexities behind strongly held opinions. Instead of simply responding to the Casey Review and listing what we agreed with, what we disagreed with, and our recommendations, we started with the experience of the group members.[13] Is segregation a problem and if so, why? Does a call to become more integrated threaten our sense of identity, will we lose something of ourselves? If there is a sense of not being listened to on the lack of opportunities for, say, Black young men or Muslim groups, how can these voices be heard and acted upon? What models of integration have worked? How can we learn from history, particularly that of Northern Ireland?

The discussions and resulting document were sometimes quite personal and raw, but they rang true and offered the Government (as well as academics and others who were interested) a glimpse into the lived experience of the groups identified in the original Review. It opened up the topic to members of the group and to the public servants who read the document, which imagined a Britain that was integrated in a positive way and where opportunities were open to people from all backgrounds. It could deal with the complexity of religion, race, gender and class and the diverse hopes for a better future because this is the everyday experience of the groups.

Effective response to emergencies

London Boroughs Faiths Network[14] (which brings multifaith groups across London together) takes the lead on training and exercising for the Faith Sector Panel of London Resilience[15] – we are all too aware of the dreadful fire that engulfed Grenfell Tower. London Resilience prepares for major emergencies such as an outbreak of pandemic flu, a widespread flood, an attack, a severe power cut. It is a new kid on the block when it comes to public sector organisations and is keen to engage with community groups, including places of worship.

Initially, the conversation was around communication – if an emergency takes

13 The Christian Muslim Forum's briefing on *Integration and Opportunity* was launched at Westminster Abbey on 24 April 2017; see: http://www.christianmuslimforum.org/index.php/news/612-westminster-abbey-integration-and-opportunity.
14 London Boroughs Faiths Network, available at: www.lbfn.org.
15 London Resilience, available at: https://www.london.gov.uk/about-us/organisations-we-work/london-prepared/about-london-prepared.

place, how do we (the professionals) get the message out to you (the public)? Slowly, it became clear that if a bad strain of flu incapacitated and killed a significant proportion of the population, the public services would have a tough time coping. When do you place restrictions on big sporting events? At what point do you close the schools? Where could bodies be stored when there were too many to cremate or bury? The priority was not so much understanding the funeral practices of Hindus, Muslims and different types of Christians, but that the city would need to enlist the help of volunteers and their buildings to avoid panic and disorder.

Effective two-way communications between the authorities and local communities need to be facilitated by people trusted by both – key people who understand the language of the emergency services ('first responders', 'sitrep'), how decisions are made and who are also trusted by their own communities to be telling the truth. A plan is now afoot to create a network of such people, linked in to London Resilience and its officers, so that, should the need arise, there is something in place. The religious input has not been so much about ritual dos and don'ts, but about the capacity to reach, through trusted networks, large numbers of people who are often disconnected from the ambit of local statutory bodies.

Religious groups have extensive experience of dealing with catastrophe, death and bereavement, and can supply the patience and love that people need under these circumstances, something that all the public services put together would struggle to provide following a major emergency. Again, the religious groups have something to offer which does not take the place of public service but complements it.

Peacebuilding

The Olympic Truce is an ancient custom from the original Olympic Games which allowed competitors to travel to and from the Games without danger. All wars were called off for the duration of the Games. It was revived in 1992 by the United Nations[16] and member states voted to observe an Olympic Truce every four years.

In the run-up to *London 2012*, this idea caught the imagination of the faith-based London Peace Network[17] which promoted peacebuilding events throughout the Olympic period. This included the opening up of Islamic centres to visitors on the International Day of Peace (now taken up by the *Visit My Mosque* scheme), a

16 See: http://www.un.org/en/events/olympictruce/.
17 See: https://lbfn.org/london-peace-network/.

linking project between Pakistan and the UK,[18] recognising the deep connections between the two nations and understanding that British Sunni Muslims of Pakistani descent have the experience of being in the minority in this country but are in the majority when they visit friends and family in Pakistan. This allows them to understand better the minority communities in Pakistan, many of which suffer discrimination and hardship.

The London Peace Network has continued its work and in 2016 produced a film[19] associated with the Mayor of London's #LondonIsOpen campaign, showing places of worship across the capital opening their doors. This has been shown again recently after the attacks on Westminster and London Bridges, demonstrating that London's religious communities remain open and welcoming, not closed and fearful.

Practical compassion

Fear is something that can affect the relationship between LGBTI groups and religious organisations. A small project funded by the Arcus Foundation[20] is taking place across several European capitals, bringing LGBTI people together with religious people, particularly those from religious minorities, with a view to recognising the human rights of each group.

I was involved in one workshop with about a dozen imams, all of them male. In Islam, as you know, marriage is highly valued and it is distressing if an adult son or daughter seems to be uninterested or avoiding a decision. One of the scenarios discussed by the imams was one of a father coming to them with concerns about his son and that he had heard rumours about his sexuality. A very sensitive conversation then took place amongst the imams, without challenging the mainstream view of homosexual behaviour in Islam, of the consequences of encouraging the son to marry in spite of his reservations: the impact on a future wife and any children and the risk to the happiness of all concerned.

Working with the grain of integrity and compassion, it was possible to have a nuanced discussion which respected firmly held beliefs and opened up a space for practical considerations. LGBTI groups in other countries are becoming aware of

18 For more information, see the film *Pakistan: the Pride and the Promise*, available at: https://www.thersa.org/discover/videos/pakistan-calling/2013/04/ pakistan---the-pride-and-the-promise.
19 #LondonIsOpen Places of Worship: https://www.youtube.com/watch?v=bExx8ZzfAnw& feature=youtu.be.
20 Arcus Foundation: https://www.arcusfoundation.org/.

the discrimination faced by refugees and members of minority religious groups
and recognising how they share some values and experiences.

A good city

Back to city life. The Diocese of Southwark in south London commissioned a
study[21] on the developments, mainly of high-end glass and steel gated apartments,
along the waterfront of the River Thames, some of the largest regeneration projects in Europe. Only a stone's throw from the river are council estates with families who have lived in the area for generations and which also reflect successive
waves of migration. The Church has been present there probably since Roman
times and has founded hospitals and schools, pioneered social housing (the work
of Octavia Hill), offered practical and pastoral support and encouraged the arts
(Emma Cons & the Old Vic) and commerce.

The Diocese brought developers, local authorities, arts institutions, urban theologians and architects together with the Archbishop of Canterbury[22] to use their
imaginations and to ask: 'What makes for a good city?' Who decides, and who
cares, if the riverside is going to be effectively off limits to large sections of the
existing population? Do people who live in the same area need to know each other,
or even meet? Who holds the collective memory of a space?

The smart and moneyed people moving in to the new apartments are mainly
of working age. The advertising shows couples in their thirties.[23] But what about
everyone else? What happens when children are born? What happens when people
get old? As the report states, 'parishes deal with the collective hopes and fears
of children, pensioners and community groups as well as individuals of working
age.'[24] As with discussions on dementia (as we heard during the 2017 general election campaign[25]) and social care more generally, religious language and practice

21 Battersea to the Barrier, 2015, see: https://batterseatothebarrierdotorg.wordpress.com/.
22 Kate Allen, 'How to Build a Community in Areas of New High-End
Developments', in *Financial Times*, 8 July 2016, available at: https://www.ft.com/
content/9f50d750–3e17–11e6–8716-a4a71e8140b0.
23 For an example of One Blackfriars marketing,
see: http://www.thedrum.com/stuff/2015/01/08/
bizarre-one-blackfriars-luxury-london-development-ad-invokes-twitter-mockery.
24 Catriona Robertson, Battersea to the Barrier, London's Creative and Flourishing
Waterfront, 2015, available at: https://batterseatothebarrierdotorg.files.wordpress.
com/2016/02/battersea-to-the-barrier-booklet.pdf.
25 Paul Vallely in the *Church Times*, 2 June 2017, available at: https://www.churchtimes.
co.uk/articles/2017/2-june/comment/columnists/mrs-may-is-looking-weak-and-wobbly.

upholds the value of human life even under the most difficult conditions. Religious communities, at their best, are able to support people through tough times; their rites of passage have marked the joys and sorrows of generations.

At Lambeth Palace, bringing this sensibility together with the shorter-term planning and investment cycles for major developments proved to be an enlightening and interesting experience for all concerned. The developers and architects wanted this level of discussion, this knowledge base, this intelligence about how communities work and a longer perspective to be part of the process. Come to the table, they said. From 'how many units' and concerns about the bottom line, the discussion often revealed the reasons that town planners, architects, developers had chosen their professions – they were creating the living spaces of the future. But opportunities for this kind of value-based conversation are infrequent and the opportunity to combine imaginations across the disciplines and with religious groups are almost non-existent.

Solidarity in the face of terror

The three recent attacks in Westminster, Manchester and London Bridge have shocked and horrified us all. Faith-based hate crime, according to the Metropolitan Police,[26] has never been higher. Anti-Semitism and anti-Muslim hate crime has risen across Europe.

There is a good relationship between many police forces and the religious communities they serve, partly through consultative groups such as Independent Advisory Groups, partly through the remains of neighbourhood policing and partly because local places of worship are well organised into a faith forum[27] or similar and are therefore easier to engage with. Fear of extremism and its links with religion, most evident on social media and in press headlines (some statements come very close to infringing religious freedom), and a backdrop of violent conflict in the Middle East and a continuing refugee crisis present a challenge to religious groups. There have been strong responses by religious groups, particularly those working together,[28] in condemning the attacks and refusing to accept divisions in society. The Great Get Together celebrated the life of Jo Cox MP and encouraged

---

26 Statement on hate crime in London, 7 June 2017, available at: http://news.met.police.uk/news/statement-on-hate-crime-in-london-245032.

27 Borough faith forums in London: https://lbfn.org/whos-who/.

28 Inter Faith Network for the UK statement following the terror attack at Manchester Arena, Ma7, 2017, available at: https://www.interfaith.org.uk/news/manchester-arena-attack-statement.

people from different communities to come together for a picnic, street party or iftar. However, vigil fatigue is a concern and a conversation is needed about how we respond if attacks continue.

The globalisation of the market focuses on those who are economically active. Without claiming to be unique in this, religious traditions (particularly when understanding the role of race, class and gender) have a wider sense of value than financial gain and tend to be close to the lived reality of people's lives through their widespread local centres, rites of passage, pastoral involvement, teaching and shared community life. The value of trusting relationships and a concern for human dignity take their place alongside fiscal probity.

By working creatively across differences with other religious, civil society, academic and governmental bodies, religious groups can offer smart, strategic and realistic ways forward on some of the perplexing issues of the day. These are informed by centuries of history, rooted in today's lived realities and infused with values and principles re-imagined to address heightened global tension, changing economic pressures and their impact at national level and in local community life.

Bibliography

Allen, Kate, 'How to Build a Community in Areas of New High-End Developments', in *Financial Times*, 8 July 2016, available at: https://www. ft.com/content/9f50d750–3e17–11e6–8716-a4a71e8140b0.

Dillow, C, *The End of Politics: New Labour and the Folly of Managerialism* (Petersfield: Harriman House, 2007).

Contributors

Mohammed Gamal Abdelnour is a faculty member at the Al-Azhar University of Cairo and a Senior Teaching Fellow at SOAS, University of London. He wrote a PhD thesis for al-Azhar on the Revivication of Islamic Theology and is currently writing a thesis on Salvation between Ash'arism and Catholicism at SOAS.

His Eminence Archbishop **Anba Angaelos** was enthroned as the first Coptic Orthodox Archbishop of London in 2017, having served as General Bishop of the Coptic Church in the United Kingdom since 1999. He has been awarded the Order of the British Empire for services to international religious freedom.

Eileen Barker, FAcSS, FBA, OBE is Professor Emeritius of Sociology with Special Reference to the Study of Religion at the London School of Economics. She has been studying minority religions and social reactions to these since the 1970s. In 1988, she founded INFORM (www.INFORM.ac), an educational charity that helps enquirers by providing information about minority religions.

Kamran Bashir teaches Religion and History as Adjunct Faculty Member in the Department of Humanities at Camosun College, Victoria, British Columbia. He holds a doctorate in History from the University of Victoria. Focused on the larger study of Islam in South Asia, his research investigates Muslim scholarship of the Qur'an and the life of the Prophet Muhammad.

Craig Calhoun is Professor of Social Sciences at Arizona State University and Centennial Professor at LSE. His books include: *Neither Gods Nor Emperors: Students and the Struggle for Democracy in China*; *Nations Matter: Citizenship, Solidarity, and the Cosmopolitan Dream*; *The Roots of Radicalism*; and *Does Capitalism Have a Future?* They have been translated into 21 languages.

John Casson was British Ambassador in Cairo from 2014 to 2018. He has worked as a diplomat on four continents, and as a policymaker in 10 Downing Street and HM Treasury. He studied History and Theology at the University of Cambridge.

Abby Day is Professor in Race, Faith and Culture in the Department of Sociology, Goldsmiths, University of London, where her teaching, research, writing and supervisions cover sociology of religion, media and religion, and critical criminology. Her recent research interests focus on gender, generations and the cross-cultural/religious meaning of 'belief'.

John Fahy received his PhD in Social Anthropology from the University of Cambridge in 2016. As a Research Fellow at the Woolf Institute, and based in Georgetown University in Qatar, he led a three-year research project that looked at interfaith engagement in Delhi, Doha and London. He has published widely on the anthropology of religion, ethics, interfaith and religious diversity in India and the Persian Gulf.

Caleb Gordon is currently in his second year of a PhD at the University of Manchester, originally from Alaska, by way of Yale Divinity School. He is looking at the relationship between theology and environmental ethics, whether our aesthetic experiences of environment are ethically significant, and the implications of a theological approach to aesthetic experience.

Mena Mark Hanna is Dean of the Barenboim-Said Akademie and Professor of Musicology and Composition. His research and teaching interests include Eastern Mediterranean chant, music of the 20th and 21st centuries, composition and electronic music, and classical music performance structures and postcolonialism. He received his DPhil from Merton College, Oxford.

Emmanuel Karagiannis is a Senior Lecturer in the Department of Defence Studies at King's College, London. He has published extensively on political Islam in the Middle East and Central Asia. He is the author of *The New Political Islam: Human Rights, Democracy and Justice* (Philadelphia: University of Pennsylvania Press, 2018).

Thahir Jamal Kiliyamannil is a third year PhD student in the Centre for Comparative Literature at the University of Hyderabad, India. His doctoral research analyses the engagements of Muslim community with the constitutional politics in South India, focusing on transformation of identity and religious discourse.

Jenna Reinbold is an Associate Professor of Religion at Colgate University. She studies religion and law, religion and human rights, and secularism. Her book, *Seeing the Myth in Human Rights*, received the 2018 American Academy of Religion Award for Excellence in the Study of Religion in the category of Analytical-Descriptive Studies.

Catriona Robertson is Director of the *Christian Muslim Forum*. A graduate of the University of St Andrews, her intercultural work takes her to local communities in Europe, North Africa, the Middle East and the Indian subcontinent. Her writing appears in books and online. She convenes the *London Boroughs Faiths Network*.

Megan Shore is an Associate Professor at King's University College in Canada, and Coordinator for the Social Justice and Peace Studies Program. Her research focuses on the role of religion and faith-based organisations in contemporary issues of justice and peace. She is the author of *Religion and Conflict Resolution: Christianity and South Africa's Truth and Reconciliation Commission* (Farnham: Ashgate, 2009).

Mona Siddiqui, OBE, is Professor of Islamic and Interreligious Studies and Assistant Principal for Religion and Society at the University of Edinburgh. Her research focuses on classical Islamic law and ethics and Christian-Muslim relations. She is internationally renowned as a public intellectual and is a regular broadcaster for the BBC.

Khushwant Singh studied Ethnology, Educational Sciences and Social Anthropology. He completed his MA in Heidelberg and MRes in London both with distinction. Since 2006, he has been working in the field of international development cooperation. Singh is a founding member of the interfaith Frankfurt Council of Religions, and served as its president for four years.

The Revd Canon Dr **James Walters** is Founding Director of the LSE Faith Centre which works to promote religious understanding and interfaith leadership among LSE's global student body and in government. He is also a Senior Lecturer in the LSE Marshall Institute, an affiliate of the Department for International Development and Chaplain to the School.

Ophir Yarden is a Senior Lecturer at Brigham Young University's Jerusalem Center, teaching Jewish and Israel Studies there and at several Christian theological colleges in Jerusalem. His other research centres on secularised expressions of Jewish identity in Israel and Israel's civil religion. He is active in efforts to improve Jewish-Arab relations.